Praise for
These Walls Between Us

"This is a powerful book with an important lesson that we all must learn in trying to understand others—a book that both Blacks and whites should read so that we can enter into a productive dialogue with each other."

—Reverend John Reynolds, author of *The Fight for Freedom: A Memoir of My Years in the Civil Rights Movement*

"Unique, fascinating, and complex, Wendy Sanford's wonderful memoir is so rare and engaging that I read the book continuously over twelve hours without wanting to stop."

—Peggy McIntosh, senior research scientist and former associate director of the Wellesley Centers for Women and author of "White Privilege: Unpacking the Invisible Knapsack" (1989) and *On Privilege, Fraudulence, and Teaching As Learning: Selected Essays 1981–2019*

"White privilege is like an invisible thread that maintains the status quo. Thank goodness Wendy Sanford is doing the work that only she can do!"

—Byllye Avery, founder of Black Women's Health Imperative

"Wendy's story demands just recognition of domestic workers, Black women, and women of color for the essential yet invisible role they play in caring for so many families. Wendy's story calls on all of us to intentionally dismantle the walls that have kept us from recognizing and actively combating the white supremacist culture that shows up in our own homes."

—Stacy Kono, executive director of Hand in Hand: The Domestic Employers Network

"This tender and evocative story about friendship across racial and class lines is an important guide for living into this time of racial reckoning. Sanford's unflinching honesty, insight, and wisdom had me saying, out loud, again and again, 'Wow, that is so true!'"
—Catherine Whitmire, author of *Practicing Peace: A Devotional Walk through the Quaker Tradition* and *Plain Living: A Quaker Path to Simplicity*

"The politics are crystal clear at all levels, the characters are fascinating and it's a superb read! Sanford presents the humanity of the characters, in all their contradictoriness, while remaining unrelenting in her condemnation of systemic racial and class violence. White people are all complicit in racism, and all responsible for taking it down, relationship by relationship. This memoir shows how tortuous and slippery that is . . . and yet, between humans who will recognize one another as such, always possible."
—James Seale-Collazo, Faculty, Escuela Secondaria, University of Puerto Rico

"*These Walls Between Us* is a deeply researched and unflinchingly thoughtful account . . . I find Sanford's work uplifting in its openness. She seeks to educate, not castigate, and the narrative force of her story is compelling in its own right. This book is a clear-eyed and riveting gift to those of us who would rather try to repair than ignore this country's tattered history of exploitation. In less accomplished hands, this might be an exercise in hand-wringing and self-doubt, but Wendy Sanford is a confident and authoritative narrator who makes this timely book at once accessible, gripping, and instructive."
—Robin Hemley, author of *Borderline Citizen: Dispatches from The Outskirts of Nationhood*

"An emotional glimpse into a lifetime anti-racism journey. Non-profit board members, government leaders, and executives from all sectors will be transformed by Wendy's journey and her painfully earned pearls of wisdom on the effort to become an anti-racist white person."

—Sue Gallagher, Chief Innovation Officer, Children's Services
Council of Broward County, FL

"Ms. Sanford's story is a necessary read for today's young white people, especially college students interested in Africana studies, gender and women's studies, and sociology courses. Above all, this remarkable book is a moving testimony for all who believe in fairness and racial healing."

—Pam Brooks, Associate Professor, Africana Studies Department,
Oberlin College, and author of *Boycotts, Buses, and Passes:
Black Women's Resistance in the U.S. South and South Africa*

These Walls Between Us

A Memoir of Friendship
Across Race and Class

Wendy Sanford

SHE WRITES PRESS

Published 2021
Printed in the United States of America
Print ISBN: 978-1-64742-167-0
E-ISBN: 978-1-64742-168-7
Library of Congress Control Number: 2021905883

For information, address:
She Writes Press
1569 Solano Ave #546
Berkeley, CA 94707

She Writes Press is a division of SparkPoint Studio, LLC.

Book design by Stacey Aaronson
Photo credit for dedication page: Elisabeth Morrison

Notes of a Native Son
Copyright © 1949, 1950, 1951, 1953, 1954, 1955 by James Baldwin
Reprinted with permission from Beacon Press, Boston Massachusetts

Excerpts from "Like One of The Family" by Alice Childress © 1986. Used by permission of the Williams and Woodard families and SLD Associates LLC, sarah.douglas@sldassociatesllc.com. All Rights Reserved.

"Antebellum House Party" from HOW TO BE DRAWN by Terrance Hayes, copyright © 2015 by Terrance Hayes. Used by permission of Penguin Books, an imprint of Penguin Publishing Group, a division of Penguin Random House LLC. All rights reserved.

All company and/or product names may be trade names, logos, trademarks, and/or registered trademarks and are the property of their respective owners.

Names and identifying characteristics have been changed to protect the privacy of certain individuals.

To Mary Norman and Polly Attwood
Beloved companions in the journey of my life

"Unless the white community breaks its silence and determines that race is not a peripheral issue, but an issue central to the things that we say are valuable to America . . . the finest movement in the world will not cause racism to cease."

—REVEREND JAMES LAWSON

I know that "simply to be white is to be racist" is the catchphrase some liberals use these days, but when will they begin hearing what supposedly they know?

—CLAUDIA RANKINE, *Just Us*

If you walk on eggshells,
I won't be able to talk to you the way I do.

—MARY NORMAN

Contents

Introduction

I GREW UP IN THE NORTHEAST UNITED STATES, AMIDST white people who thought ourselves a world apart from the white supremacists of the Ku Klux Klan—the violent, radical fringe. And yet, I grew up embedded in racist violence myself, just of a variety that was polite and normalized in American life, in which every institution advanced white people at the expense of people of color. I also toddled my first steps into a fraught zone between my white mother's blue-blood, owning-class family and my white father's hard-scrabble-farm Georgia roots. I channeled both my mother's assumptions of superiority and my father's urgent, resentful aspiration to rise.

My parents united in the project of training me to become a white, upper-class, wealthy woman. They only half-succeeded. As an adult, I thrived in the women's health movement, joined the Quakers, immersed myself in writings by people of color, and fell in love with a woman. I am grateful to the many magnets that drew me outside my family's elite bubble and landed me in a more humane life. Most centrally, I am grateful to Mary Norman, whose friendship is the magnet that has mattered the longest.

More than sixty years ago, in the mid-1950s, a young African American teenager named Mary White traveled north from Virginia to work for my family as a live-in domestic worker during our summer vacation. Mary was fifteen, I was twelve. As the Black "help" and the privileged white daughter, we were not slated for friendship. Employers like my mother used the word "friend" to manage domestic workers, not to connect with them. Soon, however, came the dynamic social movements of the 1960s, '70s, and '80s: the civil rights movement, multi-racial feminism, and liberation theology. These movements opened friendship as a possibility between Mary and me. We stepped into that opening. Across the stark differences of race and class between us, we began to shape a bond.

Some thirty years after we met, in the late 1980s, Mary declared that we should write a book about our friendship. She, more than I, understood how many rules of the dominant culture we had violated in our journey towards becoming friends— unwritten rules of domestic service, carefully policed barriers between white and Black, between rich and poor. "No one will believe our story," she said. At the time, we had been sharing novels and essays by Toni Morrison, Paule Marshall, Alice Walker, Audre Lorde, and Alice Childress. Especially electrifying for us both was Anne Moody's *Coming of Age in Mississippi*, which Mary said came the closest to expressing her own experiences growing up Black in the rural South. I had worked with a team of women as coauthor and editor of *Our Bodies, Ourselves*, a feminist resource on women's health and sexuality. All this made Mary's suggested writing project seem possible. We even fantasized being invited by Oprah to appear on her new-at-the-time TV show.

These Walls Between Us is not the book Mary and I imagined we might write together. The book would not exist without Mary, based as it is on innumerable conversations between us—by phone, in person, via email, and, in later years, via texting. Mary has read and commented on every draft, but *These Walls* is very much my story. It focuses on my often-stumbling journey towards seeing Mary more fully across the socially constructed barriers between us—that is, towards being a truer friend. It is written with a white readership in mind, to invite white readers to join me in exploring our relationship to white supremacy culture.

It's 2020 as I finish this book. Mary is eighty years old, I am seventy-six. On weekly phone calls, we carry on about politics and family like the observant, caring old women we are. As we vented about the Trump presidency, Mary said of the book, "I think of the climate we are living in now, all the hateful things mostly young white males are doing that fall into the category of hate crimes, putting a wedge between people. The people who elected President Trump want to take the country back to the good old days. This book can show what those days were really like."

For my part, I hope *These Walls Between Us* will also be a testament to the power of love that has kept us, each in our own way, reaching across the obstacles arrayed against our becoming close. I hope that it will inspire readers to examine the barriers and possibilities in their own cross-racial and cross-class relationships.

White People Swimming

I JUMPED UP WHEN I HEARD MY MOTHER'S STATION WAGON scratching along the prickly bushes that crowded the driveway of the seaside rental in Nantucket, summer of 1956. I'd been so moody and mopey that morning that my mother had accused me of "treating this nice vacation like a prison sentence." She'd driven alone to the ferry dock in town to pick up her new summer helper.

The screen door to the kitchen squeaked open, slammed shut. "Damn that door," my mother said.

A quiet, shy voice. "I can fix that right up for you, Mrs. Coppedge."

I slipped into the kitchen to find a slender teenager with dark brown skin, her body shapely in a black skirt and sweater. "This is Mary," my mother said.

I thought I saw a quick, shy "hello" pass through Mary's large, brown eyes, before she started looking around the kitchen. She scanned the rack of pots and pans, the counters and the double sink, the clothes washer, the long pine table with a built-in bench along two sides. She looked back over her shoulder to the empty clothesline outside the screen door. I hadn't looked at all these things together before. When she finished her inspection, Mary straightened her back and looked resolute. Years later she would tell me she'd been summoning courage. She didn't know how to work a gas stove. She worried that my mother would be upset by this. She felt alone.

I darted forward to tug at the handle of Mary's suitcase. I wanted to help her take the bag to her room, but I couldn't lift its weight. "Let me do that," Mary said matter-of-factly. She reached down and eased my fingers aside.

This first summer vacation on Nantucket was a long time ago now—and an experiment. My mother's upper-class family had a legacy of lengthy, expensive beachside vacations. My striving, corporate-lawyer father could finally afford a month-long rental on a secluded Nantucket beach. Friday evenings, he would fly in for the weekend, braving the relatively new commercial airlines and the island's notorious fog. My energetic eight-year-old brother would go to overnight camp on the Cape, so that my mother wouldn't have to amuse or contain him. Twelve years old and more bookish, I'd spend the month with my mother. As another perk of my father's increasing affluence, my mother would have "help." I imagine my mother calling around to her friends in Princeton, New Jersey, where we lived, seeking the name of a "good, hardworking girl." A young Black woman named Betty Phipps, who did domestic work for my godmother, recommended her niece from Elk Creek, Virginia. On the morning I'm remembering, Mary White's arrival marked the perfection of my parents' plan—and a step forward in Mary's own aspirations.

Mary carried her heavy suitcase into the bedroom next to the kitchen, and I followed. Mary's room, like mine, had two single beds. The quilts were faded, the walls yellow pine. Two brand new shapeless white cotton uniforms hung on the closet door, price tags still attached. My mother had bought them sight unseen, guessing at Mary's size. I didn't wonder at the time whether Mary had worn such uniforms before (she hadn't) or how she felt, seeing them hanging there like rules and regulations. While my room looked out over the ocean, the view from Mary's bedside window featured the empty laundry line strung between two poles in the back yard. Her north-facing window looked out on Nantucket's signature *Rosa rugosa* bushes, densely green and thorny, with occasional pink blooms. On tiptoe, you could glimpse the sea.

Mary lifted her suitcase to the spare bed. There was a flumping sound as the mattress sank. I leaned against the doorway and watched.

"Can I help?" I asked.

Mary widened her eyes and shook her head no.

"Can I stay?" I did not consider that Mary might want privacy.

She shrugged almost imperceptibly. "If you want to," she said.

We looked for a while at Mary's suitcase on the narrow bed.

"Want me to open it now?" she asked.

I nodded. I must have known, without anyone telling me directly, that Mary wouldn't feel free to say no. She sighed, snapped open the two metal clasps, and slowly lifted the top. I spotted a few clothes—a nightgown, dark slacks, and what looked like a lightweight navy-blue jacket. Then the weight: two bottles each of an unfamiliar brand of shampoo and conditioner, a six-pack of orange soda, and a brown AM-FM radio with the cord wrapped neatly around. Mary lifted the radio out like a baby and set it gently down on the bedside table.

"Nice radio," I said.

She startled at my voice. "Oh!" Slowly she drew her eyes away from the treasure. "It was a gift."

"For what?" I asked, curious to the point of intrusion. I gave my gracelessness no thought.

She blinked. "High school graduation," she said. She turned her head so that I couldn't see her full face.

Mary seemed young to have graduated from high school. Decades later, she would take me to the one-room, uninsulated building in Independence, Virginia, the only school that the state of Virginia had provided for Mary and the other local Black children to attend. "We were all in this room," Mary told me then, "everyone at some different level of learning, with the big stove in the middle, and the teacher going back and forth between the groups. It was not a good time." I could picture Mary, clustering with her fellow students around the pot-bellied stove in winter, burning hot on one side of her body and bone-chilled on the other. With no extracurricular activities, few books, and one teacher for students from five to fifteen, Mary quickly mastered everything the school could offer. There was no expectation, in that era, that a young Black woman needed further education. The only jobs open to her were like the one Mary was starting with my family. Virginia finished schooling Mary long before she received the education she wanted or deserved.

I hung around in Mary's doorway, not thinking that she had just traveled nine hundred miles and might be tired. In what would become the pattern for many years ahead, Mary turned her attention to me. "You having a good time here so far?"

I was about to complain that I didn't have any friends yet, when my mother called from the living room. "Mary's had a long trip. Why don't you let her unpack in peace?"

Mary was at her door in a split second. "I don't need more time, Mrs. Coppedge. I'm ready to do whatever you want." As she headed into the kitchen, I turned to plug in her radio. In a small vase on the bedside table, I noticed three daisies and a wild rosebud that my mother must have picked and placed there that morning.

My mother and her friends called their servants "girls," as a marker of their own superiority. And yet, though she was only fifteen, Mary was not free to be a girl. The limits our society placed on her were rushing her into womanhood. Mary's family back in Virginia counted on her earning power. She was already in the labor force. She did not have the luxury of being a child. Nothing in my affluent and exclusively white world could help me understand the relentlessness of the work Mary had done already in her short life and would be doing for us. Mary would wash and clean, straighten and replace, cook and prepare. Mary's work, and the work of women like her, helped sustain my childhood and my enjoyment of it.

In the purposeful ignorance of white people both then and now, I asked Mary little that summer about her journey to my mother's kitchen. Years later, after I learned to inquire and to listen, Mary described the nine hundred miles she traveled to the remote Nantucket beach. Her mother, Alice Johnson, put her on a train from Wytheville, Virginia, to Trenton, New Jersey, where Mary's aunt Betty Phipps had moved some years earlier in search of better work. Phrases like "long train ride" and "first time away from home" fail to capture the indignities of Mary's trip. Racist regulations at that time forced Mary's mother to put her on a train car designated for Black people. The dining car was open to whites only, Mary told me, so her mother sent her with a "peanut butter and jelly or baloney sandwich and a slice of cake, maybe a candy bar." Many hours later, Mary's Aunt Betty met her at the Trenton train station and took her home. Mary reports that this break in the journey north felt welcoming and protective after the abuse and insult of segregated transport.[1]

The historic Great Migration in the United States was made up of African Americans like Mary's Aunt Betty, and then Mary herself, who moved north and west to escape the Jim Crow South, hoping for better employment and a freer life. Mary, like others who'd gone before her, received welcome and help from family members already arrived, a job secured by a relative, and practical advice. Mary remembers her Aunt Betty's advice: "Mrs. C. is a very nice woman and will be good to you—just do what she asks."

The next day, to launch her young niece into her first live-in job, Aunt Betty drove Mary to my family's home in Princeton. My mother, who was already on Nantucket, had hired an off-duty police officer, Norman, to drive Mary seven hours further north, to the ferry dock in Woods Hole. From my mother's perspective, hiring a white, off-duty cop was a resourceful strategy for safely transporting Mary, who was very young, unfamiliar with the North, and unaccustomed to travel. I imagine my mother had no thought that Mary might be afraid of this man.

---

[1] The National Museum of African American History and Culture in Washington, DC, exhibits a railway car from the long era of segregation. Stepping on, one notes immediately the stark differences in comfort and décor between the whites-only and colored-only sections of the carriage. Mary's first trip north came months after the Interstate Commerce Commission finally ruled that racial segregation in public transportation violated the antidiscrimination section of the Interstate Commerce Act. Many states, however, were slow to comply.

And yet, the all-white police departments back home in Elk Creek and Independence, Virginia, did little to make a girl like Mary feel safe. White police officers enforced the Jim Crow regulations created to limit and control Mary's family and other Black citizens—they could not be counted on to protect Black people from white violence. None of us could know, at the time, that, over decades of supplementing their incomes by moonlighting for my parents, Mary and Norman would come to count each other as valued friends. Mary's first burden of service to my family, however, was to climb into an unknown car and travel seven hours through unfamiliar landscape with an unknown white policeman. "It was a long ride to Woods Hole with Norman," Mary remembers. "He hardly had ten words for me, so I was just looking out the window wondering, 'What am I doing? Will I be okay so far from home?'"

As Mary stood on the Woods Hole boat dock waiting to climb the gangplank to the huge, high-sided Nantucket ferryboat, she experienced another facet of migration: the first shock of aloneness in an utterly white world. Mary had reason to feel wary, venturing by herself among so many white people. For Black people at that time, as could be said for today, being among unrestrained white people was dangerous. The previous summer, a white woman in rural Mississippi claimed that a fourteen-year-old Black boy visiting from Chicago treated her rudely. Her kinsmen abducted the boy, Emmett Till, and brutally tortured and murdered him. Till's mother insisted on putting his mutilated body in an open casket, and *Jet* (the African American magazine) published the gruesome photo. News of what today is known as racial terror lynching flew through the Black community, motivating countless Black activists already poised to launch a national movement for civil rights.[2] I imagine the collective trauma of this murder traveled with Mary on her journey north, perhaps even more so because she and Emmett Till were the same age. Emmett had ventured far from home. So, now, had Mary.

The boat's horn blasted. Enormous engines rumbled beneath Mary's feet. The ferry churned into the waters of the Woods Hole harbor. Mary had never been on a boat nor seen the sea. She did not know how to swim. Where Mary grew up, the Elk Creek ran along the main country road for miles. Spring rains swelled the creek over its banks, flooding out the road and endangering those, mostly Black, who had to travel on foot. Water was a peril to be watched and feared. Mary's three-hour ferry ride across Nantucket Sound was not something to enjoy, but a crossing to be anxious about. As she said years later, "I knew that if anything happened, that would be the end." Mary remembers a miserable ride: "The younger folks looked and sniggered at me, while some of the older ones smiled, and others just looked through me. The horn was such a loud and piercing sound. After we started to move, I thought, *Oh god, I am going to be sick. Mama, I am sorry, I want to go home.*" I picture Mary sitting stiffly and anxiously inside the stuffy steamboat lounge, holding her hard-sided suitcase tightly as the boat pitched and rolled on choppy swells. Now, I ache when I think of the white kids sniggering smugly at Mary, yet I know that I was as ignorant as they were.

Mary lugged her suitcase down the narrow gangplank to the

[2] The goal of terrorists is to instill fear and to inhibit confidence and initiative; Mamie Till defied that goal. She chose an open casket funeral, so that her son's mutilated face would inform the world about white men's brutality to African Americans in the USA. Despite her courageous act, the two tried for murdering Emmett Till were quickly acquitted by a jury of all white men. Fifty years later, in 2017, the tragedy took on yet another dimension: Emmett Till's accuser, Carolyn Johnson, confessed that she had fabricated the "incident."

Nantucket dock, an immigrant from one world to another. Trying to be brave as she stood alone in the rush of white travelers,
she wondered if anyone would remember to meet her. Soon my
mother arrived in the family station wagon, surveyed the crowd
of arriving passengers through her big dark glasses, spotted the
one Black teenager, and headed towards her new helper with a
welcoming smile.

"I followed her to the car," Mary says now. "She kept up the
happy chatter about the island, and what I would do, and not to
worry. I remember saying I didn't know how to cook much.
'That's fine, darling,' she said, 'I will show you.'" Safely in the car
with her suitcase full of home, Mary felt fluttering worry about
the job ahead. I picture her sneaking glimpses through the car
window as her new employer drove deftly up and down across
the rolling moors and scruffy vegetation of an unfamiliar landscape. I doubt that Mary saw another person of color on that
drive. I would later appreciate that the land my mother was driving Mary through was stolen country, former Native land,
transformed by colonizers' greed into the heart of whiteness.

When I tell white people that I grew up in the 1950s, there is a
knowing look. Oh, the conservative, conforming '50s. Bobby
socks and American Bandstand. Eisenhower, the president who
had helped us win a terrible war; middle class women, smiling in
their homes, tending their shiny new appliances; Elvis Presley
shocking and thrilling female America with his gravelly, sexy
voice, his gyrating hips. Oh, the '50s. White veterans had been
able to buy homes through the GI Bill and were forming families, building equity for the future. An ad on the era's brand-new
TVs showed a white family in Sunday clothes, walking together

along a leafy suburban street, heading for church: "The family that prays together stays together." In a communism-wary Washington, dangerous senators and the FBI scrutinized progressive men and women of all ethnic and racial groups—writers, actors, artists, activists—looking for shades of red.

For Mary and her family in this same decade, the main theme of public life was not "I like Ike" or swooning over Elvis, but the struggle against Jim Crow—the panoply of quasi-legal rules and practices that constricted their safety, freedom, and livelihood. In the years just before Mary came to Nantucket, African Americans pursued major milestones in the struggle. In 1956, the first Black student entered the University of Alabama; Autherine Lucy was confronted by hate-filled riots that university trustees blamed on her presence. The university expelled her within months. A year later, in its historic *Brown v. Board of Education* decision, the U.S. Supreme Court at last declared segregated public schooling unconstitutional. In the winter of 1955 came powerful nonviolent resistance by those dependent on buses in Montgomery, Alabama, where Black citizens were charged full fare and told they had to move to the back, closer to the fumes. In a step long planned by ministers and other activists of Montgomery, Rosa Parks refused to give up her bus seat to a white rider. Her arrest sparked the yearlong Montgomery Bus Boycott, which was in full force during the summer that Mary first came north.

When we met in my mother's kitchen that summer, Mary and I came from different countries.

My mother began teaching Mary how my father liked his coffee, his pork chops, his steak. She taught Mary to fill the ice bucket from eleven a.m. forward and to make sure the liquor cabinet always had enough booze. Mary fixed the squeak and slam of the kitchen door. She set up the ironing board permanently in her room, where she pulled the green shades down over nearly shut windows. My mother had instructed Mary to dress for duty from breakfast through dinner, except for two hours each afternoon and Thursdays and Sundays after lunch. During her time off, Mary often did the ironing. Occasionally she sat on the edge of her bed to read, sipping from a single orange soda poured over ice. My mother was delighted to find that Mary was a reader. A loan of a thick hardback, with a tall stone castle and a flowing-haired white maiden on the cover, soon waited on the bedside table beside Mary's radio. "I wasn't allowed to read those love books at home," Mary remembers. "With my grandmother, I'd have to hide in the bed with a flashlight under the covers reading true confessions magazines. In Nantucket, as soon as your mother finished one of her books, she gave it to me. Learning all of that made me feel grown up. I didn't bother her by wanting to go anywhere on my day off. I just wanted to be in my room reading. It worked for both of us."

On the hill where Mary grew up, whole families grew and were nurtured in a few small, low-ceilinged, well-kept rooms, in homes smaller than the one my parents called a beach "cottage." In Nantucket, Mary encountered cabinets full of specialty foods, closets packed with store-bought clothes, a liquor cabinet bristling with bottles, and the diamond jewelry my mother wore each evening to dinner. Thinking about the immense class differences between our families, I asked Mary recently what details she reported to her mother after that first summer. She told me, "I said, 'Mommie, you should see all the pretty dresses and the perfume. And guess what, they eat lamb chops.' When Mrs.

C. asked me, 'Mary, do you eat lamb chops?' I thought I would die on the spot. I said, 'No, Ma'am, we don't eat that.'" Lamb was too pricey for her family, Mary says today, and, besides, she remembers her young aunt Dot saying that lambs cry like babies when they are slaughtered.

Mary says that when she first saw the inside of my family's house in Princeton that next fall, when she began going there weekly to do domestic work, she remembers "being in awe at all the beautiful things, the marble in the entrance, the high ceilings in the living room. I had only seen such things in magazines." Mary noticed, also, the luxury of a family living together in a house large enough to hold them. Mary had lived most of her life in her grandmother's home. Though her grandmother was solid and loving, Mary's own mother lived as far away as ten miles without a car can be. My family could afford to live under the same roof. We could take a long vacation together. We could hire Mary to help make our vacation seamless and uncluttered, with no requirement to clean up after ourselves. I did not register for many years that our luxury was special, and rare, and required money that most families did not have.

A later exchange Mary had with my mother revealed how little my family knew of Mary's reality. She told me, "I remember a Friday a few years later in Princeton, when I said, 'I am so glad today is payday because I was broke.' Your mom said, 'You have no money?' At that time in my life, I didn't have any money at all, not until I got paid. Your mom said, 'How horrible! No money—I can't imagine not having any.' The look on her face was disbelief. I don't think she could process such a notion." The people Mary encountered in my family didn't know material want, didn't know self-reliance, didn't know making do.

≈

One morning during Mary's first week in Nantucket, I stood on the rickety wooden steps leading down to the beach. My mother was lounging in a beach chair, out on the sand where the dune grass ended, facing the ocean. Her long, tanned legs stretched out in front of her, glistening with oil; a silk scarf secured her blond hair against the breeze. To me, she looked glamorous, like a Hollywood star. Beyond her, swells lifted and set the green water in motion under the sunlight. In the cottage behind us, Mary vacuumed. All through my childhood, vacuuming was a comforting sound, signifying that someone was taking care of us and all was well.

I flopped down next to my mother's chair in the warm sand and sniffed the familiar perfume of her sun tan oil, the fresh mint in a tumbler of iced tea stuck in the sand nearby. "Finished the next Nancy Drew," I whispered. She kept reading.

When I couldn't resist pulling at a string on the fraying edge of the chair's canvas seat, my mother turned to me, her eyes hidden behind big dark glasses. "This Nantucket experiment includes plenty of mother-daughter time . . .," she began sharply, then stopped and changed her tone. "And we've been having it, haven't we, sweetheart? We've had swims, and walks, and a shopping trip." She took off her dark glasses to plead with me. "You'll have a better time if you go meet some other twelve-year-olds. I'm sure there are loads of them just a five-minute walk away, all having a perfectly lovely time and not depending on their mothers. Your father will most definitely not like a lot of moping and heavy breathing in the offspring department."

The prospect of hunting for playmates made me crouch closer to my mother's warm skin. As she returned to her place in the novel, the morning stretched before me, as long and as unoccupied as the empty beach.

"Want to swim?" I said after a while.

"I do not want to swim," my mother said into her book. "This is my last chance at any peace around here. Tomorrow by the time I get my hair done, shop for groceries, and buy flowers for the table, it will be time to worry about your father's airplane getting in. And then he'll be here." She stopped. "I mean, of course it will be lovely to have him."

From the dune behind us, we heard Mary call softly across the sand. "Can I freshen up your iced tea, Mrs. Coppedge?"

My mother turned to smile at Mary, who stood at the top of the wooden stairs in a baggy white dress—the uniforms my mother had purchased drowned Mary's slender body in shapeless white. "No more tea, thank you, Mary," my mother said, "but you are very thoughtful. Why don't you come on down to the water?"

Mary held onto the splintery banister as if the steps threatened to float out to sea.

"Have you been to the ocean before, Mary?" my mother asked.

"Only on the ferry, Ma'am." Mary took a step backward and squinted out at the expanse of moving green, letting her eyes go once, quickly, all the way to the eastern horizon.

My mother laughed. "I hope you will come to love the ocean the way Wendy and I do."

Recalling this moment now, I realize that my mother assumed, based on her own experience, that Mary could swim. My mother also assumed that Mary would want, or feel free, to swim from a beach open only to wealthy white people. By now, I understand this viewpoint as white solipsism: We imagine that everyone shares our experience and our preferences. We fail to see beyond ourselves.[3] By now, I know that learning to swim is a function of leisure and access—time to practice and a place to swim. Across the South during Mary's youth, most public beaches and pools were closed to Black people. In our bubble of white solipsism, my mother and I did not consider that Mary might not have learned to swim. We had not learned about the Middle Passage, either—how generations of Africans had been kidnapped and transported by white shippers across the ocean to be enslaved in the U.S. and the Caribbean. We lacked a way to imagine that the embodied trauma of those crossings might still linger in a young African American woman's apprehension of the sea.

My father took a photograph on that Nantucket beach a few years later, during a summer when Mary's first cousin, Linda Johnson, came in her place. In the photograph, Linda Johnson is in her early twenties. She stands uncomfortably on the sloped beach, squinting into bright sunshine. Her back is to the ocean. Her uniform stands out, glaringly white. I doubt that Linda Johnson wanted her picture taken at that moment; she was working and not in her own clothes. Mary's summer position—sometimes passed along to her younger family members—might have been a decent job as domestic service went, but, from the perspective of time, Linda's discomfort in front of my father's camera suggests that posing for him in this way was a trying burden.

My father pasted the photo into his scrapbook of Nantucket summers. Next to the photo, he wrote: "Linda Johnson does not like to swim." I imagine he chuckled over the caption, thought his humor archly witty. Today I hear, not just a dis-

---

[3] In a powerful 1979 essay called "Disloyal to Civilization," poet Adrienne Rich defined white solipsism in this useful way: "not the consciously held belief that one race is inherently superior to all others, but a tunnel-vision which simply does not see non-white experience or existence as precious or significant."

paraging joke but the myopia of privilege. Dad seemed to assume that Linda could swim and was choosing not to. He ignored (or was ignorant of) the factors in Linda's life that may have kept her from learning to swim. And, what if she did know how to swim? Exactly because Dad had succeeded so well in his goal of vacationing in an elite, white enclave, he must have known that Linda was not welcome to use the beach and water for her own pleasure. On that beach, Black people were tolerated only in glaring white service uniforms. Linda Johnson was not allowed to swim.

A friend's college-age son once worked a summer job at a Nantucket hotel. When I asked this young white man at the end of that summer how the island had struck him, he lifted tanned hands in the air, palms up. "White people swimming," he said. He nailed Nantucket. White people in bathing suits strolled long, sandy beaches, refreshed themselves in the chilly Atlantic Ocean, and played in frothy surf that tumbled in from Portugal. A century earlier, a prosperous free community of Black whalers and sea captains had lived on Nantucket, owning homes, starting their own school, building businesses and a church, and leading the island's abolition movement. After the whale oil market went bust in the mid-nineteenth century, many of the island's Black residents left to seek opportunities elsewhere. Having lost the sources of income provided by the booming whaling industry, those who remained experienced increasing poverty and illness, and continued to suffer the racism of white Nantucketers. By the time that Mary came to Nantucket in the mid-twentieth century, Black and brown Nantucketers worked as maids, construction workers, and garbage collectors, while white people swam.

My father's photo and quip do not, in the end, tell anything about Linda Johnson, may she rest in peace. They speak of my father's limits, and my mother's, and mine, before I began to learn how much I didn't know.

On the private beaches of my youth, or in the Pretty Brook private pool in Princeton, I didn't notice that I swam only with white people, let alone wonder why. As I consider this question today, I land, with a queasy feeling, on the pseudo-science of eugenics. Shortly before my birth, Hitler exploited eugenics to assert the supremacy of the Aryan "master" race over Jews, homosexuals, and Romani people—and to legitimize genocide. Eugenics in the United States has long fed the myth that Anglo-Saxon white people are genetically—and thus physically, mentally, and morally—superior to non-affluent immigrants and people of color. According to this lie and scare tactic, swimming in the same water as Black people threatened to make white people sick. Beneath this lie was fear of miscegenation. Health became a convenient rationale for exclusion. I say "convenient," because, as Black medical sociologist Dorothy Roberts observes in her groundbreaking book, *Fatal Invention: How Science, Politics and Business Recreate Race in the Twenty-First Century*, eugenics has nothing to do with health: "In reality, eugenics enforced social judgments about race, class and gender cloaked in scientific terms."

The lies of eugenics featured in my own upbringing. My mother's aristocratic mother used to refer to people from the lower classes—New York's Irish and Italian immigrants, for example, and the Black people who came to the city from the South during early waves of the Great Migration—as "the great unwashed." My grandmother wore gloves every time she left home and taught me to do so, as though there were dirty people out there from whose grime and germs I must protect myself.

❧

Within a week of Mary's arrival in Nantucket, this became a new normal for my vacationing family: Mary in the kitchen, Mary making beds and vacuuming, Mary in her room at the ironing board, a sea breeze sucking and flapping the shades. Peeking discreetly through a slightly opened living room door to see what my mother needed, Mary entered the main part of the house only to clean or to bring or to take away. She performed her job so well—and so invisibly—that my mother quickly found her service to be indispensable.

The work of sociologist Judith Rollins helps me understand more critically many aspects of my family's relationship to Mary's role that first summer, and helps my memory turn a sharper edge. Graduate of Howard University and Brandeis University, and recently retired as Professor of Africana Studies and Sociology at Wellesley College, Dr. Rollins began her career with a prize-winning 1985 study titled *Between Women: Domestics and Their Employers.* In her research for the book, she interviewed white employers and Black domestic workers in the Boston area and took several domestic jobs in white families, herself. This was in the 1980s, nearly thirty years after Mary's arrival in my family's summer kitchen, but the dynamics that Rollins writes about ring true. Take, for example, the way my parents warmed to Mary's sweet willingness. Rollins says, "[T]o maneuver oneself into a satisfactory position—one not overly physically demanding, with more than minimal material benefits and with job security—one must have a pleasing personality as well as, if not more than, good housework skills." Mary's pleasing personality was absolutely necessary to her success in the job.

When Rollins posed as a domestic worker for her research,

she was stunned to find that members of the employers' families talked, joked, even fought, in the same room where she was at work as if she was not present. They acted as though she were invisible, not present, not a human being. The deadly antecedents of this invisibility come clear to me in a contemporary poem by Terrance Hayes. In "Antebellum House Party," Hayes conjures wooden furniture as a many-layered metaphor for the scandalous fact that plantation owners regarded, and treated, enslaved Africans as inhuman objects. "To make the servant in the corner unobjectionable / Furniture," Hayes's speaker begins, "we must first make her a bundle of tree parts / Axed and worked to confidence." I recoil from the brutal image of a human being *axed*. I think, *My family was not brutal like that*. But being unobjectionable is exactly what my parents wanted from Mary. To succeed in domestic service, a person must axe away anything that might draw attention.

The enslaver in Hayes's poem wants his workers to be invisible. Furniture, he says, "Can stand so quietly in a room that the room appears empty." My parents valued Mary's invisibility, her gift for doing her work without drawing notice to herself. They would have said that they saw her as a human being, but they wanted her, like furniture, to be invisible. Hayes's poem even foretells breakfast in my family's rented beachside living room that summer: "Boss calls / For sugar and the furniture bears it sweetly." I remember how often my parents praised Mary for being a "sweet girl," and so willing. Her seamless invisibility made her work eminently satisfactory, her presence a guarantee of normalcy in the many summers to come. A century may have divided Mary's service from the inhumanity of chattel slavery, but these haunting parallels reveal the institution of domestic service to be damningly unchanged.

∾

My father arrived on schedule from New York's LaGuardia Airport to Nantucket that first Friday evening. He visited briefly in the kitchen, looking tall and distinguished in his gray suit, his wavy brown forelock neatly combed and his intense gray-green eyes friendly. When he was introduced to the new member of our household, he spoke in the lilting, infantilizing tone he reserved for young children. "Mary White—what a nice, simple name for a pretty little colored girl," he said. "Mrs. C. tells me you are doing a fine job." His words could have landed with Mary as kind intention or clueless condescension—or both. The spatula shook in Mary's hand the next day as she fried the corned beef hash and tomatoes for my father's first lunch. She'd spent all morning getting ready. Three times she washed the hard, yellow plastic plates and cups and dried them with a fresh white dish towel. I thank Judith Rollins's work for informing me that, though the woman of the house may give the instructions, the women who do domestic work always identify the real boss. As I remember Mary's nervousness serving my father for the first time, I take her trembling hands as signs of a reasoned apprehension, a well-founded worry about pleasing him.

I was playing solitaire at the kitchen table when my mother came out to say that the first lunch had been perfect. Next weekend, she said, she and my father would have a small dinner party on Saturday evening. Mary wiped and re-wiped the counter and said, "Yes, Mrs. Coppedge," but she looked like she was going to worry until then.

"I can help!" I said.

"I trust that by next Saturday you'll have plenty of friends to be busy with," my mother said.

"You should be out having fun," Mary said.

The two of them stood side by side, looking at me together, agreeing with each other about what I should be doing. For the next thirty years, the bond between Mary and my mother would both feature and exclude me, stirring my jealousy and troubling my ethics.

two

Where We Came From

MARY AND I ENTERED MY FAMILY'S NANTUCKET KITCHEN IN 1956 from different doors, each of us a fresh sprout on a family tree. For decades, Mary knew more about my family than I did about hers. Studying my family was part of her job description. Ignoring her life was part of my training. It's taken me years to piece together the history of the family and community that helped to shape Mary. Here's what I've learned so far, rendered through my white gaze.

Mary's great grandfather Reece Cox was born to enslaved parents in Grayson County, Virginia, in 1858, five years before the Emancipation Proclamation ended the institution of chattel slavery. As was the practice in that brutal institution, Reece Cox bore his enslaver's last name. Mary's great grandmother, Mary Blevins, was born ten years later, just over the Grayson County border in North Carolina. She was born into freedom: her mother, Cintha Blevins, had been enslaved. In truth, although the Emancipation Proclamation freed enslaved Africans in 1863, many Southern enslavers delayed acting on emancipation for as long as they could get away with it. They paid almost nothing for the freedmen's labor. So, although Mary's great-grandparents were legally free, they grew up, married, and succeeded in making their family under conditions only marginally different from enslavement.

In 1884, Reece Cox and Mary Blevins married and settled in Grayson County. They were farmers, like their parents, and lived for many years as sharecroppers on the land where Mr. Cox had been enslaved. A photo on a website called Find a Grave presents Reece and Mary Cox in 1900. (Find a Grave is a resource that serves family members searching for death and burial information about distant or long-ago loved ones.) Reece and Mary Cox are seated, with the four children born to them by that time. Mr. Cox, who is forty-two, wears a dark suit, as do the three young sons standing soberly behind. Thirty-two-year-old Mary Blevins Cox, her hair pulled back tightly from her face, wears a high-necked dress in a dark, heavy material. Standing between her parents, as if supporting herself with an arm draped across each lap, is a two-year-old daughter dressed all in white. This is Verna, future grandmother to twentieth-century Mary. As in most photos from that era, due in part to the limits of early camera technology, no one is smiling. Mary Blevins Cox's expression is dead serious, resolute, even severe. Little Verna's look is so serious as to be almost a scowl. Reece and Mary Cox and their children seem to be saying: "Life is hard, work is hard, but we are here, and we will survive."

This photograph from more than a century ago is a reminder that Mary's great-grandparents belonged to the very first generation in which African American families could count on staying together. For three hundred years, slaveholders had destroyed Black families for profit—selling children away from mothers and wives from husbands; working parents to within an inch of their lives; raping women and forcing them, like live-

stock, to bear children. This portrait of Mary's great-grandparents, taken just thirty-five years after Emancipation, records,
asserts, and celebrates the family's ongoing and intact existence.[1]

A later photo shows "Reece Cox, circa 1904, in front of the
Independence Courthouse." Reece Cox sits in a wooden chair
looking directly at the camera. He wears a dark suit with a vest
and a small watch fob with a thin, looping chain. His large
hands, crossed in his lap, look capable, worn, and ready for action despite the formality of the pose. He is about forty-five
years old. In three years, his wife Mary Blevins Cox will die. She
will not yet be forty.

Verna Cox grew up to marry Dailey Phipps, a local man who
worked, like Verna's father, for the white landowners who had
enslaved his family. After the marriage, Verna Cox Phipps did
domestic work for the same landowners. This arrangement cre-

---

1 The work of historian and photographer Deborah Willis has helped me to understand the
role of photography in African American communities after the Civil War. Deborah Willis
is a former curator of photography at the Smithsonian Institution and professor of
photography and imaging at New York University's Tisch School of the Arts. One of her
master works, *Reflections in Black: A History of Black Photographers 1840 to the Present*,
introduces the context of this portrait of Mary's ancestors. The person behind the camera
may have been one of the growing number of Black photographers in the second half of the
nineteenth century. Maybe he traveled through Virginia's Grayson County as an itinerant
photographer or ran a studio in a nearby town. Clients ranged from rural to urban, from
middle-class community leaders to poor farmers and domestic workers. These
photographers worked to counteract racist images created by their white counterparts.

Willis observes that the low cost of photography at the turn of the century "made the
portrait available to many." Like many poor farming families who struggled for food and
shoes and shelter, Reece and Mary Cox probably scrimped in order to pay for this sober
record of their family's enduring existence. They had survived enslavement. Their children
were with them and none were at risk of being sold off. Willis points out that most of the
portraits taken at that time were not intended for publication or public presentation.
African American clients "merely wanted to have their likenesses preserved for future
generations." The survival of Mary's family photographs through more than a hundred years
would accomplish that very aim. Reece and Mary Cox built a family that survives to this
day; Mary's grandchildren, one a 2016 Rutgers University graduate, can view the ancestors
whose perseverance made their own path possible.

ated a heightened financial vulnerability for the couple, and further extended the shadow of enslavement, harking back to many centuries when every member of an enslaved family was forced to labor for the plantation master. In the early years, Dailey and Verna Phipps lived in a small cabin in one corner of the white family's farm. Mary Norman remembers her mother, Alice Mae Phipps, talking about being invited as a child to play with the white Phipps children while her mother Verna Phipps did her work, how the white mother checked Alice all over to make sure she was "clean," and how insulted Alice felt by this inspection. No wonder the Black Phipps family moved off the white Phipps family's land as soon as they could afford to do so.

In a step that made a lasting contribution to the family's long-term survival, Mary believes that one of Verna Phipps's older brothers wrote his sister into his life insurance policy. When he died rather young, Verna and Dailey Phipps were able to purchase a plot of land with a small house on it, on a steep hill on the outskirts of the town of Independence, Virginia. Later, one of Verna and Dailey's older sons went into the military quite young, and sent his "allotment" home each month. By saving all that he sent, his parents were able to build a somewhat larger house, though still with no running water or electricity. Owning a home and arable land enabled Mary's grandparents, by working day and night both at home and for their white employers, to make a marginally better life for themselves and their eight children. Perhaps because of the sheer workload, and because he endured the first decades of white retribution and terror known as Jim Crow, Dailey Phipps died relatively young at 60.

≈

Mary was born in 1940 in Independence, and spent most of her childhood living with her grandmother Verna Phipps, whom she called "Mamaw." Soon after giving birth to Mary, Alice Mae Phipps had gone to find work in New York City, leaving her baby in her mother's capable hands. Mary has a dim memory of traveling with Mamaw by train all the way to New York to visit her mother, how tightly Mamaw gripped her hand.

Although Alice Mae Phipps had joined the northward current of the Great Migration, she soon chose to come home. While in New York, she fell in love with George Johnson, a World War II vet from back home in Grayson County. They came home to settle a few miles from Independence, in a rural hamlet called Elk Creek. He worked in dry cleaning, and she followed her mother into domestic service. Countering the pattern of most banks in the country after the War, a local white banker who liked and respected George Johnson made it possible for him to get a loan to build a house. Young Mary was told that the small house in Elk Creek, a ten-mile walk from where she lived in Independence, would have no room for her. The George Johnsons started what would become a family of six children. Mary grew up in Verna and Dailey Phipps's home with her youngest aunt, Dot. In her early teens, Mary got to spend more time with her Johnson kin than she had as a child, but she would always feel like an outsider.

After Dailey Phipps's death, Verna Phipps continued to work full-time in domestic service for a white family in Independence while growing her family's food on the rocky, hillside acreage. To make ends meet, she sold eggs and milk to neighbors. Mrs. Phipps depended greatly on the work of the two children who remained in her household: her youngest daughter Dot and granddaughter Mary. Mornings, Mary had to tend the farm animals before school—the cow, pigs, and chickens. She hated the henhouse most of all, and remembers offering to do every other job if Dot would only clean the henhouse. Weekdays, Mary headed a mile down a steeply sloped country road to the uninsulated single room that served as a schoolhouse for the town's Black children.

Once she turned eleven, Mary cleaned house and did ten loads of wash every Saturday for a nearby white family. Mary describes this work: "You run the clothes through, rinse them in two tubs of water, put them through the wringer, hang them out on the line, then you run the vacuum cleaner, then it's time to get the clothes off the line, then you fold them, then you start ironing . . . maybe fifteen or sixteen shirts." Saturday nights, Mary, Dot, and Mamaw laundered and pressed their own clothes for church the next day. Young Mary learned early on how to iron her Sunday hair ribbons. Sunday morning, no matter how weary the week had made any of them, Mamaw marched her charges out the door to walk the six miles to Oak Grove Methodist Church. Mary grew up at that church, a youngster chasing around the patchy grass with her friends after services, a preteen whose first kiss came at a church picnic. Many Sundays, the minister drove them home and stayed for dinner. Mary recalls with no little resentment that he always ate the best part of the chicken.

Mary grew up with her Mamaw at the height of Jim Crow restrictions on Black people in the South. "In Independence, there were white-only water fountains," she says. "It was the back door at a restaurant if you wanted to get a hot dog or hamburger, the back of the bus station if you were going somewhere, back of the bus for the ride." Mamaw prided herself on growing their food and making their clothes so successfully that they barely had to shop in town at all; she was proud to be able to keep what money she had away from the racist storekeepers. "It was a hurtful time," Mary remembers, but she remembers, too, that her grandmother and mother protected her from many of the hurts of racism and poverty. "They were actresses," she says. "They could have been in the movies."

Verna Cox Phipps, the fiercely scowling child in that early photograph, was a memorably strict mother and grandmother. Mary tells me, "Whatever my grandmother said, that's what it was." Mamaw prided herself on an impeccably clean and orderly house, set exacting rules, and punished a disobedient girl's infractions. More than once, Mary and Dot secretly skimmed the cream off a jug of fresh milk that Mamaw had put aside to sell, and made themselves ice cream. When customers complained of thin milk, Mamaw whipped the two culprits with a switch cut from the pear tree. (Mary remembers the ice cream as thrillingly delicious.) A few years later, Mamaw sent Mary as a chaperone for teenage Dot on a rare date. When the two tried to tiptoe back into the house way past curfew, Dot quite inebriated, they found Mamaw awake and alert by the wood stove, with the switch in her hand. "I sometimes wonder whether religion or my grandmother had the most influence on me," Mary says. "You feared the wrath of either."

Mary has told me of pleasures, too. In rare free moments, she liked to lie across her Mamaw's bed and gaze out the window to search for shapes in the clouds. Rainy days, she daydreamed on the same bed, listening to the sound of rain on the tin roof.

On cold nights, she cuddled up to her grandmother's warm body and long flannel nightgown. And she enjoyed her clothes. "I always had pretty dresses, because my grandmother sewed; she made me dresses out of the very colorful feed sacks that the pig's grain came in back then." Mary's three older aunts, who doted on her, saved up to give her pretty store-bought dresses. To this day, Mary is a stylish dresser.

There were frights, as well. Mary dreaded escorting Mamaw to the outhouse in the night, startled at every sound in the looming mountain darkness. She dreaded the long black snakes that lived in the banks on either side of the steep, lonely walk down the hill to the school bus. The snakes always seemed to be racing after her, ready to bite. To help her granddaughter feel safe from the snakes on her way to the bus, Mamaw walked with her down the first part of the hill, and then stood, waving, on a small promontory where Mary could spot her for the rest of the descent. When Mary trudged up the hill after school, there Mamaw would be, standing on the special spot, encouraging Mary in the climb. This is one of the ways Mary learned faithfulness. Stern Verna Phipps was faithful—to her children, to Oak Grove Methodist (where the congregation honored her as "Mother"), and to the growing granddaughter in her care.

Another fright lurked indoors. In her Mamaw's house, a photograph of Mary Blevins Cox, her great-grandmother, hung in a closet under Mamaw's stairs. "I used to be afraid of that closet all the time," Mary says. "You know those old oval frames, how the person sits there with her hair all pulled back? She was very pale, with eyes that seemed to follow you. I used to be so scared of that picture. I hated going in that closet as much as I hated getting eggs from the henhouse." Whether or not the 1900 family photo on Find a Grave is the same one that caused young

Mary to race past the closet, holding her breath, I imagine that her great-grandmother looked as fierce and determined, as somber and strict, as she does in the photo online—stern enough to frighten a child. And Mary says, "Those old photographs are so sad. My grandmother barely escaped all the things her mother went through. It was just awful."

My parents, Roy and Nina, came from two very different families, both white, but foundationally different in class status and wealth. The fault lines shaped their marriage—and my life.

In 1849, a white farming couple in Rome, Georgia, welcomed the son who would become my father's grandfather. Zachary Taylor Coppedge, they named him, after the then U.S. President. In his teens, Zachary served in the Confederate Army. He was "paroled" at the end of the Civil War, when he was just sixteen years old. I have wanted to imagine my great grandfather conscripted, forcibly dragged away to war as no more than a boy, but he may have volunteered eagerly to defend white southerners' right to enslave Black people. A decade later, Zachary married Dora Virginia Wood, an impoverished white orphan who had been worked abusively by the family that took her in. Farming was hard, and Zachary was a heavy drinker, so Dora took in sewing to support their three sons. Two of their sons, including my grandfather, "married up," raising their own social standing by marrying daughters of prosperous Georgia businessmen. I've learned from Georgia cousins that Dora never much liked her sons' well-off wives. Bitterly proud of her decades of work as a seamstress, she deemed them spoiled and lazy. The two women tried to win her affection through store-bought gifts; she returned the items for cash.

My father's father, Roy, could reportedly add columns of five-digit numbers in his head. The family story is that, with this skill, he worked his way up from stock boy to president at Mc-Crory's, a now defunct dime store chain that originated in the 1880s in Pennsylvania—though I imagine his rise in the company may also have been helped by his having "married up." He and Norma Jones, the daughter of a country doctor from LaGrange, Tennessee, followed his job around the South and landed at last in New York City with their two children. One was my father, Roy Junior.

At sixteen, my father began his own climb. He got himself from a Bronx high school into an Ivy League college, a step for which his father could offer no guidance. At Dartmouth, he majored in sociology but later told me that he rarely attended class; instead, he went to movies, played bridge, and set out to devour the classics of English literature on his own. Mastering the canon of writings by white British men turned out to be good training for a rise in social status. At another Ivy League school, Columbia Law, he immersed himself in U.S. law, which was essentially British law applied to the U.S. scene. He emerged a well-shaped Anglophile, his lineage retuned for a future he intended to engineer for himself. Then, as Hitler threatened England's shores, and the United States dallied about whether to go to war on her behalf, Roy trained to become an officer in the U.S. Army. He would be stationed in London during the war, where he would eagerly soak up the tradition-bound conservatism of old Tory Britain.

My mother's family was patrician and wealthy. Her grandmother, Lavinia Riker, was born in 1866 at "Oak Hill," an estate in Newtown, Queens County, Long Island. She came from a long line of prosperous Dutch colonials, who first arrived in the settlement called New Amsterdam (soon to be called New York) in the seventeenth century. My early Riker ancestors brought with them acquisitive European codes of ownership and profit that were inimical to the values of shared community that were predominant in America's indigenous people. And so, like so many white settlers in the so-called "new" world, they became wealthy. The Riker family claimed, fenced, farmed, and gave their name to an arable island in the East River. Long before Lavinia's birth, the Riker family sold their island to the city of New York. That Riker's Island became the site of a wretched state incarceration facility known for multiple abuses of its inmates, who are mainly Black and Brown people, is a revealing irony.

In the 1880s, Nina Riker married James Remsen Strong, a fellow WASP aristocrat, in an elaborate society wedding. Edith Wharton's novels of New York's upper classes at the turn of the twentieth century give me a sense of the opulence of Nina and Jim's wedding and their ensuing life. Nina and Jim enjoyed large Victorian homes in New Jersey and on the Cape Cod shore, a staff of ten servants, family tours of Europe (steamer trunks and all), a large white sailing yacht with a full-time paid captain dressed all in white, and one of the earliest motor cars. Into this old-money opulence came my grandmother, Charlotte, and, a generation later, my mother, Nina.

When mutual friends introduced Roy, the rising young lawyer and military officer, to Manhattan debutante Nina Riker Van Vechten, with her golden hair and prominent ancestors, her daring blue eyes, and her love for a good time, he fell for her and she for him. I imagine Dad felt ready to "marry up" into my mother's upper-class world. His future mother-in-law did not agree. Charlotte was a social snob of such a high order that she never entirely approved of her own husband's pedigree. I imagine that Dad squirmed under her aristocratic disapproval like the beetles she plucked off her prize roses and dropped into killing kerosene. Before long, my dad would begin to resent bitterly the very upper-class cachet that drew him to my mother. Still, a society photographer preserved my future parents' wedding day, as they burst through church doors onto Park Avenue in December 1941—Nina like a movie star with her creamy satin train, her wavy blond pageboy and good teeth, Roy striding forward in a British-style morning coat that he had rented but aspired one day to own.

Three days into my parents' Bermuda honeymoon, the bombing of Pearl Harbor sent the country into war and my newlywed father to the Blitz and terror of nightly air raids in London. The fallout of my dad's experiences during World War II may have impacted our family life as much as the fault lines of class.

three

Learning the Habits of Dominance

AFTER THE NIGHTMARE OF WORLD WAR II, MOST WHITE
families who could afford to live on one income settled into
gendered role divisions—fathers away all day at work, mothers
tending the home, children groomed for success. My family did
the same. Roy returned from the war physically whole and still
striving. Soon he began commuting to a Manhattan law firm
from Princeton, New Jersey. In that ivied college town, he and
Nina set out to raise me and my new baby brother according to
her aristocratic traditions and his urgent aspiration.

While stationed in London as a U.S. Army officer in World
War II, my father had become even more of an Anglophile. In
the family, he touted what he called "the King's English," though
he never adopted the airs of a British accent. He was a stickler
for diction, insisting that my brother and I choose exactly the
correct word, and never mispronounce. Perhaps to sound more
British, my family said *tomahto* instead of *tomayto*; as a child, I
wondered why we didn't say *potahto*. When I became a feminist
and health activist in my twenties and first spoke to my father
about the sexual harassment of women, he interrupted me. "It's
HAR-assment, my darling daughter. Not har-ASS-ment," he

said, enunciating ASS as though I'd said a dirty word. Through my life, he would fend off many unsettling ideas by focusing on my diction.

I started school at Miss Fine's, a private day school for children of Princeton's affluent white families. There, and throughout my schooling, I got straight As in reading, writing and "proper" diction. This pleased my father. In language, I found an affinity with him that was more perfect than I knew. In language, I carried his humbler genes into the upper class.

Boarding school for tenth through twelfth grades in Maryland continued my education. Sending teenagers to boarding school was a practice copied from England, where upper-class boys as young as nine or ten had long been sent away to be shaped into the future elite. Even in the purportedly classless United States, the preparatory schools of fifty years ago prepared an elite few for a life of "high" culture and social privilege. Prep schools honed young men into future CEOs and judges, directors of institutions, presidents of colleges and nations. The stated desire of St. Timothy's School in Stevenson, Maryland, the boarding school to which my parents sent me, was to shape girls into "Christian gentlewomen."

St. Timothy's in the 1950s was, for me, a training ground in white privilege. I lived and learned with girls from wealthy, white, and mainly Protestant families from Chicago, New York, Baltimore, and New Orleans. The teachers and dorm mothers were all white; the servants all Black. The teachers did not invite us to wrestle with Maryland's centuries as a plantation economy dependent on chattel slavery. They did not teach about Harriet Tubman and Frederick Douglass—two legendary Maryland-born activists who spearheaded anti-slavery resistance before and after the Civil War. They did not prompt us to connect the

Civil War, which we studied in history class, to the Black people who served us—women who labored in the steaming hot school kitchen, and Fred, the friendly driver who regaled us with spirituals in his deep bass voice on Sunday mornings as he drove the school's sky-blue bus to the local Episcopal church. Nothing in my schooling led me to realize that most of the serving staff were only two or three generations away from the chains and brutality of enslavement. To be successful in their jobs at the school, Fred and the cooks were required to smile, which they did, and to be kind to us, which they were. No one told us that their great-grandparents may have been flogged to within an inch of their lives for not picking their daily quota of tobacco, the crop that made Maryland's plantation owners wealthy. No one told us that, when Fred and the kitchen staff went to the nearby town for shopping or recreation, American apartheid banned them from every public establishment defined as for "whites only"—soda fountains, movie theaters, transportation, restrooms.

My tenth-grade English teacher assigned an anthology of noted British and (a few) American essayists. All were white men. She instructed us to choose an author and to imitate that writer's prose style in an essay of our own. I twined my filly legs beneath the gray wool skirt of my school's winter uniform and leafed through the anthology, looking for a voice I wanted to try out for myself.

Five years earlier in Harlem, a part of the very city in which I was born, thirty-one-year-old James Baldwin had written "Notes of a Native Son." Baldwin's essay—now one of the best known in the English language—could have offered me not only a powerful prose style to emulate but also a way of understanding my complex, contradictory father. In words that would sing for me decades later with their mix of knowing, estrangement, and anguished love, he wrote of his own father: "He could be chilling in the pulpit and indescribably cruel in his personal life and he was certainly the most bitter man I have ever met; yet it must be said that there was something else in him, buried in him, which lent him his tremendous power and, even, a rather crushing charm." Studying "Notes of a Native Son" in tenth grade could also have schooled me in the racism at work in my home state of New Jersey. Of his first job—at a wartime munitions factory there—Baldwin wrote, "I learned in New Jersey that being a Negro meant, precisely, that one was never looked at but was simply at the mercy of the reflexes that the color of one's skin caused in other people."

If Baldwin's essay had been in my tenth-grade anthology, I doubt that I would have chosen him as my guide. The truths about race, class, and family that he conveyed with such lyricism and power contradicted the schooling my parents had secured for me. In my schools, Western civilization—the doings of affluent and influential white men, from the Greeks onward—marked the apex and entirety of human accomplishment.

I selected Sir Francis Bacon, a seventeenth-century Londoner. My chaste lips pressed tightly against each other in concentration, I mastered semicolons and dependent clauses, exposition and argument, multisyllabic words, and more semicolons. I practiced writing whole paragraphs that were one long sentence. I got an A. For years afterwards, I thought I wrote a little like Sir Francis, and this made me proud.

My father's attention to language, and the education he and my mother secured for me, launched my love of writing. At Radcliffe College, I majored in "English"—a field that, in the late 1950s and early '60s, focused on white, British men. To my father's chagrin, however, I would soon venture outside any canon he had known. Within ten years, I would be writing completely differently. As coauthor and editor of *Our Bodies, Ourselves,* a book on women's health and sexuality, I would work collaboratively rather than seeking to make my own name. I would write about orgasm and the profit motive in health care. Soon I'd be writing love letters to a woman. I would betray the King's English—or at least the king.

The King's English, however—the language and thinking of imperial Britain—continued to shape my thinking. Years later, when a Black friend sent me a column she had written for a local newspaper, I felt distracted by what I saw as grammatical errors. "Will readers take her seriously?" I wondered, imagining every reader a stickler like my father, like myself. I brashly, inappropriately offered to edit future essays for this highly popular essayist; she declined. To this day, I correct my family and friends' grammar, even when they don't ask. I inform my spouse when she mispronounces—once, "nuclear" and another time "rhododendron." She bristles at my assumption of superiority, my effort to correct and control her. My father's ghost still hovers at my shoulder, listening for the sounds of "proper" English via Anglophile and patriarchal distinctions that do not serve me well.

In the imperial British way of thinking that my upbringing fostered in me, dichotomy rules. Right, wrong. Superior, inferior. Light, dark. Male, female. Win, lose. Hierarchy rules, too. In family and church, in government and kingdom, in a well-ordered world, those on top of each sacred dichotomy claim the right to wield power over the rest. And, to demand order: "Speak one at a time, please, no interrupting each other, or I can't understand you." When I do not work actively to uproot much of what my family and schooling taught me, these hierarchical and elitist ways of thinking structure my personality, my aspirations, and my ideas. I emerged from my schooling with a large dose of internalized superiority and a habit of dominance.

Ironically, as far as I might think I have come from my father's training, I circle back to him in the end. My father and I both reformed ourselves through reading—he the English classics, and I a new African-American canon. I have found my own passions and rarely now read works that were on my father's agenda. But, like him in his years of intense upward mobility, I read to remake myself. I read to fill the silences and omissions of my childhood. Perhaps unlike him, I read to become a citizen of the multicultural world that is our life in this country.

In the very gendered 1950s white America, my own grooming for "success" meant learning to be an educated and graceful companion for the (upper-class, white) man they trusted I would one day marry. To this end, my mother's role was to teach me "good taste."

My mother was unwaveringly stylish. (She and Mary would always have this in common.) In her early twenties, Nina joined other Manhattan socialites in Bundles for Britain, to gather relief supplies and money for our long-time ally in the face of Hitler's air attacks. Among her treasures after her death, I found a 1985 *LIFE* Magazine retrospective on World War II. On page twenty-four, there is a shot of my mother circa 1940, her shapely young leg propped up, counting donated shoes as they tumbled down a chute. The camera caressed her slender body and stylish dark suit. In my time, feminists would decry the fact that males are encouraged to be active and instrumental, while females are supposed to be passive and ornamental—a dichotomy that works to the detriment of women's agency and power. But the word "ornament," though apt in many ways, does not convey the purposeful seriousness of my mother's approach to her wardrobe —and to mine. She communicated a sense of heritage to be honored and honed—the watchful presence of the generations of women in her family who had taught her, as she was teaching me, to dress and carry herself with the refinement and care that signaled our supposed class superiority.

I remember my mother saying, "That dress is just too Witherspoon Street," referring to the section of Princeton where immigrant Italians and Black families lived. She used "Witherspoon Street" to signify bad taste in the same coded way with which people today say "urban" to mean troubled, dangerous, poor, or, simply, Black and Brown communities. When she said that a dress was "too Witherspoon Street," I pictured tired wooden houses leaning close together, dark-skinned old men and women sitting on unpainted stoops, young boys playing, running, chasing, laughing, and yelling, scaring me when my mother used their street as a shortcut.

Private schooling offered me no help in understanding the Witherspoon Street neighborhood that was my mother's codeword for our family's superior taste. At the end of World War II, shortly after my birth, Congress passed the GI Bill, which gave returning soldiers a chance to borrow money at low interest in order to invest in good housing for their families. However, white GIs gained this access to Levittown and similar suburban developments, while Black GIs did not. Banks continued to refuse Black people loans for houses in economically advantageous areas, just as banks always had. Better paying business and union jobs still went to white workers, poor paying and dangerous jobs to Black workers. The racist policies and practices in government, banking, and business gave white people "a leg up" and left Witherspoon Street residents to fend for themselves. I learned none of this.

Growing up in the comfort and isolation of an affluent, wooded college town, I also learned nothing about communities as defined by neighborhoods—nothing about neighborhood life. I would not, until years later, learn the sustaining strength of a community where old people sit out on stoops, visiting together and watching out for the children's safety.

Poor taste, according to my mother's measure, was not limited to "Witherspoon Street." When I was seven and entering second grade, a thrillingly large box arrived for me in the mail. By then, my father's father had worked his way up to the presidency of the McCrory five and dime chain, and the box was from my granddaddy. In between layers of tissue paper, my mother and I found a treasure of dresses. Red, orange, yellow, purple, and blue. Flower imprints, ruffles, long sashes, shiny patent-leather belts. One dress, my absolute favorite, sported a cluster of little red-painted plaster cherries at the waist.

I exclaimed with delight, but my mother didn't. She placed the box on top of the new clothes dryer down in the musty basement. As soon as my father came home from work that night, I led him down there to see my new treasures, but he lifted two or three of the dresses partially out of the box and let them fall back again. He didn't get to the one with the cherries.

I looked up at my tall father, still in his business suit and overcoat. "Can I try them on now?"

Dad sighed, as though tired from his commute, and looked to my mother for guidance.

"Are these the kinds of dresses that your friends wear?" my mother asked.

"They are more beautiful," I said. But it was my bedtime, she replied, and too late to try them on.

All the rest of that week, I inched down the steps into the basement to touch the dresses. Mom had bought me a woolen kilt in a real tartan plaid for school and cotton blouses with Peter Pan collars. But for me, the dresses from my grandfather were more colorful, more enticing.

I imagine that one evening while my little brother and I slept, my mother and father negotiated. Perhaps they agreed that dresses from a five-and-dime store were too "tacky" for me to wear at the elite Miss Fine's School. Or, perhaps my mother's dismissal of the gift galled my father—his dad had given the best he had. In the end, Dad joined my mother in a united front. Neither of them asked or cared about my opinion.

One day the box was gone. My mother told me she had given the dresses away to little girls who needed them more. I ran up to my room, slammed the door, fell onto my bed, and kicked against the mattress while I cried. I thought of my granddaddy, tall and round-bellied in his suspenders, how he let me sip Coca Cola from the chilly green bottle when he came home from work. My granddaddy would be sad if he knew that another little girl would get to bounce those bright red cherries in her hand on her way to school.

Sixty years later, the memory of my granddaddy's box of dresses sends me back to examine the training in social class that I received in my affluent white family and schooling, as I fought to stand stably in the crosswinds of my mother's privileged certainty and my father's edgy aspiration. This upper-class training is inextricably implicated in the story of racism and white supremacy in my life.

Americans don't like to address social class. Policy makers, and the media, have long assumed—or pretended—that our country is free of class distinctions. (In 2011, activists in the Occupy Wall Street movement would point out that the wealthy one percent of Americans live large on the sacrifices of the other ninety-nine percent.) In my childhood as a WASP, being upper or upper-middle class was about money, yes, but also about taste, culture, refinement, education in the "classics," high art. We didn't think specifically about class. We just thought ourselves superior.

As a child, I did not mix or mingle with children who were not white and wealthy. I believed what I had been implicitly taught: that anyone not like me was to be avoided, and that children who were dark-skinned and exuberant, especially boys, were a danger. As my mother sped our capacious, state-of-the-art family station wagon through the working-class Witherspoon Street neighborhood, I rolled up my window against imagined harm. My mother seemed to believe herself more cultured, more intelligent, better dressed, and simply just "better" than anyone we saw on those short-cut side streets. Feelings of superiority and feelings of fear are kin to each other and have the same effect: closed windows, closed minds.[1]

The WASP aristocracy into which I was born was on the wane as I came of age in the 1950s and '60s. WASP solipsism—

---

[1] I absorbed classism through my parents' teachings on language and taste, and through their assumption that being upper middle class (upper class, for my mother) made us superior to other people. In my life-long wrestling match with that internalized sense of superiority, Dr. Barbara Jensen has become a savvy coach-in-print. After growing up in a white working-class farming and factory family in Minnesota, Jensen worked her way through college and graduate school, earned a doctorate, and became a counselor and college professor. She wrote *Reading Classes: On Culture and Classism in America* from the rich and stressful borderland between her upper-middle-class academic life and the working-class family she respects and loves. Her deep regard for the ethos and strengths of her own working-class culture, and her analysis of key forms of classism in the U.S., continue to inform and challenge me.

our inability to see beyond our own narrow world, our tendency to use ourselves as the measure of excellence—would continue to misshape our perceptions, but our power was declining. There may already have been a defensive element to the WASP sense of superiority during my youth, a suspicion of upcoming displacement. In fact, laying a claim to superiority at all may be a defensive gesture.

I puzzle over how much my mother's dedication to good taste was a defensive move in itself. Her class standing was considered unassailable, but her gender opened her to risk. She told cautionary tales about female friends or acquaintances who had "let themselves go." As a girl, I didn't know what this meant, but she seemed to mean anything and everything from a "tacky" wardrobe to having too many children. Given how swiftly a woman could find herself thrust outside a safe and privileged circle, I suspect that fear may have helped to fuel my mother's lessons in the rules of "good taste."

four

Fog

ON FRIDAY MORNING OF MY FATHER'S SECOND WEEKEND commute to Nantucket that 1956 summer, beads of moisture quivered in the tiny squares of every window screen. As Mary and I ate our morning Rice Krispies, fog billowed outside the kitchen windows. Mary stood at the counter to eat breakfast, as if to be ready for my mother's next command, while I sat at the long wooden table. Standing while her employers sat was one of many forms of deference required of Mary that I did not notice at the time. As a domestic worker, Mary was to answer questions but never start a conversation, enter the main part of the house only to clean or serve, call my parents by their last name while they called her Mary. I could not, as a child in that kitchen, have named the required acts of deference, but certainly I internalized them. Much later, sociologist Judith Rollins named what I had witnessed—required behaviors that "underline the inferiority of the domestic worker."

My mother burst into the kitchen in her bathrobe, hair undone, pale lips. "What does your radio say, Mary? Is this fog going to go on all day?"

Mary dipped her head as though she had done something wrong. "I'm afraid so."

"Christ!" My mother swung around and slammed the kitchen door behind her.

When she opened the door again, a bobby pin held a limp curl off her forehead, and her lips glistened with red. "I apologize to you both for slamming the door like that. I've been awake half the night worrying about the airport getting fogged in."

The three of us looked out the window to the dripping clothesline. The nearest bushes were cloaked in gray mist. In my shorts and bare feet, I felt a chill.

That night, fog did close the Nantucket airport, and my father's flight from New York landed on Cape Cod. Dad caught the last ferry to the island. Long after I slept, my mother drove to meet him. The next morning, in the sunny kitchen, Mary reminded me not to slam the fridge or clatter the spoon in my cereal bowl. She whispered that Dad had been too tired to eat the dinner she kept ready for him. "He said he just wanted a drink and bed."

When we finally heard Dad in the living room, Mary smoothed her uniform and turned to the coffee pot on the stove. Her trembling hands rattled the cup on the saucer. She pulled a plate with toast and bacon from the oven. "Could you open that door for me?" she asked. My mother wanted the doors to the back of the house to stay closed: "It's a small house, and we don't want everyone on top of each other." She wanted the "help" to stay out of sight.

Peering through the narrow crack in the doorway after Mary entered the living room, I spotted my father's pale knee, the green and yellow squares of his madras shorts. Mary set the breakfast tray down on a low table by the sofa.

"Very nice, Mary, very nice," Dad said, almost in sing-song, like she was a little girl. "Are we keeping you busy enough out there in the kitchen?" he asked, chuckling.

Mary returned to the kitchen with a shy grin. She slid the butter knife into suds she had ready in the sink. "Your father is funny," she whispered. I didn't know what to say. To me, Dad seemed often crotchety, critical, quick to anger.

"Go on in and tell him good morning," Mary said. "He's fine," she added. Already, she'd adopted my mother's habits: measuring and explaining my father's moods, calibrating risk, studying surface behavior for possible fault lines or quakes. Already, Mary tried to please Dad into behaving well, so that we could all have some peace.

I entered the living room, with its wide pine floor boards, raftered ceiling, and picture window out to waves rolling across the world from Portugal. "Have a seat, little one," my father said. He patted the green cushion beside him, and I sat. He lit up a Camel and ran a hand over wiry brown hair that was starting to go gray at the temples. "Christ, what a trip I had last night. Do you like flying?"

I half nodded, half shook my head, waiting to see if he liked flying or not.

"Well, I don't," he said. "Never have. And circling over an airport in fog thick as pea-soup?" He looked quickly in the direction of the bedroom he shared with my mother. "It doesn't bring out the best in me."

When Mary came for the tray, he thanked her and said, "You seem to be doing an awfully good job out there, Mary." After she left the room, he shook his head. "You meet a nice girl like Mary—pretty, neat, intelligent—and you wish they could all be like that." He pointed to an article he'd been reading in the *Times*. "We're witnessing the downfall of the American system of public education, Wendy. These damned-fool liberals—hearts on their sleeves, blinders on their eyes. They are dooming the whole system by trying to educate the Negro."

In the future, I would remember Dad's racist views and find myself self-righteous, tempted to pin him down like a splayed specimen on a board: the racist. Humility would ease my urge to condemn him. Dad learned his erroneous views from white relatives and teachers who benefitted from living in a society built to favor white people. They wanted the same for him. White skin privilege was an advantage he neither recognized nor wanted to lose, and he wanted the same for me.

Dad tapped the face of his watch and frowned at the bedroom door. "9:30 a.m.," he announced. "Damned golf course on this island jams up by ten on a Saturday. I don't know why in hell your mother can't—"

The door opened. My mother zipped up her golfing skirt as she moved towards the kitchen. "I know," she said in my father's direction. "I'm hurrying." My mother returned from the kitchen with a glass of milk, and headed back to the bedroom. No lipstick yet. To appear on the golf course without lipstick, without a trim white skirt and tanned, smoothly shaven legs, would have violated the rules of her own position in life as a former debutante and wife of a rising professional man. She internalized this requirement so fully that she would have been horrified not to appear beautiful—even on a golf course. Dressing for golf was part of her work.

"Nina?" my father's voice, peremptory. She stopped, her back to us. "Three and a half minutes," he announced.

She didn't turn around. "Yes sir," she answered, the way privates spoke in army movies, only she was being sarcastic.

My father re-opened the newspaper roughly, snapping his elbows back. "A man works all week and travels two hundred miles in pea-soup fog so his wife can sun herself by the ocean, and she can't get ready for a goddamned golf game."

I sat straighter and watched him cautiously. I was one of the ones he got stuck in the fog for.

"Jesus Christ, Nina," he shouted towards the bedroom door. "A man needs the patience of a saint around here."

Later in the month, Dad took a week-long vacation. He and my mother played golf each morning, then had a swim and pre-lunch cocktails. "Relax is not a word I'd ever use for Roy," I heard my mother say to a friend on the telephone, "but he's getting some rest and a little fun." She had seemed more relaxed when he was in New Jersey.

Late one afternoon, she passed my bedroom door, carrying a newly pressed cocktail dress from Mary's room. In homes where servants work, freshly pressed clothes appear as if by magic. Lying on the spare bed in Mary's room earlier that afternoon, I had watched Mary fit the bodice of the silk cocktail dress over the narrow end of the ironing board, nose the iron expertly into the corners, lift the dress to check for wrinkles, pause to blot perspiration from the nape of her neck. As working-class writer Tillie Olsen famously observed, the lives and literature of the wealthy ignore and belittle the women who stand over the ironing board.

In my doorway with the cocktail dress, my mother said, almost nostalgically, "We've had some lovely times here, haven't we, Pumpkin, just the three of us?" I didn't think she meant my father. That day, "the three of us" included Mary.

Just a few years ago I asked Mary, on one of our weekly phone calls, what she remembered most from that first Nantucket summer. Her birthday, she said. She turned sixteen on July 20. "You called me out from my room into the kitchen, and there you all were," Mary remembered, "even your father, singing 'Happy Birthday.' You'd bought me a real bakery cake with white frosting and little chocolate sprinkles."

In my effort to understand Mary's lifelong loyalty to my parents, I come back to this cake, and our singing.

"I had birthday cakes before," Mary went on to say, "but that cake was special. I had never had a cake so prettily decorated. I'd only seen them in books, and this one was for me."

Thanks to Mary's skill, dependability and willing presence that first summer, and to my family's almost childish readiness to lean on her, we had grown to rely on Mary. Awkwardly clustered in the kitchen, without candles, we celebrated her. In that small moment of kindness, we gave Mary a sense of being loved. As one domestic worker said to Judith Rollins, "I was getting a little bit of love there. It did give me a sense of belonging. And I needed that."

On the day before my brother was due to arrive at the Nantucket beach house from overnight camp, my mother complained that Copey's arrival, with all his little-boy energy, couldn't be more poorly timed. My father was just beginning to relax, and now this.

"It's your last two days of vacation," Mom said to my father, as though he were to blame for her discomfort. "I'm not sure I can bear it."

That night, there was no breeze, no sound of surf splashing and sliding on the beach below my window. I woke suddenly to loud, angry voices stabbing the silence. Fast footsteps in the living room. A thump, a cry. A door slamming. Then, nothing. My heart pounded as though I'd been the one yelling, shoving, shouting, crying out. I lay flat in my bed, trying to settle back into calm. When I couldn't wait any longer to use the bathroom, I inched the bedroom door open and tiptoed into the dark of the back hall, praying that one of my parents wouldn't be passing through.

"Oh!" cried Mary, as we bumped up against each other in the dark. She grabbed the hand I put up in surprise.

"Sorry!" we both whispered at the same time, peering towards each other through the darkness. There were no more sounds of my parents' battle, only our breathing and listening.

For many years, Mary and I would not talk about the fights that punctured the nighttime quiet, but we shared a kind of witness. The next morning, unlike some other mornings, my mother had no visible bruises, but thumps and cries from the night seemed to echo through the house.

On Saturday, Copey arrived from sleep-over camp, tanned, lanky, and baseball-obsessed. That evening, my mother wanted me to take him to my friend's house. "He is most definitely not going to stay here in the living room with us. Mary's fixing a nice dinner before we go out for a nightcap. Tonight is not a time for small childr—"

Dad stirred. "Little fellow, we'll have a game of catch tomorrow morning, what do you say?"

I fled to my friend's house before Copey could tag along. I returned later to find my parents' car gone and the kitchen lights blazing. Mary was leaning against the kitchen counter, breathing hard. Copey looked dazed. Apparently, while Mary was in her room, Copey had put a hot dog in the oven, turned on the gas, left the kitchen for a while, came back, and lit a match. The gas exploded into a brief, intense flame, shriveling and blackening the tip ends of his forelock of sunshine hair.

"I never, ever should have gone into my room and left him alone in the kitchen. I know they'll send me home." Mary pressed her lips tightly together, trying not to cry. Soon she collected herself, set me to opening the kitchen windows against the acrid smell, and fetched her scissors. She sat Copey down, tucked a dish towel around his neck. Back home, she told us, when the children in her family needed haircuts, a man named Clay walked down out of the mountain with his scissors. She'd learned from him.

Mary had just expertly clipped off the last singed ends from Copey's forelock and swept up the hair when a slow sweep of headlights arced across the yard.

"It's them!" Copey cried out, and the three of us scrambled out of the kitchen. At the last second, Mary grabbed the charred hot dog from the oven and shoved it to the bottom of the trash. We piled into Mary's room, eased the door shut, and stood in the dark. The front door opened. Footsteps came, stopped in the kitchen. I sank to my knees and put my head on the end of Mary's bed. We held our breath.

Finally, the footsteps went away. Copey and I slipped out of Mary's room into the dark hall. "Goodnight," we all whispered. "Goodnight. Goodnight."

By the time I got up the next morning, Copey was gone to the harbor, searching for friends. "Just four weeks away, and so independent," I heard my mother say to herself, as though she needed to rearrange her thinking. This became my brother's survival strategy in our family: finding people who enjoyed his company more than our mother did.

Five minutes before Sunday lunch, Copey wasn't back yet. Still blue but no longer quite brilliant, the sky had shifted ever so slightly, as though someone had pulled an invisible gauze veil across, leaving less light by one gradation. My dad, who had to eat promptly and get to the airport for his commute home, looked from his watch to the driveway with growing agitation. No Copey. When Dad scowled, you sensed the anger in him, ready to erupt. Copey was going to get it.

We heard fast running before we saw Copey's newly trimmed forelock bobbing above the bushes. He tore around the open stretch of grass by the car and bounded up the single step to the deck. "We were sailing," he exclaimed. "The wind died, and the fog started coming in."

Mom shot a worried look at the ocean. "Can't see a single drop of fog out there," she said. I looked at Dad to see if Copey was still in trouble, but, just then, Mary came to the door to announce that lunch was ready. Copey slipped into the house, unscathed.

Mary served lunch, passing the platters of food to each member of the family in turn, waiting in the kitchen for my mother to knock on the door when she wanted Mary to clear the plates or bring dessert. "Very nice, Mary," my mother said to her. "You have learned a lot this summer. I hope it comes in handy for you. I can't bear to think you're leaving us in just a few days."

Halfway through dessert, an unfamiliar car nosed into view outside the dining room window and drew to a halt. "Who in

God's name is that?" my father said. Drifting alongside the mystery car, we could see a first wisp of fog, and another. Soon a whole cloud of fog drifted in, ghosting the bushes beyond the clothesline.

My father fumbled in a nearly empty cigarette pack. "Find out who's loitering and get them out of here."

My mother tapped on the kitchen door. "Mary! There's a strange car in our driveway."

Mary entered and said, in a small voice, "Those are my cousin and her friend who are working on Nantucket this summer, come to take me to town the way we said."

"Oh, Mary, not *this* afternoon. I can't bear it. Mr. Coppedge's flight is at 4:00 p.m., and look at that fog out there!"

Mary had spent three weeks in an all-white world, far from every person and place she'd ever known. Her cousin brought her a chance to be with family for a few hours, to be off duty, to be herself. But my mother, on edge about the foggy commute and my father's building anger, let her own drama supersede any promise she had made to Mary. In *Between Women*, Rollins talks about moments like this. Live-in domestic workers vented to her about the illusory promise of time off. "Some of the employers felt Thursday and Sunday also belonged to them," claimed one woman. Another expressed the rage of a person repeatedly cheated: "Women who hire domestics feel they've bought a slave. She becomes a possession. They don't feel the domestic as a person, that she is human." In the tangle of intimacy between the woman who employs and the woman who serves—as Rollins puts it, "between women"—many employers take advantage of that intimacy to require extra work. Rollins calls domestic service a "profoundly exploitative" occupation for this reason. "What might appear to be the basis of a more humane, less alienating work arrangement allows for a level of psychological exploitation." My mother cried, "Not *this* afternoon," knowing that Mary understood full well the tough afternoon Mom would face if Dad was fogged in.

My father was not tangled in this dynamic between the two women, though he reaped its benefits. As the breadwinner, as the man at the top of the hierarchy of gender that governed so many families back then, he felt free to intervene, and he did. "If you have given Mary the afternoon off," he said sharply to my mother, "let her take it."

"Would you mind your own business, Roy, and let me—"

"Nina," he said, bringing his eyebrows into a single dark line and enunciating carefully. "Let her take the afternoon."

"I don't have to go if it's not convenient," Mary said. If she backed away any farther, she'd be in the kitchen again.

Dad's scowl included Mary this time. "I don't want any argument from you, either, Mary. It is decided, god*damn* it."

Mary looked stricken. What Dad said wasn't as caustic as his usual outbursts, and he was on Mary's side, anyway, but she looked as though he had slapped her. I felt surprised by how frightened she seemed. Sixty years later, I understand that, for Mary as a Black person, angry white men meant danger. Mary could have no idea how this situation might turn out, or how she should respond.

My mother took a deep, put-upon breath. "Copey, you help Mary clear. Wendy, go out and tell Mary's cousin she'll be ready shortly."

The rusted black car sat like a beached whale in the drifting fog. As I approached across the wet grass, two people watched me through closed windows. The driver was a dark-skinned man in a baseball cap. The woman next to him was older than Mary, but bore a resemblance. I figured she must be Mary's cousin. She rolled down her window to smile at me. "Are you Wendy?" she asked. Utterly unfamiliar with Black people not in a servant role, I must have looked uneasy, because the woman made a special effort to put me at my ease. "You're just as pretty as Mary said."

"Thank you," I said. I thought I should say something back. "Mary's pretty, too."

She looked over at the man and smiled. "We think so."

I stood awkwardly, feeling I should ask them in but not knowing where they could go besides the kitchen.

Mary's cousin read my mind. "Just let Mary know we'll be out here," she said. As she closed her window, the man leaned forward to turn on the radio.

In a few minutes, Mary came out of her room with her black skirt and sweater on, smelling like cologne. "Don't leave Copey behind this time," she whispered to me, and was gone.

It was nearly dusk before Copey and I walked back barefoot along the sandy road. Copey seized a dried-up crab claw and tried to carry a dead beetle between the pincers. He had gone bankrupt in a marathon Monopoly game, but he hadn't minded.

Just as we reached the back door, we heard our mother's voice through an open window in her bedroom. "I dropped the damned tape, Mary, can you find it? Watch out, there could be broken glass anywhere." We turned to see Mom's face framed in a splintered windowpane. "Maybe I dropped it out the window," she said.

"I'll get it!" Copey cried. He lunged towards the hydrangea bush.

"Stay out of those bushes, you little ass," our mother said. "There's glass out there. You'll cut yourself to shreds."

Mary came up next to my mother with the tape, still in her black sweater and skirt.

"I don't know what I'd do without you, Mary," our mother said gratefully. "Doesn't look like rain, but I do think we should cover this hole up tonight, don't you?"

Inside, Copey and I found Mom clutching the lid of a shoebox, with varying lengths of Scotch tape sticking out ineffectually from the edges. Her cheeks were flushed, her eyes red. A half-finished drink sat sweating on the telephone table without a coaster. She waved us back. "Out of here, kids. I've dealt with enough today without someone getting badly cut. Bedtime."

"It's not really . . ." Copey started, but I grabbed his arm and pulled.

A few years later, a young man who'd been part of my beachside pack of friends told me he'd overheard his parents talking about the broken window. Heard them say, as fact not speculation, that my father's shoe shattered the pane that foggy Sunday afternoon. Hurled as a missile of his anger at the inconvenient fog, maybe even aimed at my mother. I did not see my father throw the shoe, so I can't say for sure that the rumor was true, but I can say this: The bruises that my mother hid so diligently, so protectively, suggest a man whose ready and explosive rage could turn a richly polished, lace-up leather city shoe into a weapon.

Mary heard the sounds of my father's violence that summer, saw the shattered glass. Judith Rollins observes that domestic workers have "a level of knowledge about familial and personal problems that few outsiders do." She reports "scathing judgments" from the domestic workers who spoke to her, often in the form of "cynicism and humor displayed in their derisive imitations of their employers."

I have never heard Mary express cynicism or derision towards my parents, though, many years later, she said to me that "he was mean to her." Like the women in *Between Women*, Mary would come to measure the dramas of my family by her own moral compass. As one woman said to Judith Rollins, "When I was younger, I did . . . wonder why they could have it all and we didn't have any. But I don't anymore, because as I got older and took a good look at them, I realize material gains don't necessarily mean you're happy. And most of those women aren't happy, you know." Wise words. My mother's unhappiness would shape Mary's ongoing work for my family, and, in many ways, the trajectory of both our lives.

By the next morning, the jagged hole in the window was securely covered over. Mary had clearly taken over the patching job from my inebriated mother. Standing side by side to survey the window together, the two seemed satisfied with their work. I got the feeling that Mary knew how the pane got broken, because Mom put an arm around Mary's shoulder and said, "Mary, you are a good friend."

You are a good friend. These words stay with me. In my mother's elite and highly segregated world, Mary was not the kind of "friend" with whom she went to the movies, or had cocktails, or played bridge. Mary was a companion when there was no one else and, like many a lonely employer in *Between Women*, my mother appreciated this. But she did not treat Mary like a friend. Mary, for her part, gave far more than companionship. That foggy evening in Nantucket—for the first, though far from last time—Mary helped my mother tape over the splintering violence in her marriage. She secured my mother's fragile shelter of reputation and self-esteem. Mom knew that Mary would tell no one about the domestic incident, especially no one in my mother's gossipy community of summer people. The illusion of my mother's good marriage could stay intact, if only in my mother's heart. I say that Mary would tell "no one" because, if Mary called her own mother, as she did almost daily throughout her life, and mused or cried over happenings in the Coppedge family, that would be, to my mother, the same as telling no one—no one in my mother's world, no one who counted.

Copey and I hide behind a bush outside the kitchen door, trying to muffle our laughter. Copey has his crab claw again, and I've grabbed a clump of wet seaweed from the beach. Mary is in the kitchen, Dad has gone back home to New Jersey for good, and our mother has gone out for farewell cocktails.

We slip into the kitchen and begin a low howl that is our idea of scary.

"Hi, you guys," Mary says. We approach her at the sink, still howling softly. "What's this?" she says, suddenly suspicious.

"We bring you creatures from the deep," I intone, and draw the clump of slithery seaweed from behind my back.

She gasps and turns to get away—right into the opening and closing crab claw.

"Creatures that want to eat you up!" Copey wails in falsetto.

Mary starts to laugh, but screams despite herself. "Stop it!" she cries, as we howl on.

She escapes out the screen door and runs away from us, towards the purple and orange summer sunset.

Copey and I stop chasing Mary when he and I are laughing too hard to run any more. We fling the creatures into the bushes. My memory offers up the three of us strolling breathlessly, side by side, back to the cottage in the gathering dusk.

Something in the nostalgia of this memory arrests me now —especially the companionable stroll back to the house. Not every reading of the crab-claw romp supports nostalgia. In one reading, two children tease a young babysitter in good-natured fun. Another reading, however, shows two white children amusing themselves by trying to frighten a young Black woman whose history, though they are kept carefully insulated from knowing this as a fact, includes many kinds of white violence. Her role as a servant restricts her freedom to respond. She is expected to play with these children, to indulge their pranks, and, at the same time, to monitor them and keep them safe. They come at her from both sides, brandishing dripping seaweed and a crab claw from an ocean she fears and avoids. They chase her up a shadowy road.

The end of Mary's stint for that first summer in Nantucket had come. "Time was up," Mary remembers. "Time to go home. What seemed like forever had finally ended. I was being told by Mrs. C. what a good job I had done, and how quickly I had learned. I was happy to be done. I had missed Mom." Mary felt satisfaction, too. "How proud I felt bringing that check home. In those days, it was a lot of money."

My parents decided that the month-long vacation in Nantucket had been a success. For the next thirty years, they would rent that same house, on that same long, empty Atlantic beach. For the next thirty years, we were white people swimming. Each year, my mother begged Mary to come. Mary managed to make the trip many times. If she couldn't, she sent a family member in her place—like Linda, the young woman whose photograph by the ocean my father captioned with such callous irony.

Fog would remain a presence by that beach—drifting in to dampen clothes on the line and turn potato chips limp and soggy, shrouding the roads and bushes and summer shore. Mary remembers, "I did love the ocean, so blue, looking as if it touched the sky. I also liked hearing the waves hit the beach. But I didn't care for the fog. It was so eerie."

My family's illusions of superiority were a kind of fog, shrouding the available light of human relationship. The ambient fog of alcohol permeated our days and nights. As white people, we drew around ourselves a comfortable fog of ignorance about Mary's life, and about Black people in general, even though we all shared a country, and an uneasy past. Try as I might to remember that summer accurately, nostalgia and wishful thinking fog my memory.

I believe also that the fog arising from racism and classism in that summer enclave distorted our experiences of love. My family was relatively kind as employers go, though selfish and demanding as any. During that summer and in the succeeding years, Mary came to interpret my parents' kindness, and their dependency, as love. She had always longed to live with her mother. Here was a family who needed her. She came to love my mother that summer, and would do so for the rest of her life. "As to your mother," Mary texted recently, "she was like my mother. I had that sort of attachment to her, or maybe I wished that she was my mom back in those years. I loved her very much."

At the end of her novel, *The Bluest Eye*, Toni Morrison delivers a truth in the voice of her narrator: "Love is never any better than the lover." My parents did come to love Mary, and would love her for the rest of their lives, but the limits to their love were both culturally prescribed and staggering. Theirs was a segregated love. Mary's was more whole.

five

Dream Wedding

MARY'S ROLE IN MY 1964 WEDDING ON NANTUCKET, AND the wedding itself, took on a starkly different aspect for me fifty years later, when I read *Between the World and Me* by Ta-Nehisi Coates. The 2015 National Book Award winner is a searing, book-length letter to Coates's teenage son about brutal realities in their lives as Black Americans. Coates chronicles multiple assaults on his body and his life as a young man trying to stay alive in one of the poorest sections of 1980s Baltimore. Profiled by police and targeted by armed teenagers on the street, he also found no refuge in school, the place where young people should be educated and protected. Coates found himself utterly barred from access to the middle class American (read, white) Dream.

The Dream, Coates writes, "is perfect houses with nice lawns. It is Memorial Day cookouts, block associations, and driveways. The Dream is treehouses and the Cub Scouts. The Dream smells like peppermint and tastes like strawberry shortcake." This is the Dream touted by advertising and Hollywood, the Dream that white middle- and upper-class Americans either appear to live, or strive to attain. What's more—and what skews the moral arc of my own life—Coates understands that the dangers and deprivations that characterized his childhood actually sustain the (white) Dream that excluded him. "Fear ruled everything around me, and I knew, as all black people do, that this fear was connected to the Dream out there, to the unworried boys, to pie and pot roast, to the white fences and green lawns nightly beamed into our television sets." Marxists have long argued that prosperity for the upper and middle classes depends on the existence of a deliberately impoverished underclass. Coates puts this more directly, more boldly, and in contemporary American terms to which all of us bear witness. The Dream, he warns his son, "rests on our backs."

I grew up securely inside this Dream of access for me and exclusion for others. I was one of the "unworried" children. I worried, yes, about the slammed doors and whimpers of family violence, but I did not fear for my bodily safety on the streets of Princeton, New Jersey. I had no reason to doubt that I'd get a full academic education. And I had no inkling that this ease in my own life actually required the dilapidated housing of the Witherspoon Street section of Princeton, no idea that my comfort and sunny prospects depended on the poverty and ragged education that sent Mary, at fifteen, into domestic service. Recalling the events of my wedding week, I understand now that I married within my family's upper-class version of the very American Dream that, as Coates would argue so cogently fifty years later, thrives for white people by excluding people of color.

When my Harvard boyfriend graduated and proposed marriage halfway through my sophomore year, I said yes in the next breath. An honors student at Radcliffe, I listed English literature as my course of study, but truly I was majoring in Alfred. My parents fretted briefly about our youth, but Alfred was a prep school graduate from a prosperous, landed white family in eastern Tennessee, with a waterfront home in the town of Nantucket. His social standing reassured my parents that we would thrive.

Like many in her social set back then, my mother viewed a proper wedding as a portal through which a young woman took the all-important step to a successful life: marriage to a man "from good stock" who would "do well." And so, she resolved to create a perfect Nantucket summer wedding. Dad wired his London tailor for a navy-blue blazer with antique brass buttons that shone with the luster of generations. Poised at what would be the peak of his success as president of a large liquor corporation, Dad reserved the company jet to fly select guests in for the wedding. Perhaps because his own father had worked his way up from stock boy to department store CEO, Dad prided himself on being able to give me the kind of wedding that he aspired to—and that my mother took for granted.

As part of the grand plan, my mother called Mary. Twenty-three years old, married, and with a two-year-old son, Mary did day work at that time, cleaning house for my mother and other Princeton families. Mary had no plan, herself, to return to Nantucket the next summer. The previous August, she'd brought her new baby boy, Dennie, to the cottage for two weeks. While she labored to give my parents their accustomed vacation, the baby slept in a crib beside the ironing board in Mary's room—with the door closed, as my mother required. As the summer ended, my mother didn't beg Mary to promise to return the following August. Little Dennie would be a toddler by then. Having him underfoot, my mother said, wouldn't do at all. With my engagement, however, my mother believed that only Mary—with her diligence, stamina, and sweet service—could help her with the heavy lifting a wedding would require. She begged Mary to come—and to leave her child behind. Mary said yes. If Mary had other plans, she changed them. I asked no questions. This blissful ignorance, this disregard, is part of the Dream.

I've understood, over the years, that Mary could not have said no to my mother without risking future work. A ready yes to whatever my mother asked of her—this was an unspoken job qualification. Mary says, of the time, "How do you say no to your mother? It was an impossibility. She was so frantic about the wedding. She said she couldn't deal with it unless I was there. That's why I came." Involved for nine years already with my family, in the charged intimacy that Rollins names "between women" who share a household as "boss" and "servant," Mary knew that my father was likely to be volatile and even dangerous as the wedding approached. She knew that my mother needed her kind companionship (and possibly the protection of her presence) just as much as her physical help—an emotional net that my mother did not mind brandishing in order to get what she wanted.

Mary sacrificed her own needs in coming. As she told me years later, "I really didn't want to leave my boy. He was at that stage of 'don't you go anywhere without me.' I had no babysitters, had never even been gone from him overnight. When you have your first baby, you think that no one can do the right thing but you. But your mother said she just could not cope with all the things to do if I were not there. After wondering what to do, what to do, and my mother agreeing to keep him, I came." Like so many new mothers, Mary was certain that no one could care for her child the way she did, and so her next words are particularly chilling. "When I got back home to him, some of the closeness was gone."

My family didn't blink at Mary's sacrifice of irreplaceable time with her baby. Throughout the "dream wedding," we would continue to act in ways that epitomized the racism and classism of the time. We would continue to treat Mary as a helpful, indeed desperately needed, adjunct, rather than a full human being.

Mary flew to Nantucket a week before the wedding, and my mother sent me to pick her up. "Mary's coming for *you*, you know," my mother said. I hear in this a convenient fantasy that Mary was so invested in my happiness that she wouldn't want to miss helping out with the big day. Perhaps my mother used the story to condone, for herself, pressing Mary to leave her son behind. As I headed out the door for the airport, Mom called out, as though reassuring us both, "Mary loves us. And we love her." To build a friendship with Mary that merited the claim of love, I would have to open my eyes to everyone's humanity, find my way to the edge of the (white) Dream, and wake up.

Driving to Nantucket's small airport, downshifting and revving the engine to manage the road's narrow curves the way my fiancé had taught me, I thought about Mary. During most of the past seven summers, Mary had encouraged my adventures. She met me when I slipped into the kitchen at night after a date, poured us glasses of milk while I grabbed the crackers and jam for a whisper session at the kitchen table. Now, she would help me get married.

Beyond the weathered shingles of two low buildings and a small flight tower, bright orange windsocks bobbed along a runway that ran through scruffy moors to ocean surf at one end. I stood by the low picket fence as a freshening southwest breeze blew the scent of salt and bayberry bushes through my hair. The front section of a *Boston Globe* fluttered on a bench before me.

In July 1964, the Republicans had nominated arch-conservative Barry Goldwater for the presidency—the candidate of my parents and their friends. Two days after my wedding, the Democrats would gather in Atlantic City for their own convention. A small headline in the *Globe* that I scanned lazily, waiting for Mary, announced that an all-Black delegation chosen by hundreds of newly registered Negro voters in Mississippi was poised to demand recognition as the state's true delegation. On behalf of the newly formed Mississippi Freedom Democratic Party, leader Fanny Lou Hamer voiced her outrage at the violence met by Black Mississippians when they tried to register to vote. Hamer, an agricultural worker and daughter of sharecroppers, argued strategically that the all-white and anti-civil rights "official" delegation to the convention reflected a flawed and illegal selection process. A struggle on the floor of the convention loomed. One day, I would study Fanny Lou Hamer's life-long dedication and brilliant grassroots strategy and feel humbled and inspired. At the time, I was mildly interested in the drama unfolding in Atlantic City but far more thrilled by my impending wedding.

The plane landed, taxied in. Mary appeared at the top of the rolling stairway in a smart navy-blue dress and bolero jacket outfit that looked like something my movie-star mother would wear. Her lips were a rich red. Holding her back erect, she carefully negotiated the narrow stairway in high heels. In the seven years since her first arrival in the Nantucket cottage as a skinny girl far from home, Mary had grown both shapely and elegant.

Self-centered as I was that summer, I was happy to see Mary, and felt suffused by sense-memories of her warm and kind presence. I jumped up and down, waving like an exuberant child.

We fell into each other's arms. Mary smelled of perfume and cigarettes.

"You are so wonderful to come," I said.

Mary stepped back. "Why wouldn't I?"

"I don't know. Your family. Your work." I said these to mark the sacrifices Mary was making for me, but she just took a deep sniff of the piney, salty Nantucket air.

"Smells as good as ever," she said. As we walked to the car, Mary turned to me. "You're so thin you make me jealous."

"You're thin, too," I said.

"Not me. Since I had the baby, I can't get rid of this extra inch." She frowned and gave her thigh a pinch. "Want a manicure?" she asked suddenly, when she caught me checking out her nails. She held her hands up with a flourish. "I could give you one for your wedding!"

I scanned my hastily clipped nails and craggy cuticles. "No thanks," I said. Alfred wasn't a fancy dresser, and neither was I. He moved through the elite Ivy League world with an informality and unbothered ease that displayed embedded and unquestioned social privilege. I could not have explained this at the time. I knew only that his informal way of carrying himself made me feel at ease, myself, and I didn't want a manicure.

As we settled into the car, Mary flicked a speck from her dress and smoothed the linen fabric over her knee. I remembered, then, my mother's double closet in Princeton, how the dry-cleaned dresses hung pressed and ready in a long line of clear plastic bags. I could see my mother selecting the navy sheath, stepping into it in stocking feet, pulling it up over her silk slip, reaching back for the zipper. She'd let me close the snap at her soft neck before she took the bolero jacket from its hanger and hurried to catch the train for a theater matinee in Manhattan. My mother must have passed the smart linen jacket-dress along to Mary.

Mary looked smashing. She wore the second-hand dress stylishly and with flair. Mary was studying (and emulating) my elegant, blond, stunningly dressed mother, paying attention to everything I didn't care to learn. To me, style was a snare that tied my mother to my father. Tending and enhancing her beauty, as she did devotedly, did nothing to protect her from his rages. I was ripe for the upcoming era of hippie beads and long, shapeless skirts sewn from South Asian bedspreads. Mary says today, "I so admired your mother, who was tall but still wore high heels. I love clothes. She taught me fashion, how to dress, what not to wear, when and where."

In *Between Women,* Rollins argues that employers give second-hand clothes and items to their domestic workers, not only to nurture a useful loyalty but also to assert their own superiority in taste and material abundance. Gratefully accepting those gifts becomes another part of job performance. As one domestic worker said, "I didn't want most of that junk. But you have to take it. It's part of the job, makes them feel like they're being so kind to you. You have to appear grateful." To my skeptical mind, the fact that my mother's linen sheath and bolero jacket looked fabulous on Mary does not erase the condescension at work in the "gift."

Mary fished around inside her shoulder bag. "Will it bother you if I smoke?"

I shook my head and told her I'd given it up.

"You *smoked*?"

"My first semester," I said, feeling a little proud. "Every time I have a drink, I want one."

Mary shot me a look that said, "You *are* growing up." She lit a Salem, drew in a big puff and exhaled, closed her eyes, and leaned her head back against the seat.

I could see circles now—dark smudges of droopy skin under her eyes that showed up when she wasn't smiling. "You tired?" I asked.

"A little, but don't worry," Mary said. "Coming to Nantucket is nothing. This is a vacation."

Whatever Mary called her time with us, I knew that she *worked*. Perhaps working for my mother by the beach truly was a vacation for Mary, a break from traveling to different white women's homes each day, even a break from the needs of an active two-year-old. But Judith Rollins reminds me that, to be successful, a domestic worker must convey both an enthused willingness to work and a sense of taking pleasure in the job. This, Mary did. *This is nothing. This is a vacation.*

Mary sat up straighter in the passenger seat. "Can you believe I waited so long to ask you about Alfred? Aren't you so excited? A year on a sailboat!"

In a year-long honeymoon, Alfred and I planned to take an ocean-going sailboat through the canals of Belgium and France and to sail in the Mediterranean. I would postpone my junior year at college for the trip. At the time, I was too deep in the Dream to recognize—as I do now—that the expensive honeymoon was a glaring exhibition of money and privilege. I realized that the trip was "rare" in terms of being a great idea, a creative adventure, but I was not aware how much disposable income, what ample pockets of my fiancé and his family, our trip required. I was far too deep in the Dream to ask who might have made good use of half, even a tithing tenth, of the money our trip would cost. And so, I repeated to Mary, with relish, every detail of our plans. I'd like to be able to say that spelling out, for Mary, the details of this fabulous affluence made me uncomfortable. I don't remember such discomfort at the time. For those of us who are lost in the (white) Dream, utter ignorance of another person's reality is actually possible. Mary, who had come so far to help me marry, was invisible to me.

Mary smoked a cigarette as I detailed the honeymoon plans. When I ended, she lit up another cigarette and inserted the dead match carefully between the pack and its cellophane. She started to speak, but began coughing instead. "Did you promise to finish?" she managed to ask, slapping her chest to quell the spasm.

"Finish what?" I asked.

"College," she said.

"Promise who?"

She looked away. "Your dad."

"I'll do my junior and senior years of college married. Dad says it would be a waste of his money if I didn't."

Mary exhaled sharply. Smoke blew back in the window, and she tried to wave it out with her hand. Usually so straight-backed, she slumped in her seat. Not knowing what I'd said to cause this shift, I tried to change the subject. "How's . . . your little boy?" I asked. I was chagrined to find that, even after spending a week with Mary's baby in the cottage the summer before, I couldn't remember his name. "He must be crawling by now!"

"Walking!"

"Oops, I knew that. And . . . your husband?" I couldn't remember her husband's name, either, which goes to show that acting friendly is not the same as paying attention.

"Oh, him," Mary said flatly. "He's the same."

"Tell me all about being married," I said, like a cheerleader. "By next week, we'll both be married ladies."

Mary sat up in her seat. "There's the ocean!" she called.

"Do you like it? Being married, I mean."

She turned slowly back to me. "I guess."

"You guess?"

"He works, I work. We have the baby." Her red lipstick was disappearing, and a sheen of perspiration dampened her skin. I swung the car into the sandy driveway as if on cue, veering away from the glimpse of marriage that she offered without enthusiasm, without joy.

"You and Alfred will have a wonderful life," Mary said as my mother stood up from her deck chair and crossed the wooden porch in her pink, floppy hat, smiling and waving. "I just know it."

There's a lot of hype about marriage in the United States, a lot of fairy-tale promising and dreaming. Truth is, we all find out that marriage is tough. Mary didn't have a "wonderful" marriage. My mother didn't. But they both thought, or hoped, or pretended, that I might. *I just know it,* Mary said. My married life, unlike hers, promised to unfold within the (white) Dream. Half a century later, Ta-Nehisi Coates—in *Between the World and Me*—would make clear just how much my Dream of white ease and privilege depended on Mary's exclusion.

Coming home from town at midday the next day, passing outside the open windows of the dining room and kitchen, I heard my mother and Mary talking. My mother was speaking in her conversation voice—not the voice she used when reviewing Mary's tasks. Through the window, I could see Mom in her usual spot at the dining room table, leaning back comfortably against the wall shared by the kitchen. My mother used that seat so she could tap on the wall at dinner, telling Mary when it was time to clear the table or to bring more food. Usually shut, because my mother liked it that way, the door between the dining room and kitchen was now wide open. Passing by the kitchen window on my way to the door, I could hear Mary saying something back to my mother. Not "Yes, ma'am," or, "Will you have more iced tea?" but one relaxed, casual sentence, then another. Mary sat with her own lunch at the kitchen table. Back to back, dining room to kitchen, my mother and Mary were having lunch and talking. With a testy and critical husband and a self-involved daughter, my mother seemed to be benefiting from Mary's listening and kind attention. The unwritten rules of domestic service, and toxic dividers of race and class, put the kindest person in the house on the other side of a wall.

Mary jumped to her feet when I entered through the kitchen door. "Please, finish your lunch!" I said, but Mary remained standing. As I joined my mother in the dining room, Mary swung the kitchen door slowly shut behind me. The brief moment of informal exchange between my mother and Mary—their lunch "together" on opposite sides of the kitchen wall—had ended.

Three days later, my father arrived. My mother came through the front door ahead of him with a look that forewarned me. My mother always worried about my father's state of mind and spirit, and enlisted Mary's help in tending to his mood. My mother's attitude during our summers was: "He's worked hard. He's been successful. We should give him the nice vacation he deserves." This summer, in particular, his successes were paying for my wedding.

"How's the bride to be?" my father asked. He dropped heavily into his usual chair and took two long swallows of the drink my mother brought to him. "You are both staring," he said finally— and not in a friendly way. "Do I have horns?"

My mother turned to her own drink, and I rearranged the magazines on the coffee table several different ways until she frowned at me to stop. "Daddy got some bad news today," she said. "Granddaddy's heart is acting up. He and your grandmother can't come to your wedding."

"Christ, I knew this would happen," my father said. "Mother and Dad would get down to the wire and back out, and there we'd be with ten thousand Van Vechtens and not a single lousy Coppedge."

"That's not fair, Roy."

"What's not fair about it?" he said dangerously.

"Your sister and her husband are coming. Besides, the other night you were worrying about what to do with your parents for a whole weekend."

He took another gulp and set his glass down with studied care. "Don't get me wrong, my darling daughter," he said with a mock bow in my direction. "I'm happy for you to have just exactly the wedding you want." He honed the word "exactly" like the tip of a dart he was preparing to throw. "But you must realize that there are costs."

The dart landed: My grandparents' disappointing absence was somehow my fault. I slid to the edge of my chair. "I'm sorry, Daddy, I . . ."

He held his cocktail glass in the air. "I'm empty," he announced.

My mother shot him a dirty look and started up from her chair, but Mary appeared at the kitchen door. "Shall I make your cocktail, Mr. Coppedge?"

Dad turned around with what looked like the start of a smile, and I thought maybe Mary's friendly offer had eased his mood. But he soured quickly. "Shouldn't a smart girl like you be studying math instead of cocktail recipes?" he asked. He sounded friendly enough, but Mary flinched and took a step backwards.

My mother stood abruptly and went to the bar. "You are a mean bastard, Roy Coppedge," she muttered, though I didn't understand why.

That night, when I escaped to help with the dishes, Mary didn't fool around the way we usually did, bumping our hips against each other to see who would win a place at the sink. Methodically and almost stiffly, she sudsed and rinsed.

"Did Dad hurt your feelings?"

She ran a plate through hot water. "He had every right to say what he did."

"But why?"

Mary did not answer. She drew the dish towel from my hands.

Promising to give Alfred a rousing goodbye to single life, his friends threw a bachelor party for him in town. From wild stories I'd heard, I imagined flowing liquor and bare-breasted women. The idea made me miserable. My parents invited me to join them for dinner with nearby friends, and I welcomed the distraction.

Before we left for dinner, my parents drank a cocktail "for the road." They seemed congenial enough with each other but, in the car, the mood turned.

"Mary thinks you're upset with her about college, Roy," my mother started out.

"What makes you think that?" my father snapped.

"College?" I asked, but my mother shook her head for me to stay out of it. Later that night, Mary would tell me about the year my parents paid her college tuition, and how she struggled, and failed, to pass math. As tension ratcheted up between my parents in the car, I didn't know the subject, though I was painfully familiar with the feel.

"You hurt Mary's feelings, Roy. You cut to the quick with that math remark."

"Feelings? Preposterous." My father shook his head. "It's such a waste, a smart girl like that not finishing college. I had hoped that, with help from us, Mary could prove herself an exception to the generally lousy record of Negroes in American education."

"She may still finish—"

"With everything going against it? Nina, are you nuts? She had her one chance, and she muffed it."

"She cares what you think, Roy."

"Who are you, Jane Addams? Florence Nightingale?"

"Could you just tell her you're not upset—"

My father braked the car so abruptly that we all lurched forward in our seats. "I'll tell Mary whatever I goddamn want to," he shouted.

My mother had a certain way of fixing her head and looking out the window when she felt aggrieved but was trying not to get into further trouble. Finally, she said, in a small voice, "Maybe there's a silver lining. If Mary finished college, she might stop cleaning houses, and she wouldn't be able to help me."

"Christ, Nina. What do you want for Mary anyhow?"

"I was just thinking that she needs the work now, with the baby and everything."

"That's just the goddamn point! She missed her chance to do better than cleaning house for you and your precious friends!" He accelerated up to the rear of a Jeep in front of us and slammed the brakes again, spraying sand in all directions. "Damn it all to hell!" he yelled, and lurched us into our host's driveway.

As I recall that scene, I want to hear in my father's angry outburst only that he cared about Mary, cared about her chances in life. But racism distorted his caring. He believed the lie that Black people were intellectually inferior to whites, and therefore not as educable. Also, like many white people who find an "inferior" person they choose to patronize, he wanted Mary to be an "exception" to the negative assessment he'd made of her race. Paternalism also distorted his caring—he wanted to throw money at Mary's problems and feel good about himself. Ignorance, too —he chose not to see the challenges facing Black people in an education system that criminally underserved them. Dad showed, too, the arrogance of class. Accustomed to power and control, he was angry and frustrated that Mary missed an opportunity he credited himself for creating for her. Any caring Dad had for Mary was distorted, finally, by the patriarchal power that had permitted him, with his cocktail recipe taunt a night earlier, to hurl the dart of his angry disappointment at a person who had only, ever, served him and tried to please.

At the time, I thought, *Pretty soon I won't have to drive with them anymore.*

Ahead of us, on a broad wooden deck overlooking the Atlantic, two women in pastel print dresses lifted cocktails to their lips. Two husbands in bright madras jackets fanned smoking charcoal in a grill. My parents were putting their smiles on.

I told them I felt sick. "Maybe it's butterflies about the wedding," I said. "I have to go home."

My mother turned in surprise. "You have no to way to get home, young lady."

"I'll walk."

She frowned skeptically. "You said you were sick."

My parents' eyes met. All the aggravation that had careened around inside the car on the drive over merged as they turned to focus on me.

"For Christ's sake," my father began.

I thought they would forgive me anything during my wedding week. But my mother threw a "do something" look at my father, and he raised the back of his right hand as if to strike me. As I cringed, my mother's "do something" look evaporated. "Roy!" she cried. He dropped his hand to the steering wheel, shaking his head like he couldn't believe what a thankless and rude daughter he had.

I clambered out of the car and fled, my high heels crunching on the broken oyster shells of the driveway. In the flimsy bright dress my mother had bought me, I ran like a silly non-runner, heels out, toes in, breathing hard, until I reached the sandy, one-lane road that led back to the cottage. Then I thought of Mary. All those summer nights, she had been waiting for me in the clean kitchen with milk and soda crackers.

Dusk had settled towards night by the time I tiptoed up to Mary's open window. Pulled all the way down as usual, the green shade flapped lazily against the screen. Her light was off. No sound from within. I veered away and headed along the raised wooden walkway towards the ocean.

Mary was sitting at the top of the splintery steps that led down to the beach, leaning back against the same railing that she had grasped so nervously seven summers earlier, when my mother said so casually, "Come on down and see the ocean." I watched Mary take one slow puff, then another. Her cigarette glowed like a firefly against the night sky. The day's wind had died down, but the waves still sloshed and sucked as they reached the sand.

"Hi," I said.

Mary scrambled to her feet with a little cry, dropped her cigarette to the step, and stomped at it. She put a hand on her chest, breathing hard. "You nearly gave me a heart attack!"

"I wanted to be home. I thought we might . . . I don't know. . . ." I settled on the step just below Mary, hoping she would sit down again, hoping she would stay. Like my mother when she and Mary ate lunch "together" across an actual wall, I craved Mary's kind companionship and gave her little choice in the matter. I felt glad when she settled back onto the wooden step.

"The stars are bright like this back home," she said at last.

"In New Jersey?"

"Oh no. No, no. In Virginia. In the mountains. There are no street lights down home, only millions of stars."

"Do you wish you still lived there?"

Mary seemed to sink into herself in the dark. "I couldn't make a living like I do in Trenton," she said soberly. "But Mommie has my boy down there this week. Little Dennie is in the mountains."

"Do you miss him?" I asked, and the way she caught her breath made me sorry I'd asked. Of course, she did. "You miss your husband?" I asked.

She shook her pack of cigarettes, then returned it to her hip pocket. "I miss him, and I don't."

I waited to hear Mary explain what she meant, but she said no more. "Do you think I'll feel that way about Alfred someday? Missing and not missing?"

"Oh, no," she said, definitively. "That won't be your kind of marriage." We looked out at white foam edging the dark waves, each having our thoughts. "You worried about that bachelor party?" she asked.

I told her about naked girls jumping out of cakes.

"You're so beautiful, he won't look at anybody else. Don't worry," Mary said, then added, as though speaking to herself, "There's plenty else to worry about later on."

"Like what?" I asked.

As if she knew I wouldn't really listen, Mary didn't answer. "What should I fix for your dinner?" she asked.

"Please, stay!" I said. I wanted to keep our talk going. I wanted Mary to tell me something about herself. Or, so I thought. "Did Daddy upset you the other day, about studying math instead of cocktail recipes?"

There was a silence. "The math was my fault. I wasn't smart enough. I didn't know my numbers."

"Why would Dad have an opinion about that?"

"They didn't tell you?" Mary asked, then she told me the story. When Mary was eighteen, her grandmother wrangled her a Methodist scholarship for a junior college in Tennessee. Despite her scholarship job in the women's dorm, cleaning up after her careless classmates, and so little spending money that she had to save up for toothpaste, Mary liked college. She was sorely disappointed when, the next year, her stepfather became so ill that she had to stay home to earn money. "Three summers ago, while I was up here in Nantucket working, Mr. and Mrs. C. called me into the living room. Your dad said, 'Mary, we think you should complete college, and we're going to write a check for this year's tuition to that school you've been going to. You're a smart girl, and we want to see you go on with your education.'" Mary sighed heavily. "I failed two math classes that year. I never did graduate. I wasted your dad's money. He's right to be upset with me."

I wish I'd responded to Mary's story with what I know now.

She "didn't know her numbers" because the segregated Virginia public education system had utterly failed her. And my father was bent out of shape because, when white employers give money, strings are attached—expected gratitude, expected service, expected results. He had no right to make her feel bad about college. Instead of saying any of this, I listened passively while Mary recited, like a fated litany, "I moved to New Jersey to live with Aunt Betty, got married, did day work, got pregnant. And here I am."

"And here you are," I repeated. Mary had responded openheartedly to my invitation and told me something about herself, but I didn't know what to say next. My mind drifted towards the bachelor party. I was absent from the very conversation I thought I wanted.

"You stay here and enjoy the stars," Mary said, finally. "I'll fix your dinner." She pulled herself up by the splintery railing to head for the kitchen. I remember her departure with a pang of loss. We would not attempt another real conversation for many years—and rightly so. I was not fit, at the time, for friendship.

In the living room on my wedding day, Mary worked to fasten the sixty tiny cloth-covered buttons on my white silk wedding dress. Just as a "simple" island wedding had turned out to be a big production, my dress featured sixty buttons down the back for someone else to fasten. My mother had started at the top and Mary at the bottom, but Mom gave up as soon as the tight buttonholes threatened her manicure.

Picking up the day's *New York Times* while Mary and my mother tended to me, Dad found news that made him swear under his breath. The Democratic Presidential convention started in two days, and the Mississippi Democratic Freedom Party was still fighting to be seated. "Mary," Dad said, in the voice he used for bantering with little children, "a nice girl like you doesn't know any of those Mississippi troublemakers, do you?"

Mary was lifting the delicate lace veil that my aristocratic Riker great-grandmother had worn in the 1890s. Smiling shyly past the bobby pins in her mouth, she shook her head.

"Good girl," Dad said, as Mary settled the bridal veil on my hair. "We wouldn't want you part of the mess that group is going to make by barging into the convention. Would we?"

Mary slipped a bobby pin delicately through the veil to secure it. "I don't follow all that, sir," she replied.

My mother draped the veil gently over my shoulders. "Leave Mary alone, Roy. She is too busy working and being a good wife and mother to get involved in politics. Aren't you, Mary?"

When my parents praised Mary that day for not joining civil rights protests, they persisted in a long and unholy tradition. White America has always loved the lie of "happy" Black workers—on the plantation, in minstrel shows, in the kitchen. Not at the ballot box. Not in arenas of power. Not determining their own lives. During the centuries of enslavement, enslaved Africans who didn't act happy (or at least cooperative and unthreatening) risked brutal punishment. My father's threat was more indirect, but a threat nonetheless: "We wouldn't want you part of the mess in Atlantic City," he said. No troublemakers employed by this family.

"I don't follow all that, sir." Mary had given my father the reassurance he wanted. In *Between Women,* I find that wearing a mask of deference and giving answers that in some way "satisfy" the employer are a domestic worker's "necessary survival strategies." Mary made a strategic choice not to respond to my father's question with direct information. She did not tell us whether she paid rapt attention to the civil rights movement as she grew up, whether she listened to her gift radio for news of marches and sit-ins, whether in her heart, or with her body, she had ever participated in a protest. Ministers preached civil rights in Black churches across the South at that time; Mary chose not to mention whether she'd been touched or affected by those messages of righteous anger and faithful resolve. This is how she kept her job.

Years later, Mary would elaborate on her response to my father that day. "The few Black people where I grew up were all far apart, people too spread out, people too poor and had too much work to do. There was no time for that [activism]. Your parents wouldn't have let you do it even if you wanted to. You'd just work, save your money, and leave. You tried to scratch your living out. The thing was survival." Mary's silence with my father was about survival.

A great deal of sorry U.S. history swirled in that sunny living room on my wedding day—young Black woman, young white woman, both clothed in white, both in socially conscripted uniforms. Too much history for real exchange.

My father looked irritably from his wristwatch to the door. "The limo is three minutes late." To keep him from getting antsy, I asked what was happening at the convention. He looked over at the door that Mary had shut behind her when she slipped out of the room. "A band of Negroes has camped out, demanding to be seated as delegates. Goddamn northern liberals invade the South to register a whole new onslaught of uneducated voters, and the result is chaos."

I studied my engagement ring as it flashed diamond and

sapphire in the sunlight. "Those new voters are American citizens, Dad."

"We'd want Mary to vote, wouldn't we?" my mother added from the mirror, where she was adjusting her wide-brimmed movie-star hat. "That is, if she couldn't."

My father raised his eyes to the ceiling like my mother had said something unbearably stupid. She and I traded a look. Even on my wedding day, my father was a bully.

When the limousine pulled up to the cottage, my mother gasped and pressed her hand to her cheek. I was leaving her. "Quick, Daddy!" I said. "Take our picture."

My mother brushed at her tears and put her arm around me delicately, so as not to displace the veil. In the photograph, she is glamorous in whisper-blue chiffon that drops to the top of her tanned, shapely calves. I am shockingly young.

Fog pulled back from the beaches long enough to allow nearly all the wedding guests to arrive. The church was full, and the reception ample. In the receiving line, my father's Southern sister, Louise, adorned in thick, bright red lipstick, kissed my new husband full on the mouth. My fifteen-year-old brother drank too much of his first-ever champagne and spent the evening throwing up in the men's room. Alfred and I left the reception to hooting and guffaws from his ushers. They'd fastened a full-sized ball and chain around his ankle to signify married life as a form of bondage for the unsuspecting male. The memory is searing, but not because the ushers crossed signals and did not provide the rusty old key until the middle of our wedding night. The memory sears, because only in the (white) Dream would an implement of human suffering become a prop for a joke.

Alfred and I made promises that day that we wouldn't be able to honor. Not even a perfect summer wedding could effectively shore up our marriage against the predictable backwash of our families' dysfunctions or the oncoming tides of feminism.

As the Island Taxi carried me away with my new husband, my mother waved from beneath the wide brim of her powder-blue hat. She wore dark glasses, which meant she was weeping. I knew that the seaside cottage would feel bleakly empty to her when she got home. Then I saw Mary standing nearby in the fading afternoon. *At least Mary will keep her company*, I thought. I counted on Mary to fill my place as a light in the dim corners of my mother's lonely life. I looked to Mary, that is, to set me free.

Decades later, I asked Mary to remind me where she sat in the church at my wedding. We were relaxing together in a high-ceilinged sunroom in her New Jersey home. Her third husband had built the room shortly after they moved back to New Jersey from a stint in Florida. Louvered vertical shades angled against hot spring sunshine, creating a cool, airy brightness within. Strewn on the coffee table before us lay mementoes from Mary's decades in corrections. She lifted her legs to the table with the weariness of one who has worked for as long as she can remember.

"Your wedding? What was that—thirty, forty years ago? Doesn't that make a person feel old!" She half groaned, half chuckled, pushing at a sofa cushion to wedge it more comfortably behind her neck.

I tried to follow the thread of Mary's presence from the long buttoning through the church and the reception, to the moment when Alfred heaved the iron ball into Mrs. Nickerson's Island

Taxi and we sped away. I pictured Mary seated in a row some-where on the bride's side of the church. At the reception, she'd have been at a table in a far corner of the great, creamy-green ballroom with its floor-to-ceiling windows overlooking the bay. In my memory, she wore turquoise. She didn't dance. According to my self-serving recall, she brightened when I floated by.

"Where *did* you sit in the church?" I asked.

Mary fixed serious brown eyes on me with a neutral look. "I wasn't in the church."

"You weren't?"

"No, I didn't see any of that."

"At the reception . . ." I began, and then faltered.

"You've forgotten the time," Mary said. Measured, matter-of-fact.

The time was 1964.

"Not the wedding, not the reception," I said slowly.

Mary held a long silence. "I was outside," she said. "I watched as you came out."

For decades, I had "almost" pictured Mary at my wedding and reception. The fog of "almost" and "somewhere" hid reali-ties I didn't want to see or to feel. The lie of approximate memory protected me from knowing that we hadn't asked Mary to the wedding. Although we (too casually) said we loved Mary, my mother and I invited three hundred guests without putting Mary on the list. Our uninterrupted expectation, and Mary's ever-presence, obscured this stark exclusion. Misremembering pro-tected me from regret and from unexamined sorrow. I "forgot" that I did not invite Mary, because to remember would destroy the comforting illusion that, in that year of my Dream wedding, I had treated her as a friend.

Ta-Nehisi Coates addresses this white amnesia: "The forgetting is habit, is yet another necessary component of the Dream," he writes. "[Those who think themselves white] have forgotten the scale of theft that enriched them in slavery; the terror that allowed them, for centuries, to pilfer the vote; the segregationist policy that gave them their suburbs. They have forgotten, because to remember would tumble them out of the beautiful Dream and force them to live down here with us, down here in the world."

In the sphere of Mary's life and mine, my sloppy "approximate memory" and self-serving forgetfulness both belied my declarations of friendship and reflected—indeed, reinforced—the systematic forgetting that keeps white supremacy in place.

six

Womanhood

DURING THE LATE 1960S AND EARLY '70S, SEVERAL SOCIAL movements—civil rights, anti-war, feminism, gay rights—emerged into a sustained and embattled public presence. As my own story began to reflect all that ferment, the careful training I'd received from my parents in class and gender began to fray. During that same time, Mary became a single parent and made a new path for herself in work. We found our way through the turbulent, stressful decade, each of us, little knowing that our experiences were preparing us to meet on slightly more common ground.

Alfred bought a large, wood-framed house near Harvard Square in Cambridge, Massachusetts, where he pursued a graduate degree in architecture and I finished college. Alfred had a trove of inherited money that came to him via a trust built from money his grandfather made in the mining-car business. Each month, a check from the trust arrived to swell our bank account. I did not need to work for pay. Other affluent young wives in my social set volunteered for charities, played tennis and golf, beautified their houses, and got giddily, importantly pregnant.

I think now of a small paperback book I ignored at the time.

Soon after Alfred and I got engaged, a friend gave me *The Feminine Mystique,* Betty Friedan's groundbreaking 1963 critique of the restricted life of middle-class (white) housewives. A child of the post-war era, I had no idea that, while American men fought in World War II, women on the home front proved their skill and competence in jobs once restricted to men. After the war, employers ejected women in favor of the returning GIs, and heavy propaganda followed. Postwar ads and movies featured happy white housewives in new suburban developments, delighted by their children and their brand-new appliances. In 1957, journalist Betty Friedan surveyed her fellow Smith College graduates as they prepared to celebrate their fifteenth reunion. In words that could have been a warning to me, had I opened her book, Friedan reported that "Each suburban wife struggled . . . alone. As she made the beds, shopped for groceries, matched slipcover material, ate peanut butter sandwiches with her children, chauffeured Cub Scouts and Brownies, lay beside her husband at night, she was afraid to ask even of herself the silent question: 'Is this all?'" My friend's gift was an attempted wake-up call.

A different book—Julia Child's *Mastering the Art of French Cooking*—lay perpetually open in my new kitchen, becoming grease-smudged and dog-eared from daily use. Malcolm X was murdered early in my marriage, then Dr. Martin Luther King, Jr., and Bobby Kennedy. Years later, I would have to study these assassinations in order to learn the history of my own time, but mine was not a problem of memory. I can tell you to this day how to make Julia Child's Boeuf en Daube (chunks of beef, tomatoes, onions, rice, all in a long, slow bake). My ignorance of the real world stemmed, not from poor memory, but from selective inattention.

With no concept of a career and no need to earn money, I decided to get pregnant. Alfred and I would want a family sooner or later, I reasoned, so why not get started now? I say *reasoned.* Reason was probably the least active ingredient in the pot I stirred in my newlywed's kitchen, trying to cook up a future for myself. Ambition was a spice I'd never tasted. No surprise, then, that the soup I served up was motherhood. Alfred tasted hesitantly, wasn't sure he liked it, but finally said that we could have a baby if I wanted to—since, he said, scanning the other young couples we knew, mothers raised the kids.

In the hospital in the spring of 1969, while I breathed and panted through labor contractions, Alfred dozed in a plastic chair at the end of the bed. Later, in the delivery room, a nurse laid the bundled infant in my trembling arms. I remember the doctor standing over me, studying my face. "What's wrong?" he asked. "Aren't you happy?" I hadn't expected to feel so alone.

Nights, slumped in a rocking chair in little Matthew's room, I'd feel his tiny mouth rooting for my nipple, and worry: *Will he latch on correctly? Will I have enough?* Daytimes, I dragged myself towards his naps. While he slept, I lay on the living room floor, dreading the little sighs and whimpers of his waking.

Ashamed to show friends how lonely I was, I tried speaking to the doctor who had delivered my baby. Across his wide expanse of desk, I searched for words to tell him how I felt. The doctor laid a hand on mine. "Don't want too much," he said, patting. "Get out to a library once in a while, keep your mind fresh, but be satisfied. You are raising a new generation. You are taking care of your husband when he comes home from a busy day." The doctor's unsolicited advice on a woman's role was sexist and unprofessional, though I had no words for this at the time. Unwittingly, he propelled me towards feminism.

In the late fall of 1969, a friend invited me to an informal "course" on women's health to be taught in an MIT lounge by a group of women. The women had met at a conference on women's liberation at Boston's Emmanuel College the prior spring. In a workshop on health, they had set out to make a list of "good" Boston-area ob-gyns—doctors who treated women patients like intelligent adults. When no one in the group could put her own doctor on the list, the women decided to research women's health for themselves. They studied what questions to ask, how to become full partners in their health care, and how to judge the quality of the care they were receiving. After months of study, they were ready to teach other women what they had learned.

On a chilly November evening, I found fifty people crowded together in an MIT lounge. They were all female and, although I didn't notice it at the time, all white. Some were still dressed from the workday; some nursed babies. Several smiled and gestured for me to enter. The speaker at the front of the group was talking about masturbation. Hearing the word spoken aloud for the first time, I could feel my face heat up.

According to an article I'd once skimmed furtively in a college library, Sigmund Freud claimed that females who masturbate become fixated on an "immature" sexual organ called the clitoris and can't enjoy "mature" penis-in-vagina sex later on. The fixation theory scared me. I didn't enjoy sex. I often pretended to be asleep when Alfred rolled over to me at night, both of us in our preppy cotton pajamas. Was this because I'd "touched myself" as a girl? Maybe I was—I cringed at the cruelty of a term used in the Freud article—frigid.

In the lounge at MIT, the speaker held up a shockingly life-size diagram of a woman with her legs spread wide apart—a full-sized vulva, pubic hair and all. "See," the woman said, pointing boldly at the diagram with her finger. "Here's the clitoris. During sexual arousal, it engorges with blood just like a penis does." Laughter rippled across the room. "No, I'm serious. The clitoris has all kinds of nerve endings. It's our major organ of sexual pleasure. Not the vagina, despite what Freud says. Who knew this before?" She looked across our upturned faces. Only a few hands. "That's my point," she said. "We should know these things."

When the time came for small groups, I joined several women in a nearby classroom. They seemed to be in their mid to late twenties, like me; nearly all said they were mothers. I studied their faces, looking for signs of happiness. A woman named Paula said that she felt depressed for months after her first baby was born. She couldn't seem to get active, she said; she felt drained, worried, and afraid.

"What did you do?" I asked, hearing my own voice for the first time that night.

Paula turned to me, her hazel eyes earnest, friendly, sober. Many doctors dismissed postpartum depression as the "baby blues," she said, but the condition was caused by hormonal changes and social isolation and could be serious. She was doing research on this condition; she wanted to offer information and understanding to other women.

This was dizzying news to me. What I had been feeling had physical and societal causes. The nuclear family was a lonely place for mothers. Feeling depressed wasn't my fault. I felt a glimmer of elation, as if a heavy tarp had been lying across my spirits and these women had lifted an edge, letting in light and air.

Over the following months, I joined the women's health

movement with the energy of one sprung from a trap. I trained as a sex educator at Planned Parenthood, and helped teach the "bodies" course to new groups of women. I practiced new words in front of a mirror so I could say them naturally in public. *Clitoris. Orgasm. Penis. Cunnilingus.* And, yes, *postpartum depression.*

Postpartum depression was a turning point for me, a gateway. My life so far had brought me no conscious suffering. I had wealth and health, an able body, private education, and blond-haired, blue-eyed whiteness to smooth my path to marriage and success. Yes, my parents drank and fought, and my mother hid bruises beneath her fancy cashmere sweaters, but I kept quiet about this violence. I did not let this personal pain open a door to connection with anyone else. When caring for a new-born surprised me with its own variety of pain, I found myself in a circle of women who sought to tell each other new truths. With them, I was able to let my small experience of motherly distress "raise my consciousness" about more than my own misery. With their help, I learned that my depression was part of a larger social picture—the isolation of mothers in the nu-clear family, the loneliness of parents separated by rigid sex roles, the paternalistic sexism of many doctors to whom new mothers turned for help. I joined this circle of women to keep learning and to work for change—in medical training, in workplace support for new families, in fundamental assump-tions about what's "normal" and what's "right."

During the following decade, I'd feel uncertain and often miserable as I took steps that shattered the familiar surfaces of my life. Sometimes, thanks to the experience of talking and working with the women I met at MIT that winter evening, I could let my own small share of personal suffering point beyond my own life to a wider world.

The public story of *Our Bodies, Ourselves* has been told by scholars and activists. A collective of women without advanced degrees created a "revolutionary" resource on women's health and sexuality. The book sold, first, through a socialist press and the hippy Whole Earth Catalog and then through a commercial press. It became a best seller. We coauthors were invited to speak to medical students, women's groups, college classes, national conferences, and we appeared in interview segments on the TV morning shows. By the end of forty years, the book would have sold two million copies, appearing in thirty translations and adaptations around the world. The private story differs for each of the OBOS founders, and we have diverging takes on the public story. We agree on this, however: Year by year, choice by choice, working on *Our Bodies, Ourselves* transformed our lives.

Transformation, for me, included reckoning with social class. In an initial draft, we wrote, "We are twelve middle-class white women." I knew the claim would offend my father, whose upper-class aspirations I so embodied. Briefly, humorously, I suggested that we dub ourselves, "eleven middle-class women and one aristocrat." Getting involved with OBOS opened my eyes to social class in ways that no life of golfing, tennis, and gardening could have done. Feminism unsettled any notions I'd ever had about class—also about work, sexuality, politics, my marriage, and motherhood.

Feminism alone didn't end my marriage. My parents' troubled relationship gave me no clue to fair fighting, give and take, or working through conflict. Alfred's family taught him no more. Becoming parents exposed the fault lines, not in our love for each other but in our ability to work things out. My women's health activism and increasing allegiance to women Alfred didn't know increased our tension. He was not the only husband who feared that we feminist wives complained about them in meetings. Men may have benefited from our new levels of savvy and ease about sex, but, even there, we turned the tables: We wanted to show them what we liked, and we wanted them to listen. We sought to renegotiate who did the cooking, who took out the garbage, who took care of the children. Many marriages survived these power struggles; mine did not. My parents would blame the women's movement ("those women"). In the ending of a marriage and the shifting of a life, blame is not useful, but growing closer to those women did alter everything for me: my take on work, my experience of friendship and, yes, my marriage.

Joining with the "Bodies" women and helping to create *Our Bodies, Ourselves* was the first time in my life that I spent time with people who were Jewish. I remember arriving at Nancy's Cambridge apartment in December 1976 for a weekly Collective meeting and being surprised by the strum of a guitar and voices singing. Nancy, too, had recently divorced. I followed the music along the bravely painted yellow hallway and found Nancy playing the guitar on her bed, while her two small children swung their legs from the edge of the bed in slippered pajamas. "Dreidel, dreidel, dreidel," they sang, a catchy, buoyant tune. Members of our group perched around them. Wilma patted the space next to her for me to sit. "It's Hanukkah," she whispered into my ear. "Listen. You'll catch on."

Dreidel, dreidel, dreidel. I closed my eyes and sensed the women around me. I had history by now with each of them. Pam and I started a playgroup for our children, I'd written book chapters with Nancy, Paula, and Esther, and even begun travelling with some to speaking engagements around New England. But they were civil rights marchers, socialists, and practicing intellectuals. Those with Communist parents proudly called themselves "red diaper babies." Most all were Jewish. They had grown up singing these Hanukkah songs. They were not the kind of people I'd ever imagined as life-long friends.

The women around me swayed as they sang. Elbows raised in the air, they clapped their hands with an exuberance I'd experienced in my own family only in my mother—and only when she'd been drinking. I began to clap awkwardly, in search of the rhythm. With a swoop in my stomach and a flutter in my chest, as though a spinning top careened inside me, I understood that I might grow old with these women. I'd been moving out beyond the life I'd always known. That night I realized—in my body— that I wasn't going back.

That one of my earliest, viscerally felt experiences of difference was at a Hanukkah sing-along highlights the extreme limits of the world I grew up in. Through their loving inclusion, the working- and middle-class Jewish women in the collective opened a chink in the wall raised around me by the exclusions of my WASP and affluent upbringing. Whether I'd let more light in, time would tell.

≷

I was too distracted by my own dramas during those years to note Mary's news beyond my mother's occasional headlines. This is a pattern of domestic service: the "maid" studies every member of the family, while the employer's grown children go off to their own "important" lives. With Mary, I lost the decade. Here is some of what she has told me since.

Mary started out her married life in late 1961 doing day-time domestic work in Princeton for my mother and her friends. After she had Dennie in 1963, she improvised childcare. "Dennie was always with me at that time. I had no one that I would leave him with. My aunt was my only family nearby. So, I bought a small playpen that I kept in my car, and every day he would go in to work with me. He was a quiet child; he would play and sleep while I worked. At five o'clock, he would get very fussy, and that was it, we had to leave. I always called him my Little Clock. His place in the car going home was standing behind my right shoulder holding on tightly to my neck."

My entry into motherhood may have been shadowed by post-partum depression, but the 1967 birth of Mary's second child was difficult—and hair-raising—in a whole different way. "Four years later, here I was having another baby," Mary has told me. "Life had not been a cakewalk. Dennie was in Virginia with my mother. I worked until the day of labor, drove to the hospital around 2:00 p.m., had Greg around 7:00 p.m. The next day around 11:00 a.m. I was discharged. The nurse carried little Greg in his baby box and placed him on the passenger seat, and I drove home with one little bottle of milk. I got the girl across the street to watch Greg while I went to the store for supplies. It was not a happy time." Soon to be divorced from her husband, Mary was profoundly on her own.

Mary's life as a single working parent of two children comes alive in her description of a typical evening when her boys were young. She'd grab a nap after work, while the boys stretched out next to her on the bed watching *Speed Racer*. Dinner was "a thousand ways to cook hamburger." After the boys went to bed, she polished their little Stride Rite shoes and washed the laces. No new clothes for herself, but she made sure they had the sturdy shoes she lacked as a child. As she remembers with pride, "They never knew we were poor."

Eager to move beyond domestic work, Mary landed a job as a guard at a women's jail in 1967. I say "landed"—she got the job by making a way out of no way. She lived in Trenton, New Jersey, at that time, with her husband, four-year-old Dennie, and newborn Greg. "There was a local tavern where my husband would stop. After only a drink or two, he'd get feeling generous and buy rounds for everyone. He'd spend the money we needed for food and rent. One Friday I was waiting for him to get home, and time was passing. By 10:00 p.m. I was so angry that I went into the tavern and caused a scene. The bar's owner took a liking to me and apologized for not seeing that my husband couldn't afford all those rounds of drinks." Perhaps the tavern owner noted the impressive mix of will and courage that led Mary to march into the bar and give her husband and everyone else there a piece of her mind. Perhaps he understood how well these might serve her as a jail matron. As Mary reports, "He was very influential in the community. He contacted his connections at the women's jail, and sent me there to apply for a job." Mary pursued the opportunity with everything she had. "I studied hard, learned the procedures, took the test, and passed. I was the third

Black person who was ever hired, and everyone wanted to know how I got there."

Mary's continuing skill, dependability, and hard work convinced the jail's warden to send her to Officer Training School a few years later. In 1973 Mary became the first female officer in the Mercer County corrections system, cutting a trail for other women to follow. In 1977, Mary passed an exam that won her promotion from officer rank to that of sergeant. Soon a sergeant's position opened at the male division of the Mercer County Correction Center, a jail for men awaiting trial or serving sentences under a year. With encouragement from friends, and despite opposition from much of the all-male officer force at the correction center, she got the job. Maybe second-wave feminism was in the air in central New Jersey, prompting Mary's friends to say, as she quotes, "We know you can do it!" With her promotion, the county corrections system reluctantly advanced a qualified woman, opening the way for a new role for women in that system. "After that," Mary reports, "the floodgates were open."

Mary understands now that she played a role in the women's movement. "That movement was what enabled me to get the supervisory position, moved me into the male institution. I don't think I fully understood what was going on. I was making a contribution to women's progress but didn't even know it."

seven

Beach Walk

IN THE SUMMER OF 1978, MARY WORKED ONCE AGAIN FOR my parents at the Nantucket seaside rental, as she did most summers during a span of more than thirty years, 1956–1988. As usual, Mary used her vacation time from the correction center for the job, and I came to relax. We were two women in our thirties that summer—both divorced, both single parents. It was in no way inevitable that we would step outside our assigned roles to connect as human beings.

I arrived on the island alone, eager for time with my son Matthew. Now nine, he was spending the summer on Nantucket with his dad. After we divorced in 1975, Alfred had moved to Nantucket, to pursue a boat building business. We devised one of those "sensible" post-divorce arrangements that fails to mask the cruelty of any plan for splitting a child's life: schooling with me in Cambridge, summers on Nantucket. Early in 1978, we'd decided on a change for the coming year: Matthew would go to fourth grade on Nantucket and live with Alfred, his wife Bunny, and their new baby.

As Bunny's pregnancy had advanced, Matthew had begun to alienate his third-grade friends in Cambridge with a brittle new boastfulness. His new edginess may have been developmental, but I also thought he might be afraid of losing his dad's love and attention to the baby. It was a wrenching decision, for me, to let him go, but I wanted Matthew to know he was a full member of his dad's new family.

I drove down the bumpy, sandy driveway of my parents' seaside getaway to find them taking their ease in noon sunshine on the deck. My mother had angled her chair towards the ocean, with her back to my father. I studied her floppy pink hat, the slope of her tanned shoulders, the large insulated tumbler at her side. Chablis, I was sure. Behind her, my father took a thirsty swallow from his usual noon martini, shelled a peanut, popped it in his mouth. He'd lost his bladder to cancer surgery a few years earlier. His doctors cut him from two packs of Camels a day to none. Instead of smoking, he ate peanuts. He dropped the shells to the floor the way he once flicked ash—for someone else to sweep up. In this case, that someone would be Mary.

Each year, as my mother drank more steadily, mobility became more difficult for her. Now she clambered awkwardly from her chair and steadied herself with a hand on the white railing to greet me. Her cheek, warm from summer and sun. My father's, dry, tilted up from where he sat.

"Mary!" my mother called out. "Wendy's come!"

Four decades later, I shift my focus from the sunny deck and try to put myself in Mary's shoes at the time. Mary would have stood just inside the screen door that separated her work sphere from my family's relaxed sunbathing as thoroughly as a shield. Already that morning, she'd have swept the wide wooden floorboards free of sand, made the bathrooms sparkle, scrubbed the old kitchen sink as white as it was going to get. On a small cabinet in the corner of the living room, Mary would have piled the ice bucket high and re-stocked the wine and gin. Glasses would stand waiting, in perfect rows. For most of the past twenty summers, Mary had attended to my parents' desires, and these did not change.

That day, as Mary squinted through the screen door against the glare, perhaps she remarked to herself how odd it was that white people liked to bake themselves in the hot sun. Mary would one day tell me that she had no tolerance for direct sunshine. She remembers the mid-summer sun beating down on her grandmother's garden, the expanse of tilled soil stretching out under the heat, row upon row of knee-high plants needed to feed the family through the winter, weeds cropping up everywhere. Even wearing her grandmother's biggest hat, Mary lagged in the hot sun. Her head felt heavy, and her legs weak. She remembers begging not to have to hoe at midday, how her no-nonsense grandmother assigned garden duty anyway. One noon, Mary awoke to find herself crumpled beneath the broiling sun, having fainted to the ground between the tomatoes and the beans. Vindication! From then on, her grandmother sent her into the garden only when the sun was lower in the sky. I think now of Mary's great-grandmother, also named Mary, born in 1868. As part of a family of sharecroppers, Mary Blevins Cox would have met no such coddling for fainting in a field, no prolonged rest in the shade, no glass of iced water fetched by a worried grandmother.

Yet here were these white people in Nantucket, baking themselves on purpose.

Three years after surgeons removed his cancer-ridden bladder, my father was dapper again, doing fine, sunning himself in madras shorts Mary had pressed. In the intimacy of live-in service, Mary knew that my father spent tense hours in the bathroom trying to change the plastic bag that he wore to collect his urine. She heard, from my mother, how the tube slipped and the opening chafed, how skin infections raged on for weeks. Mary knew men in the correction center who had lost organs to cancer, limbs to the Vietnam war, feet to the ravages of untreated diabetes. These men lacked the expensive medical care that had returned my father to relative fitness. They had no private places to sweat out the struggle with urine bags and prostheses, and no servants to ease their recovery. Mary's work was to further my parents' ease. The sun beat down on them, but Mary kept them comfortable, kept their cool drinks supplied.

Although Mary focused her attention on my parents, she remembers that her sons were in her mind and heart. Not long after Mary divorced in the early 1970s, her ex-husband had died suddenly, leaving her to support Dennie and little Greg on her own. The boys were spending the summer down in Elk Creek with her mother and stepfather and all the cousins up and down Willow Oak Lane. The corn must be waist-high already, green beans picked, snapped, blanched, and canned for the winter. If, for an aching moment, Mary longed to be in Elk Creek with her sons, she brushed the thought away and reminded herself that half her relatives drove her crazy. She took this summer job to put food on the table, to make sure the boys had sturdy shoes and maybe a new football in September.

As soon as my mother called out to her, Mary stepped out into the Nantucket sunshine. We embraced in a long hug. "How many summers has it been since we were here at the same time?" I asked. "Just two?"

"Too many," my mother interjected.

My father lifted his empty peanut bowl in the air. "Don't get us wrong, Mary. We appreciate the girls you send in your place when you can't come. But no one spoils us the way you do."

Mary took the empty bowl from my father, slipped into the house, and returned with the bowl piled high with unshelled peanuts. A skilled domestic worker, Mary read signs—however silent—and did her job.

"I'll get your bags," she said to me.

I moved quickly to stand in Mary's way. "The car's a mess. Papers I'm working on, clothes all over the place." We stood up close, facing each other, breathing the same air, two women on either side of thirty-five. Already the familiar, awkward dance.

"Let Mary do her job," my father pronounced.

Together, we headed for my car.

Mary insisted on carrying my heavy suitcase, and I gave in. But she winced as she heaved it onto the spare bed in the guest room. She put a hand on her lower back and looked out the window towards the ocean, setting her eyes on the horizon. "It's nothing," she said, when she caught me looking. "Just a little something from the correction center." She dropped her hand away.

Recalling Mary's back pain that August day, as she worked and I vacationed, I realize what a harbinger that was. In more than sixty years, I would rarely see Mary free of physical pain. Mary did farm work every day of her childhood and started in domestic service when she was eleven—realities unthinkable for children from my affluent sphere. As Mary headed north to work in domestic service, young Black girls all over the South were fanning out over America: cooking, cleaning, washing, ironing—making lives like mine and my parents' more sanitary, more comfortable, more open to long stretches of enjoyment. Domestic service demanded unrelenting physical labor—kneeling, stooping, lifting, scrubbing, standing.

Since neither domestic service nor the corrections work Mary began in her thirties paid her a living wage, and since motherhood paid only in sacrifice and joy, Mary always worked several jobs—as a mother, at the jail, and as a part-time domestic worker for a number of white housewives in Princeton. Each kind of work—and the balancing act itself—demanded sustained physical effort and brought significant emotional and psychic stress. For the six decades of her working life, Mary's work would tax her body and psyche, increasingly limiting her movement and disabling her with physical pain—in her back and her neck, her knees and her shoulders. Remembering her beautiful, strong body when we first met, I don't think I ever saw Mary feeling truly well after that time. And yet, always, she pushed forward with the work at hand.

I reached out to touch Mary's back in the Nantucket guestroom, thinking I might be able ease the back spasm. Mary turned quickly, moving her body just out of my reach. Remembering the moment now, in 2020, I reflect that Mary had grown up in a place, and within a history, where a white person's sudden touch was more likely to be punitive or coercive than friendly or healing.

"You're going to have to let me spoil you a little," she said, steering us back to our more usual roles.

I thought, with horror, of my father lifting the empty peanut bowl into the air as a wordless command. I didn't want to be the kind of person who thinks it's acceptable to command service in that way, an empty bowl held aloft.

"Don't spoil me!" I cried to Mary, more sharply than I intended.

Mary took a step back, her face serious, unreadable. "It gives me pleasure, Wen," she said. Here was our familiar conundrum. Mary wanted to do her job. I felt uneasy with Mary waiting on me, and didn't want to add consciously to her workload. My resistance to her proffered help assaulted her in ways I would later come to regret. I bristled at my father's sense of entitlement, and little recognized that my own sense of entitlement to Mary's willing, friendly, comforting presence on my family's summer vacation might be as great as my father's, despite the fact that I more often said *thank you* and *please*.

Still in the Nantucket guest room, Mary and I stood briefly side by side in front of the mirror. We were close to the same height. Mary had filled out—her shoulders and hips were more substantial than before, while I was still what I thought of as worry-thin. Our faces looked weary in different ways: hers wider and puffier somehow, with dark, pouch-like bags under her eyes, and my face narrowed and tight and worried into sharp angles. In Mary, I could still see the gorgeous teenager who stood in my mother's kitchen by her hard-sided suitcase, her beautiful complexion vibrant with the resilience of youth. I was a far cry from the coiffed debutante whose wedding dress Mary had endlessly buttoned. I actually liked the change. I thought I looked less "constructed"—less like I crafted my appearance with a man in mind—and more natural. Mary and I were beautiful still, I thought. Just a little worn, just a little tired.

Mary had bunched her thick, straightened hair into a little ponytail for the workday. I was unaware, at the time, of the devilment the sea air created in Mary's hair. Salty moisture invaded every strand, inciting irrepressible frizz. I did not know the effort Mary spent fighting the frizz into submission, a battle that accounted for the stock of oil-based hair products that weighed down her suitcase that first August. Starting in the 1960s, politically oriented Black women had stopped trying to tame the nap of their natural hair into the flat, smooth look that white people considered appropriate. Afros had been the style of choice for progressive Black women for a decade—Angela Davis, most famously, wore her hair like a luminous cloud around her head. A woman of an earlier era, Mary allowed no hair to stray towards the freedom of an Afro.

In the mirror, I could see Mary's gaze take in my new, very short haircut. I'd had my long hair cut off that spring. I felt elated to be free of the thick, blond hair that had rippled down my shoulders for years, weighing me down with a prescriptive femininity. I also felt bare before the world, shorn and revealed, no screen of hair to hide me.

"How could you cut off all that beautiful hair?" Mary said, almost longingly, as though the mirror image revealed the ghost of my shorn locks.

"Wanted a change," I said, hiding behind vague elusiveness the way I used to hide behind my hair. Secretly, I called my new hair style, "lesbian short." I didn't know if I was really a lesbian, but I hoped my cropped hair sent a signal that I no longer cared about appealing to men.

"How could you cut off all that beautiful hair?" Mary's question would come back to me the next year in 1979, when I discovered Toni Morrison's first novel, *The Bluest Eye.* The book's young Black narrator, Claudia, rebels against the blond baby doll that she gets for Christmas. "All the world had agreed that a blue-

eyed, yellow-haired, pink-skinned doll was what every girl child treasured," Claudia says. She hates the fact that people with skin like her new doll enjoy ease and security unreachable to her family no matter how hard her parents work. She tears her baby doll limb from limb.

In the novel, Claudia's mother briefly offers shelter to Pecola Breedlove, a Black girl from a brutally poor and troubled family whose ramshackle house has burned down. The whole community considers the Breedloves to be profoundly physically ugly. Perhaps "ugliness" condemns the Breedloves to desperate poverty, and perhaps being so poor is what makes them ugly. Perhaps their neighbors so fear falling into deeper poverty themselves that they brand the family as "ugly" to keep misery at a distance. But Pecola takes the community's cruel and self-serving judgment inside herself; she believes she is ugly. While staying with Claudia's family, Pecola is powerfully drawn to an old, cracked milk cup decorated with a picture of Shirley Temple, the popular blond, blue-eyed child actress. She drinks cup after cup of milk. Soon, Claudia's mother, whose tight budget has no room for extra milk, sends Pecola home. There, Pecola disappears inside herself, harboring the wild hope that she will wake up with blue eyes—no longer "ugly," no longer doomed.

Through these two girls of Morrison's invention, I began to understand the power dynamics of beauty. A society that equates beauty with whiteness serves those who are white. Like Morrison's characters, I grew up in a popular culture that identified beauty with blond hair and blue eyes. I saw myself in the images of "beauty" in ads, movies, and TV shows. Adults said to me, "You're such a pretty girl." All the messages sang to me of my beauty. I wonder if anyone told Mary she was beautiful. Her mother's sisters, perhaps, the doting aunts who loved to spoil their first niece. Her Mamaw may have taken a moment from work and farming to say, "You're a pretty girl." Whatever affirmations Mary heard from those who loved her, however, any ads she caught sight of in white-owned newspapers or magazines of the time told her otherwise.

When Mary began to work for my family at nearly sixteen, I remember my father calling her "a pretty little colored girl." His implication was, "pretty *for* a colored girl," and he didn't say beautiful. As she chatted to Mary over the years, I imagine my mother went on about my "classic" beauty, inviting Mary to lament with her when I didn't make the "best" of my looks. When Mary asked how I could "cut off all that beautiful hair," I thought I heard my mother's voice. I heard the voice of white supremacy, too, though I did not know this at the time. In white-controlled America, blond hair is the epitome of female beauty, a symbol and even a source of power.

"Being married wasn't so great for either of us, was it?" I said suddenly, wanting to connect with Mary further.

Mary looked at me in startled surprise, seemed to measure how I meant the question, and began to answer. Before she could speak, however, my father's voice cut through the open window. "Wendy!" he commanded—peremptory, imperative. "Come out and see your mother."

I wanted to hear Mary's answer.

Mary gave me a little push. "Go now," she said, as though any delay would be her fault. She was at work. My parents' wishes had her primary attention.

≷

Back out on the deck again, my mother's eyes brimmed with tears as I bent over to kiss her cheek. "How *are* you, sweetheart?" she asked. Since my divorce, she had looked at me with an unsettling pity.

I gestured towards the moving gleam of the ocean and said, in an overly hearty manner, "It's great to be here."

She asked if I would be calling Matthew.

"Of course, I'll be calling Matthew," I snapped, as though she'd said the stupidest possible thing. My quick, exasperated retort brought a quiver to her bright red lips, and I knew I sounded like my irascible father. "Give me a break, Mom. My son is eight years old. He's going to live with his dad this year. It's not my favorite aspect of life right now."

"We . . ." She glanced over at my father. They were studying me, looking for signs of misery or collapse. I was glad I had decided to shave my legs. Smoothly shaven calves, at least, belonged to a world my parents knew. "We worry about you," she said finally.

"Well, don't," I said, surprised at how irked I felt, how petulant.

Alone in the pine bedroom later that afternoon, I unpacked treasures from the suitcase that had strained Mary's back. First, the hefty 1976 edition of *Our Bodies, Ourselves*. The book that was a source of pride in my Cambridge life felt like a brash intruder in the summer cottage. My parents would be aghast that I wrote about sex. *Masturbation. Orgasm. Clitoris.* They had not sent me to elite schools for this writing. Holding the book before me in my parent's seaside guest room, I felt like two different people. In Cambridge, I played my part in a revolution in women's health education. In my parents' home, I was an awkward daughter hiding more than half of myself.

I'd edited a new chapter on violence against women that spring. As I sharpened language that would enable readers to identify, survive, and fight against domestic violence, I had flashed to my mother's occasional morning-after bruises. Encouraged by the text to think beyond physical violence, I began to understand that even my father's verbal attacks were a form of abuse. Violence tore at my own family, but I could think of no way to stop it.

Next, I lifted up a manuscript from a Boston-area group called the Alliance Against Sexual Coercion. In consciousness-raising groups and public meetings at the time, women were talking openly about struggles with male supervisors, teachers, and professors who used the power of their gender and status to pressure women into sex. A woman who refused sex with a boss or teacher risked losing a job or failing a class. Women seeking to succeed in male-dominated work—from the trades to the academy—encountered hostile and humiliating treatment. Alone, women had little recourse. Together, they could fight. The Alliance women called their book, a first of its kind, *Fighting Sexual Harassment*. They'd asked me to edit their sprawling first draft. I loved this work.

I heard a sound from the doorway and turned to see my mother still in her bathing suit and pink hat, holding her bare feet apart for balance, clutching the door frame. I remember now how vulnerable she seemed, how needy. My presence was a solace, a balm, and a life raft for my mother, though I didn't want this to be true. I'd once heard her claim that she could bear anything, all year long, if she knew that she could stay by this beach in August, swim in this ocean, travel the highway of moonlight across these waters. By bearing anything, I knew she meant my father.

There was a curious equation between misery and luxury in my mother's life. She wasn't self-conscious about her affluence, as I was. She seemed to need no justification for the luxuries allowed by her wealth. Exclusive Nantucket and Florida beachfronts, annual stays in London's best hotels, household help, an ankle-length fur coat, a full liquor closet, Mary's helpful presence whenever she wanted it—my mother seemed to accept such abundance as her birthright. As she aged, however, as her marriage to my dad wore on, she increasingly expressed her "need" for these luxuries against the strains of her marriage. Each year, this equation seemed to require more of the drinks that soothed, consoled, and would ultimately kill her—big tumblers full of iced Chablis, bourbon cocktails, scotch and soda, and the whiskey that laced her beloved Irish coffees.

At that moment, however, holding herself up on the door frame, she was on a mission to make me happy. "I called Matthew for you," my mother said. "You can pick him up this afternoon."

Later that afternoon, I rapped the brass knocker at Alfred and Bunny's grey-shingled house on the town's historic Academy Hill, and Bunny opened the door. I had no illusions of getting back together with my ex-husband, so encountering his next wife did not wrench me. But when Bunny turned back into the house and called out, "Matt, sweetie, your mom's here," I almost hated her. All year, she and the new baby would win their way into Matthew's heart. They would become his idea of family.

I heard the squeak and thud of sneakered feet on stairs inside the house. Nine-year-old Matthew—blonder, tanner, taller, with a smattering of new freckles across his peeling nose—spun around the front entrance. I wondered: Would he hug Bunny goodbye? As I steeled myself for jealousy, Matthew grabbed his sports bag from her hand as though she were merely a hook for his stuff. "Bye," he said over his shoulder, throwing the bag into the back seat and hopping in beside me. Bunny's eyes met mine. She gave a small shrug as though saying, "He treats me like a piece of the furniture." As a woman, I felt empathy—as a rival mother, satisfaction.

Dinner out with my parents was uneventful in a good way—moderate drinking on my parents' part, no boozy outbursts from my father, and, for my mother, no hurt tears. Later that evening, Matthew put on his pj's and settled into bed in the corner bedroom of the seaside cottage. I lounged on the floor, leaning my head easily against the mattress. Below the open window, small waves rushed the beach and peacefully receded—ocean as lullaby. I reported to Matthew on the sailboat I'd borrowed for the days ahead, the neighbors who wanted to take him night fishing. Before leaving him for the school year, I wanted to make vivid memories together.

"I won't be here Saturday and Sunday, right?" Matthew said in a louder voice than he needed to. He pushed an elbow into his pillow and propped himself up. "My dad told you, right, about the races at the Yacht Club, how I'm going to skipper and he'll be my crew?"

"He'll have you all year," I said loudly. "I don't want you to miss the only weekend I'm here."

The year Alfred and I separated, five-year-old Matthew had

developed a brittle little cough that had nothing to do with being sick. He coughed like that now. "I don't think you should be the boss of me in Nantucket," he said.

Sooner or later, most children want to be their own boss. Capable parents select what decisions their kids can control, and at what age. They may welcome their children's input but make key decisions themselves. I remember watching in awe as my friends insisted on what they thought was best for their children, no questions asked. Being a single parent demanded a kind of self-confidence and fortitude I did not easily muster. I'd been unnerved by Alfred's move to the island, by his retreat from any united front we might have maintained towards Matthew. I often felt too confused and unsteady to assert what I wanted. Children with two parents get skilled at playing one off against the other in order to get a yes to something they want to do. When parents separate into opposing camps, divorced or no, playing one off against the other becomes infinitely easier. Matthew's claim hit me where I felt most insecure.

This is how social location matters. When a white boy, headed for a life of economic and racial privilege, declares, "I don't think you should be the boss of me," he voices the sexism of the wider culture. At the same time, he is a child, angling for what he wants.

I sprang from the floor, no sweet tuck-in, no goodnight kiss. "See you tomorrow," I said, and shut the door behind me.

Mary was in the back hall in pedal pushers and a sweatshirt, carrying her toothbrush from the bathroom. "You guys have a lovely evening?" she asked.

"I hate being a single parent," I snapped. I looked down at the gauzy dress I'd worn out to dinner. My get-up looked stupid to me—too fancy, too irrelevant. "You know what I mean?"

Mary nodded soberly. Even in the dim light of the hallway, I could see worry lines in her face. Of course, she knew about being a single parent. "Can we talk?" I said.

We turned towards the back door and tiptoed out so quietly that my mother, drinking and reading alone in the living room, did not hear us. We made our way along the unlit wooden walkway towards the dark beach and the sound of the surf.

What I remember as a smoothly tacit agreement to head out to the beach together, an easy flow of two women eager to talk, must have been a necessarily calculated choice for Mary. In my dream-state of whiteness and wealth, I did not have to think about my race or social standing as we escaped to the beach. This was "my" world. I knew that I would be safe. For Mary, the stakes in a beach walk were infinitely higher. Despite my mother's early fantasy that Mary might enjoy a swim, Mary's presence was tolerated on that beach only in service—to relay a phone message, to refresh my mother's iced tea. Mary's unwritten contract of domestic service did not include pleasant strolls on the beach. Pent up in that small room with the folded laundry and the ironing board, a beautiful beach just a stone's throw away, Mary had no safe way to enjoy the breeze and the beauty without a white person—without, in this case, me. In real and definite ways, this open beach and gorgeous ocean were closed to her.

In the Klan-infested area of the rural South where Mary grew up, a Black person venturing into the night alone risked injury or death inflicted by racist whites. Nantucket's summer residents would have disparaged the Klan as rowdy and violent. But many white homeowners on that beach and along much of New England's Atlantic coast apply exclusionary and restrictive policies. Unlike Klan members, who use sheets, knives, ropes, guns, and torches to preserve white dominance, Northerners use economic and social weapons. All are forms of violence. Maybe Mary had wanted to walk on that beach for years, but didn't feel safe. My accompaniment offered her a protective "pass"—a familiar term from the lexicon of apartheid.

Linking arms in the darkness, we threaded our way across the sand, through the sharp dune grass, over crackly piles of dried seaweed. "You okay?" I asked, once or twice. I could just see Mary's nod. Where the open beach flattened out before beginning to slant towards the water, we let go and stood for a moment, looking up at stars that wheeled far above our heads.

"Sit, or walk?" I asked.

"Let's walk," she said.

Under cover of darkness, we began a walk that daytime would not permit, a Black domestic worker strolling in a relaxed manner on the secluded, whites-only beach.

Mary pulled a Salem from her pocket and turned her back to the breeze to light it. On a smoky exhalation, she began to speak about her fellow corrections officers. "These men never had a woman superior to them in rank before, so they like to make things difficult." Recently, her fellow officers had "forgotten" to tell her about a certain set of keys that the night supervisor was supposed to carry—keys that would have made her job easier and safer. "And they do not like having a woman in their locker room," she added. Just that week, guards had plastered photos of naked women on the walls of the locker room they had been ordered to share with Mary. "Girlie photos," she said. "Ones no decent woman should have to set eyes on."

I thought of the manuscript I was editing for the Alliance Against Sexual Coercion. Mary seemed to be encountering classic workplace harassment. By refusing to advise or assist Mary in her work as night supervisor, her fellow guards were undermining her success on the job. By withholding information about the night supervisor's keys, they were putting her in danger. Although the men did not threaten Mary directly with sexual violence, lewd pictures in the locker room were a menacing message of disrespect. All their tactics seemed aimed at unsettling and unnerving Mary. I thought she'd start to cry any minute.

Mary took an emphatic tug on her cigarette. "I fixed them," she said, not crying at all. "You know that magazine that started having centerfolds of naked men? I cut out a big, naked he-man and taped him up inside my locker door. Then I opened my locker and exclaimed, 'Now there's my idea of a *real* man.'" She snorted into the night. "They stopped that funny business, I'll tell you."

Half a decade earlier, *Cosmopolitan* editor Helen Gurley Brown had introduced a bold new feature to the popular women's magazine—a male centerfold. The new spread accomplished many goals: to affirm heterosexual women's delight in the naked male body; to show men what it felt like to be treated like sexual objects; to protest the hyper-sexualized, airbrushed female nudes in men's magazines like Playboy; and, naturally, to boost the magazine's circulation. Though more capitalist than *Our Bodies, Ourselves*, the new *Cosmo* centerfold was arguably feminist.

I figure now that the "hunk of a man" Mary pinned up on her locker door might have been actor (and later California state governor) Arnold Schwarzenegger, from a 1977 issue. Or perhaps she had saved the sexy 1973 centerfold of Black football hero and film star Jim Brown. With a snip of scissors and a few pieces of scotch tape, Mary converted one of *Cosmo's* "feminist" centerfolds into a locker room ally.

Helen Gurley Brown was a complicated figure over the years, obsessed with her own sex appeal, perhaps, but also dedicated to succeeding, and helping her readers succeed, in a sexist world. I like to think she would have been delighted to know that, in the locker room of a county jail in New Jersey, a brave woman with an excellent sense of humor used a *Cosmo* centerfold to fight workplace harassment.

Soon afterwards, Mary reported, several officers dared her into a drinking contest at a local bar. Mary downed more shots of scotch than any of them and walked out of the bar standing up. "Course I nearly killed myself driving home, but I did it." Mary stopped and leaned against me to empty sand from her shoe. "They've realized I'm not going away," she said proudly. "Some of the guys I supervise have even found out I'll go to bat for them with the warden. A few started coming around to my office for coffee."

"And the ones who still don't accept you?"

"I just have to keep an eye out for what they'll try next. What? Are you thinking about that centerfold? Am I awful?"

"The guards are the awful ones," I said. Suddenly, I was on a mission to tell Mary everything I'd learned from my new editing job. The guards were harassing her, I said, and poisoning her work environment. They were illegally affecting her working conditions. The warden should protect her. Mary could take the county to court under Title VII of the Civil Rights Act of 1964, or the Occupational Health and Safety Act of 1970.

Mary walked steadily ahead during my outburst.

"This is all in a book I've been editing," I said finally. "Do you want to see the manuscript?"

Mary didn't jump at my offer. "Sure, if you like."

"You don't want to see it?"

"I'm sure the book will be helpful. It's just that I've handled them already."

"But your body is like a fortress, your back is all seized up." I said this almost accusingly, as if Mary's tense and defended back were somehow her doing. I was concerned for her wellbeing, yes, but today when I listen again—*like a fortress! all seized up!*—there is a note of complaint or even accusation in what I said to Mary, as though I resented the discomfort of worrying about her. Subtle, perhaps, but I see it as no coincidence that, shortly afterwards, Mary turned around to head back.

When we reached the wooden steps to the cottage, I feared that Mary might head straight up. She paused, however, and we both sank down to sit on the sand. After my sexual harassment rescue mission backfired, I was relieved Mary didn't rush to go in.

Sifting cool sand through my fingers, I told Mary about Matthew's plan to sail the weekend races with his father. "It's like his dad gets everything this year," I complained. Mary said nothing for so long that I wondered if I had lost her. I could feel my face heat up. My whining must sound so stupid and inconsequential to her. So wealthy. Whatever Mary had meant by her nod in the hallway about being a single parent, she didn't mean my losing Matthew to a weekend of yacht club sailboat races.

Finally, Mary said, simply, "Don't stop Matthew from doing what he loves." She seemed knowing, matter-of-fact. "His father is not going to help you. You know that."

She was right. If I fought what Matthew and his dad wanted, I'd lose. Plus, I'd be the bad guy. "How'd you get all that single-mother wisdom?" I asked.

"I talk to Mommy, and she helps me."

I wish that I had asked Mary, right then, how her mother helped her. I could have honored her mother that way, and learned, for myself, how a mother-daughter relationship unlike my own could strengthen and nourish a person. But I didn't. Perhaps I was more interested in being the savior than in being saved. A chilly sea breeze picked up just then, and the porch light glared brightly over the shadowy dune. We fell silent. Our evening was over.

Mary and I eased the screen door open and tiptoed into the kitchen, but my mother heard us anyway. "What in God's name were you two doing?" she called out loudly from the living room. "Doesn't anybody think about anybody else around here?"

Mary froze. I turned to her with a conspiratorial look, but the fear in her eyes stopped me. I hadn't imagined that our walk might get her into trouble with my mother. I slipped into the living room alone, shutting the door behind me so that Mary could return to the haven, or the prison, of her room.

A novel lay open on my mother's lap, a fresh scotch and soda on the table beside her. "The walk was totally my idea, Mom. I'm sorry we ... I ... stayed so long."

The whites of my mother's eyes were tinged red with the burst capillaries of too much drink. "You left me with *him*," she said in a vicious whisper, nodding her coiffed blond head towards the closed bedroom door.

I wondered if they had fought, if he had hurt her.

My mother left the question in the air. "You're home now, and it won't happen again. Now go to bed," she said, as though I were still a child. I leaned over to kiss her, holding my breath against the smell of scotch. She clung so long that I could not hold my breath long enough. When she let go, I fled the cloying, sick-sweet smell of her drunkenness.

Mary's door was closed.

I lifted the latch to crack Matthew's door open. A column of light from the hall fell across his face. His cheeks were flushed and moist with sleep. "I've decided," I whispered. "You can sail with your dad."

As I seek to understand what drew Mary and me together that summer, I light on Mary's loneliness and mine. As I became more feminist, and left my traditional marriage, I became more isolated in my family. The more my parents drank, the lonelier I felt in their presence. Mary faced extreme isolation as a Black person in that elite, white, windswept corner of Massachusetts. Our mutual loneliness turned us towards each other. I wasn't Mary's boss, which helped. Although deference and service to me were part of Mary's job, I had no role in evaluating her, nor did I control her paycheck. There were immense power differences between us, but none directly related to purse strings.

In an earlier era, given the absolute divisions of class and race between us, Mary's and my very different experiences of divorce and single parenting would have done little to draw us together. It's possible that my work in the women's health movement played a small role here. I was learning to recognize—and seek—common threads between women. In my rather simplistic new views at the time, women were more alike than different: we "all" had vaginas and went through monthly menstruation for much of our adult life, we "all" faced sexism at home and on the job, and we "all" sought health care from a medical system that didn't value our knowledge of our own bodies. My idealistic convictions disregarded profound differences in experience caused by racism, classism, and other systemic evils. Or, to say this another way, I did not stop to question what "we" Mary and I might actually both inhabit.

I once asked Mary why she'd been open to possible friend-ship with me, and her answer was quick and definitive: "There wasn't anyone else out there to be friends with." Loneliness, above all, opened the door between us.

At the end of our joint time in Nantucket that summer, Mary and I were verging on a slight but definite shift in our relationship. Within the constrictions of Mary's work for my parents and my own profound ignorance about the socially constructed walls that divided us, we took a small step towards each other. Whether we would continue this movement, only the future would reveal.

eight

A New Canon

DURING 1978–79—THE YEAR THAT I SPENT IN CAMBRIDGE
alone without Matthew—I devoted myself to my work and
friendships with the women of *Our Bodies, Ourselves*, as well as
pursuing seminary studies and Quaker worship. These pursuits
unexpectedly prepared me to re-enter the conversation that
Mary and I had begun the previous summer.

A few years earlier, in 1972, I had discovered Quakers. If
feminism catapulted me from the life I had known, Quaker worship offered spiritual and moral compass as I sought my way. In
the deep, accompanied silence and "expectant waiting" of
Quaker worship, I found I could wrestle with my own questions,
like *Who are you, God, if you're not the old white man up in the sky
I learned about in Sunday School?* After my divorce, silent worship gave me a chance to pray over my fears and dilemmas as a
single mother. I could remember to honor "that of God" in
everyone—including myself. I found no quick answers, but a
centering sense of sharing a spiritual quest, individually and col-
lectively seeking guidance for how to live. The social witness of
Friends also spoke to me. Quaker values—simplicity, pacifism,
integrity, community, and equality—offered an alternative to
the elitism of my upbringing.

❧

By 1974, feminism and my awakened Quaker spirituality had inspired me to pursue a ministry degree at Harvard Divinity School. There, I studied theology and ethics from dazzling feminist scholars who were part of a new, cutting-edge program on women and religion. I encountered "liberation theology," first developed by justice-minded Latin American Catholics and later a major influence in the progressive Black church. Whereas many evangelical or "born-again" Christians focus on individual "salvation" through Jesus's death and resurrection, liberation theology lifts up the example of Jesus's life and teaching—how he challenged established powers and sought justice for marginalized and oppressed people. The liberation church enacts the good news of the gospel: food for the hungry, shelter for the homeless, and justice for the oppressed. As a new Quaker and new feminist, I embraced these aspirations.

Enter Reverend Dr. Katie Geneva Cannon. The first Black woman ordained as a United Presbyterian minister, Dr. Cannon was a visiting professor of Christian ethics whose teaching became central to my spiritual formation. Dr. Cannon taught Christian ethics in an utterly nontraditional way. Novels by Black women were her texts. She highlighted Black women's moral agency in the face of multiple oppressions. We discussed ethics through characters created by Toni Morrison in *Sula* and *Beloved*, Ann Petry in *The Street*, Paule Marshall in *Brown Girl, Brownstones*, Audre Lorde in *Zami*, and Margaret Walker in *Jubilee*. Dr. Cannon's teaching merged liberation theology and "womanism," a term that leading Black feminists in the church created to center Black women's perspectives. She ran a classroom in which every voice mattered and conflict was an opportunity for learning.

～

Working on *Our Bodies, Ourselves* also turned my focus to writing by Black women. Early in my women's health activism, I'd rejoiced to find myself part of a "we" that seemed to include women of every race, class, and nationality. Surely, I thought, being female was a bond that transcended differences. The illusion did not last long. Women of color rose during the '70s to assert their own goals for a women's movement—some goals the same as mine, and some very different. The Combahee River Collective in Boston—a group of brilliant and activist Black lesbians who gathered starting in 1974—challenged white feminists' blithe assumption of commonality among women. I came to understand that the banner of "we" waved by white feminists too often prioritized middle-class and white-centered goals— freedom to work outside the home, for example, rather than a decent minimum wage, or the primacy of abortion rights over the right to decent maternal and child health care. White health activists had everything to learn about the life and death concerns of women of color—the scourge of involuntary sterilization, damage inflicted by racist ideals of beauty, and the effects of poverty on family health. The Bodies group had begun shaping revisions of *Our Bodies, Ourselves* in response to the call for a more inclusive and culturally accurate agenda for women's health. In turn, the revisions were revising me.

The 1970s brought a surge of powerful literature by African-American women, published, at least for a period, by a few mainstream and several independent publishers—some feminist, some Black. On the shelves of New Words, a vibrant local women's bookstore, I encountered the authors to whom Dr. Katie Cannon was sending us to learn about moral agency and ethics. That I had never heard of writers like Zora Neale Hurston, Ann Petry and Paule Marshall revealed the absolute inadequacy of my elite, private school, Ivy League education. Their works opened realities I hadn't known existed and fed a hunger I hadn't known I felt. I thought of this hunger as intellectual and political, the result of a long ignorance that would take years to remedy. Today, I believe my heart hungered, too. Mary's and my nighttime walk on the beach the summer before had opened a door. Beginning to read outside the white, male, European canon allowed me to keep the door ajar. I didn't know it yet, but the writers I discovered that year would challenge and continually re-inform my inherited perspective on the world.

As I began to read literature by Black women and men more widely and with more purpose, I found myself adapting the traditional spiritual practice of "devotional reading." My devotional reading for the rest of my life would feature, not the Bible and other more traditionally religious texts, but writings that increased my understandings of Black American history and culture, and also of white racism, white privilege, white supremacy. Over time, this devotional reading evolved into what I have come to call "restorative reading."

Restorative reading is an ethical practice, allowing me to access crucial information without burdening Black colleagues or friends with my blunt deficits. Restorative reading allows a white reader to become more responsible and accountable in the real world. Restorative reading helped me to become—gradually, awkwardly—a more informed and dependable person in Mary Norman's life. The writers whose books appear in this memoir taught and awakened, chastened and re-formed me. They are my teachers-in-print.

A twenty-first century update on Quakers: In recent years liberal Quakerism has broached a new honesty about racism and white supremacy. I had long idealized Quakers as courageous and dedicated abolitionists who helped bring chattel slavery to an end in the United States. This proud abolitionist history turns out to be only part of a complex truth. Until ninety years before the Civil War, some Quakers enslaved Africans, and some Quaker ship owners profited from the slave trade. Even among white abolitionist Quakers, with their principled commitment to ending slavery and their general kindness and compassion towards enslaved Africans, there was rarely an openness to mutual friendship. Indeed, until the 1850s, some meetings seated Black worshipers on a segregated bench. Contradictions continued, as chronicled in a 2009 book, *Fit for Freedom, Not for Friendship: Quakers, African Americans, and the Myth of Racial Justice.* White supremacy persists today in many Friends meetings in the United States, demonstrated not in formally separate seating anymore, but in ignorance, on the part of the white majority of Friends, about the ways that white culture dominates what we think of as "Quaker" practice. Quakers who take *Fit for Freedom* to heart keep me honest about power and whiteness.

nine

Coming of Age

WHEN I HEADED BACK TO NANTUCKET THE FOLLOWING summer, in August of 1979, Mary was the person I most whole-heartedly looked forward to seeing. I hoped we would walk the beach again. I hoped we would continue to broach the more adult relationship we had begun the summer before.

Matthew, I wasn't as sure about. In two weeks, I was to bring him home to Cambridge after his fourth-grade year in Nantucket with Alfred's new family. Matthew said he wanted to come back. A fifth-grade spot waited for him at his Quaker school. When I recalled the lonelier moments of being a single parent, however, I felt a familiar coil tighten. A better mother, I thought, would want her child back home, no question.

My parents, I actually dreaded seeing. The specter of their drinking had filled the worry-space temporarily vacated by Matthew that year. I agitated over my father's drunken bullying, the insults and blows that scarred my mother and scared me. In the spring, like so many children of alcoholics who try to stop a parent's drinking, I labored over a letter to my father. Maybe, I thought, the right mix of words could persuade him. *I love you very much. I can't bear to see you hurting your body. When you have more than a couple of drinks, you get so mean.* I mailed the letter, clinging to the belief that words could save him. Foolishly, I called to alert my mother. "How could you?" she cried, as though I'd aimed a machine gun at a litter of puppies. "That letter will kill your father!" Now that I know that alcohol affects women's bodies more easily, swiftly, and dangerously than men's bodies, now that I have lost my mother to liver disease, I marvel at the denial that caused me to plead with my father and not with her.

I settled into a deck chair on the ferryboat to Nantucket and reached into my backpack for a small blue paperback. *Coming of Age in Mississippi,* civil rights activist Anne Moody's account of her childhood and growing activism, had gripped me from the start. As the ferry rounded the first bell and began to pound into the oncoming chop, I picked up where I'd left off.

Moody grew up with her parents and siblings in a one-room shack in rural Mississippi. Their home had two beds, a table, three wooden chairs and a single tin bathing tub. In my home, my brother and I each had our own bedroom and bath. Being a child, and not learning otherwise, I had believed everyone lived that way. In getting to "know" Anne Moody through her vivid autobiography, I was learning about poverty and resilience.

I was shocked that Moody's family "ate beans all the time," that her parents had to leave four-year-old Anne and her baby sister home alone all day while they worked in the fields, and that Anne had to get a job when she was nine to help feed her family. Moody's searing inside picture of sharecropping taught me about the system that, in most of the rural South, condemned formerly enslaved families to generations of ongoing poverty. The Moodys did not own the land they lived on. After the whole family worked eighteen-hour days through the growing season, the landowner "bought" or, rather, stole, their crop for less than it was worth. Moody was never sure she'd have school clothes that fit her growing body. Later, her stepfather struggled to buy, and then farm, his own half-acre. He roused his family out into the killing heat to till and plant and weed the scraggly patch of land that was all he had been able to afford. Moody conveyed the family's desperate urgency as they waited for the weather, which was bad, and the yield, which was minimal, and the profit, which was often nonexistent.

As I read further into *Coming of Age in Mississippi*, the violence of white racism took more tangible shape in my mind. White supremacists murdered fourteen-year-old Emmett Till just a few counties away from Moody's town. Moody, who was fourteen herself, could find no adult willing to talk to her about the lynching. Not long afterwards, Moody watched a neighboring house burn to the ground, torched in the night by angry whites, nine members of a Black family trapped inside and dead by morning. She listened as a schoolmate described the gang of white townsmen who nabbed him, accused him of a petty crime he did not commit, and beat him unconscious. I could see why Anne Moody began to, as she put it, "hate people." Reading about the fear that seized her community after this rash of events, I began to understand that the purpose of racist terrorism is to force submission by instilling fear.

I'd been to expensive schools, and got As in U.S. history. I thought I knew about the world. Moody's memoir was showing me how wrong I had been.

Immersed as I was in Moody's life as the ferry rumbled across Nantucket Sound, I looked up only once or twice to scan my fellow passengers. For the first time, I noticed that the people around me were all white. I couldn't think of a single Black person I'd seen in Nantucket besides men who did menial jobs like hauling garbage and women who performed domestic service for white families. I studied the trim white mothers around me and noted, as if to hold these women at a safe distance from myself, that they sported large diamond engagement rings like the one I no longer wore. I noted how the women toted their wallets and sunglasses, tissues and compacts, in pricey "lightship baskets" woven by local craftspeople as replicas of baskets made by early whalers. I watched two boys with wind-tousled curls skid around the deck after a shiny-coated golden retriever straining on its leash. A few clean-shaven fathers sat nearby in khakis, boat shoes, no socks, reading the *Wall Street Journal.*

People like this had been my close friends while I was married; I played tennis and sailed with them, partied with them, invited them to my wedding. During the first summers after my divorce, I had rushed around visiting these old friends, wanting to make sure that they still liked me. More recently, despite their ongoing kindness to me, I had used these friends to make myself feel superior: I imagined that I was more interesting than they were—less preppy, more questioning, more open to change. But I had never noticed that they were all white.

Actually, *we* were all white. I closed my eyes, opened them again. I felt my bare white arms, neck, and face exposed to the salty air. I felt the whiteness of my skin.

Anne Moody was seven when she first noticed that her three white neighbor-playmates had lives radically different from her own. They had store-bought toys, plenty of food, and a mother who stayed home. Their outdoor playhouse was in better shape than the shack that Moody's family crowded into. One Saturday, Moody and her siblings started to follow the white children into the "whites only" section at the movies. Moody's mother snatched her children up angrily; she forced them to go home and miss the movie. Moody reflected that she had never really thought of these children as white before. "Now, all of a sudden, they were white, and their whiteness made them better than me." Already at seven, Moody began consciously confronting the impact of race on her life. She had no choice, barely old enough to read books but forced to read her social standing, her social situation. Here I was, thirty years older, scanning the boat deck and living the luxury of noticing my whiteness for the first time.

How could I never have noticed my whiteness? Easy. In the news, in school, in the movies, and in church, I saw affluent white people in charge. I swam in a sea of whiteness as immersing and total as the Atlantic Ocean. White people were the norm in my world. I was taught to see everyone else as different, or "minority," or "other." Although race is a social construct and not a biological reality, the construct called "race" served to create my family's good fortune and to hype our supposed superiority. Every aspect of the society I grew up in was structured around strict racial and class hierarchy, with wealthy white people like me at the top. Whiteness and wealth brought me privileges that I never had to recognize, or tally, or even stop to consider: private schools, large houses, expensive vacations, a future of education and possibility. That's how affluent white people can reach the age of thirty-seven, or seventy-three, or a hundred, without noticing their (our) whiteness.

Scholars of color, among them Ralph Ellison, James Baldwin, Franz Fanon, and Toni Morrison, have long argued that whiteness lies at the center of the scourge of racism. White people created the notion of white racial "superiority" in order to justify discrimination against—and the assertion of power over —everyone else. Racism is a white problem to cure. These truths first began to sink in for me as I read Moody's book.

Not until the 1990s would I begin to develop a more fully informed sense of responsibility for the power I gain by being white. By then, activists and writers in the emerging field of "whiteness studies" would take up the challenge issued by Baldwin and other Black thinkers. In a ground-breaking 1989 essay, "White Privilege: Unpacking the Invisible Knapsack," Peggy McIntosh of the Wellesley Center for Research on Women identified white privilege as "an invisible package of unearned assets which I can count on cashing in each day, but about which I was 'meant' to remain oblivious. . . . I was taught to recognize racism only in individual acts of meanness, not in invisible systems conferring dominance on my group." In *White Women, Race Matters: The Social Construction of Whiteness*, white British sociologist Ruth Frankenberg observed that most of the white women she interviewed did not recognize that being perceived as white brought them privileges. Most aspired to be "colorblind"—not to see race at all. By contrast, she argued, those who are "race aware" understand that race *matters*: being perceived as white or Black brings a host of consequences, from greater or lesser economic opportunity to political representation, from schooling to police treatment and physical safety on the streets.

Being able to go through life ignoring race is, for white people, a big part of white privilege. Only by waking up to the power our whiteness gives us and by working to change the structures that reinforce that power can white people aspire to be truly anti-racist. I am grateful that long before Frankenberg's book, long before whiteness studies, reading *Coming of Age in Mississippi* on the Nantucket ferry made me notice, for the first time, my own white skin.

I arrived at the cottage during my parents' naptime, ghosted the car into the driveway, tiptoed through the kitchen, and stood in Mary's doorway. She jammed a cigarette into the ashtray next to her radio and jumped up from where she'd been reading. She opened a window and fanned at the smoke, holding her head carefully aside to hug me.

I closed her door.

"What's wrong?" Mary asked, eying the shut door, not sitting back down.

"They may get up soon," I said, meaning my parents.

"They're fine today," she said, all reassurance. "They'll be wanting to see you."

I'd been there two minutes, and already I was asking Mary to negotiate a path between her three charges.

"I wrote Dad about his drinking," I said.

Mary widened her eyes and seemed to flinch. "Again?"

"Not 'again,'" I said, nettled. "One letter, this spring. You knew about it?"

"I guess your mother mentioned it to me."

Did Mary flinch because she'd seen my father react with cruelty to my mother? I didn't want to know.

Mary eyed the closed door again. I realized she was uncomfortable visiting together while my mother waited for me. Our more adult exchange the previous summer may have thinned the curtain of fog between us, allowing a shared glimmer of common life. Lying in wait for us in my parents' home, however, were our familiar roles: skilled, attentive server and sometimes conflicted beneficiary. The institution of domestic service was like a fixed global weather system, blowing fog between us once again. I remembered my mother's petulant and angry complaint the previous summer, after Mary and I walked the beach. *"Doesn't anyone think of anyone else around here?"* Mary succeeded in this job by pleasing my mother. I opened the door.

Lingering in the doorway, I asked Mary awkwardly whether she wanted to walk on the beach again. I turned "walk" into a code word for many things I didn't know how to say—that I'd spent the year trying to understand Mary better through reading books by Black women, that I felt strengthened by her presence. My parents knew little of the person I was becoming. I was a mature woman, with a best-selling book under my belt. I'd left a marriage to a wealthy man. With steady determination, I was reading my way out of my parents' narrow world. And yet, perversely, in the way of so many grown-up children, I brought little of my new strength home. All this fed my hope for another walk with Mary. She was the one with whom I felt like myself.

"Of course, I want to walk!" Mary exclaimed. "I couldn't wait until you got here!" She pointed to a wall calendar she had marked off with big Xs, day by day, until my arrival. "Walk" may have covered unspoken elements for Mary, too. As Mary texted to me years later, "I liked you and I was starved for some interaction with someone. It was so lonely there. It was a joy to know that you were coming. Being able to slip out of the house to walk on the beach was heavenly." Under conditions of white supremacy, my accompaniment gave Mary untroubled access to the beach, to the night sky and the sea air, even if she did have to wear a tight kerchief to prevent unmanageable frizz. Walking together put us both in the presence of another human being who was ready to listen.

Whatever went unsaid by each of us in that moment, Mary's animation buoyed me. Perhaps, I thought, spending time together mattered to Mary, too.

Up early my first morning, I found Dad in the living room with his second cup of coffee. Sunshine streamed in the picture window, the ocean just beyond. I sat down with my breakfast of yogurt and fruit. My father was often benign at breakfast. This was the safest time to be in his presence.

Dad asked how was I fixed for cash. "With the little fellow coming back," he said, "you'll have added expenses." I suspected this was his way of saying he was glad Matthew was coming back to live with me. I responded that I was being paid to coordinate the next edition of *Our Bodies, Ourselves*. I was nearly done with divinity school, I said, so those expenses would be behind me.

Dad shook his head, as though to ward off more information than he could tolerate. "What in God's name does 'divinity school' accomplish anyway" he asked, scowling, "except to make you a thorn in the flesh of your family?"

I set down my bowl and took a slow breath. I'd expected some kind of attack after my letter that spring. I wasn't surprised by the insult.

"Your mother tells me I must acknowledge your rather nasty letter," my father began. I started to speak, but he raised his hand for silence. "My Salvation Army daughter believes that she has all the prerogative in the family. I'm not surprised. Character doesn't change, after all." As insults go, this was mild for my father. Heart pounding, I waited for his rage. But he surprised me.

"I admit that I lash out at you and your mother from time to time. And I should probably cut down a bomb or two of an evening. There you have it," he added. "The confession you wanted." A solitary nod towards the truth of my childhood.

"My mother's gentle, giving spirit died with her," he continued. "I see a bit of her spirit in your brother, very little in you." He glared at me with the piercing gray-green eyes that I had so clearly inherited, then turned away abruptly, to look out at the ocean. "I see none in myself," he said.

I received the confession I'd wanted, laced with mild insult—and an unsolicited glimpse into my father's despair.

Later that morning, I plunged into the ocean and turned to watch my parents negotiate the wooden steps down the dune to the beach. Although only fifty-nine and sixty-two, they moved like old people. Stiffened by his cancer surgery, my father shuffled across the sand in madras bathing shorts that hid his tubes and plastic bladder. Seeming uncertain of her balance, my mother placed each foot with care. Once in the water, my father submerged his whole body, kicked a few times, lifted his arms stiffly in a brief crawl, then rolled onto his back. Sunlight played on tiny beads of water on the sparse, graying hairs of his chest. My mother waded until she was chest-high in the sea, sank backwards with a look of bliss, and gave a few exuberant little kicks. No seaweed today. No surf. The three of us floated, buoyed at the very edge of the ocean. White people swimming.

After my father headed back, my mother splashed her palms happily on the water as though she'd been waiting for him to go.

"How does Daddy seem to you?" she soon asked. The familiar, and always tricky, question.

"He mentioned the letter I wrote him. He was a bit insulting, but not bad."

She sighed. "He's been so tired this summer." "Tired" was my mother's code word for Dad's bad behavior. "Even our trip to London didn't do its usual magic. It's gone now, thank God, but until last week you could see traces of black and blue." My mother raised two wet fingers to her left cheek. "Your father was so infuriated with the hotel. You know how he gets. We've been patrons for a hundred years, and our rooms weren't ready. He doesn't sleep a wink on those transatlantic flights. He was bushed."

"So, he hit you," I said, appalled.

She laughed quickly. "I traipsed around London looking like a wounded prize fighter in a mink coat."

I flashed to the day, shortly after my father's cancer surgery, when his stitches had split open and he lay close to death. My mother and I took a quick break from our watch at the ICU. In a nearby park, she turned to me, the soft curly wool of her lambskin jacket drawn up against the November cold, and began to cry. "He is so mean sometimes," she said. "He's so mean." She stood alone, hard sobs shaking her shoulders. I didn't know what to say. "There he is, back there in intensive care, barely living. Tubes, machines, doctors in and out. I have to admit that part of me . . . not all of me . . . not by any means all of me . . . but I . . . Wendy . . ." Amazement in her eyes, fingers closing into fists. "Part of me doesn't want him to live."

Startled as I had been at her words, I couldn't blame my mother. I'd seen the bruises, felt the cruelty. The battles between them tore me up, churned up the turf of my own psyche. I did love my father. I did "want" him to live through this relapse, but the truth is that I would have felt guilty to admit otherwise. In my mother's emotional and physical exhaustion, she had confessed this truth.

Now, during our companionable swim, came news that he'd

hit her again—recovered in body but unchanged in behavior. "He slugs you," I said aggressively, "and you laugh it off?"

"He didn't slug," my mother retorted.

I dove down and swam away through the press of water until my lungs burned and sent me up gasping for air. Peering out through the stinging lens of salt, I couldn't find my mother. I whipped myself around in a crazy fear, half expecting to see her swimming towards the open ocean, out of reach already, heading out to drown herself. But she was paddling in towards shore.

"I have a feeling golf time is upon us," she said.

On the next evening that my parents went out for dinner, Mary and I headed to the beach as soon as they drove away. At the bottom of the wooden stairway, we turned north in the clarified light of early evening. The empty beach stretched ahead of us. We began in amiable silence, stopping occasionally to spill sand from our shoes. Then we traded reports on our children. Matthew was returning to Cambridge for fifth grade, I told Mary. I did, and didn't, want him home. His stepmother reported that he'd been tough to live with that year—cranky, even belligerent. He seemed nostalgic for Cambridge. I liked being the greener grass, but the thought of a difficult year with him scared me.

"He wants to come back? That's all you need to know. You'll get along, just wait and see." Mary gave this welcome reassurance as if she had looked into a crystal ball.

I asked Mary about the guys at the correction center. As soon as her fellow officers learned that she meant business, Mary reported, the harassment had lessened. "The guards know I'll go to the warden for them when they want a day off. They know I'll watch their backs. The inmates know I'm fair. What I say to them today is what I'll say tomorrow." More than a year into her new role as a sergeant, Mary sounded grounded and confident.

Remembering her words today, I hear the integrity and even-handedness with which Mary treated both guards and inmates. I enjoy remembering this brief, upbeat moment in her corrections career. By the mid-1980s, she would tell me of a new warden who espoused the era's increasingly more punitive approach to corrections. This "warden from hell," as her fellow officers would call him, would set out to undermine Mary's rehabilitation-centered approach to inmates, and succeed in making her work life miserable.

Gradually, along with the thump and splash of waves on the ocean shore, a sound rose up to our left, like wind whooshing through tall grass. A dune loomed beside us then, black against the fading sunset. We clambered to the top and spotted the harbor only fifty feet from where we stood. We had walked all the way to the haul-over, where harbor and ocean nearly meet—no houses, only a strip of dune and beach grass stretching north as far as we could see in the gathering dusk. We stood without speaking, the sounds of moving water before and behind us.

At the end of our walk, perhaps because the companionable stroll with Mary made me feel confessional, I blurted out, "Mom's worrying about me this summer. She thinks I'm not socializing enough." I thought nothing about how my words might land.

Mary unlinked her arm from mine. "You shouldn't be spending all this time with me."

Immediately I knew I had hurt her. I had thoughtlessly implied that, for me, "socializing" didn't include our time together. "That's not what I meant at all! I love our walks," I said, trying to repair the moment.

"Your mother is right," Mary said flatly. She sped up her pace, heading for the splintered stairs.

"She's not," I said, stumbling as I tried to keep up. But I had lost Mary.

Microaggression. This is the term that activists in the twenty-first century use for my careless comment about socializing. Microaggressions are the demeaning comments and subtle insults that Black people encounter daily, often from ostensibly well-meaning white people. Though microaggressions may appear more subtle than outright discrimination, they are a deadly part of the daily trauma of racism, and they take a cumulative toll. White people, like me, who seek to nurture friendship with Black colleagues, family members, or lovers, need to stay vigilant about this toll. We need to understand, in all humility, that we commit microaggressions all the time. We need to understand, if such a friendship continues, what an astounding amount of forgiveness may have already come our way.

Mary and I made dinner together that evening, and ate outdoors on the deck—farm-fresh zucchini and red onions, fresh-caught sole drenched in lemon butter. We watched the clock, wanting to finish before my parents returned, weaving and dangerous, to head for the ice bucket and scotch.

Before Mary and I said goodnight, I ducked into my room to grab *Coming of Age in Mississippi*. From the cover of the small blue paperback, twenty-year-old Anne Moody looked into the uncertain distance with determination and hope. I could feel the pulse throbbing in my fingers as I held the book. I'd brought Mary new editions of *Our Bodies, Ourselves* over the years and the published version of *Fighting Sexual Harassment*. I'd never before shared a book that was explicitly about race.

The idea of "race" might be a construct rather than a biological fact, but structures built around this false idea shaped the hierarchy that Mary and I would have to navigate, and possibly reinvent, if we were to have any kind of friendship. Until that point, in more than twenty years, we had not mentioned race between us. I hadn't even become aware of my whiteness until a few days earlier on the ferry. Before I could reflect on the immensity of this silence or change my mind, I knocked on Mary's door. As she let me in, I felt suddenly shy. I gave her the book quickly, saying only that I had learned a lot from Anne Moody and wondered what she'd think.

Waking near midnight, I tiptoed from my bedroom into the back hall. Mary's light leaked into the dark hallway through the crack beneath her door.

The next morning in the kitchen, I asked about *Coming of Age in Mississippi*. Mary lifted three dripping strips of my father's bacon to a folded paper towel on the counter. She studied my face for a long moment. Finally, she said, "That book was my life."

Water boiled in the small aluminum saucepan for coffee. My mind whirred. Mary and I had "known" each other for more than two decades, yet I knew nothing about her life at all.

Later that day, I stood in Mary's doorway, not wanting to say something wrong. In light of Anne Moody's life, I had questions for her. Had Mary struggled for an education in a one-room schoolhouse, the way Moody did? Had she, like Moody, started working for pay as a child? Had whites killed Black people in her town? Had she marched or organized for civil rights? Underlying my curiosity lay a question that frightened me: Moody had reported that, in her teens, she hated white people for their racist cruelty. If Mary hated white people, I wouldn't blame her, but I wondered: Beneath her friendly and mild exterior, did Mary boil with rage? At me? This was my self-centered bottom line: *at me*.

I couldn't bring myself to voice these questions. I'd grown up with the word "white" as a color for clouds, or stars. Words like "Black" and "Afro-American," I was beginning to use in the context of women's health activism, but not with Mary. I know now that, at the moment in the late 1970s when I stood in Mary's doorway, trying to speak about race, most well-meaning white people like me aimed to be "colorblind." During the brutal period of Jim Crow, many white people talked about race only to assert their own dominance. They used words like "darkie" and, later, "n-gg-r," as a way of linking Blackness to every kind of character flaw—laziness, violence, dangerous sexuality, criminality—although these qualities belonged not to Black people at all, but to white people's ugliest projections.

In order to avoid this blatant "old-time" racism, many progressive white people shied away from overt references to race. "I don't see color," they said—we said. Being "colorblind" was supposed to mean that you were a good white person, that you would not use a person's race as an excuse to oppress them. The idea of colorblindness may have been a small, brief improvement over blatant racism, but colorblindness actually implies that race doesn't matter. Colorblindness ignores the mortal hazards of being a person of color under white domination.

At the time I stood in Mary's doorway, progressive thinkers were beginning to suggest that becoming "race aware" was crucial for white people who want to be effective allies to people of color. Sociologist Ruth Frankenberg would soon argue that we should acknowledge all the ways that race matters. And yet, to say, out loud, words so long linked to dangerous slurs and put-downs felt offensive and wrong.

Mary looked up at me expectantly from where she sat on the bed. She stayed sitting, instead of jumping up the way she would normally do when my mother or I came into the room. I took this as a compliment, a sign that she was feeling relaxed with me, that I hadn't messed up yet.

"What?" Mary asked. "I can tell something's on your mind."

In a panic about saying the wrong thing, I forgot every real question I'd wanted to ask. "I'm just thinking about the harassment at your workplace. I was, you know, just wondering. You were the first woman to become an officer. Are you the only officer who is . . ." I made my lips close for the "B" and brought my tongue forward for the "l," opened my mouth into an "a" and lifted the rear of my tongue to my palate for the percussive "ck." As I said this word intentionally to Mary for the first time, I had to instruct the muscles for each movement. ". . . Black?" I said.

"Yes," Mary replied, like she was saying, *Of course.*

"Thanks," I said, and started to back away.

"That was all?"

"That was all," I said, blushing, backing up, nearly out of her room already.

Mary cocked her head and studied me. "If you walk on eggshells," she said, "I won't be able to talk to you the way I do."

My sudden awkwardness and my fear of making a mistake threatened to end any real exchange between us. I know now that, in Mary's Elk Creek family and her Trenton neighborhood, people spoke all the time of Blackness, addressed the impact of being Black on everything from a police car parked down the street, to the high cost of borrowing money, to the wary way white people looked at her growing son—just a boy in her eyes, already a tall, muscular, threatening Black youth to them. Talk about race was natural in Mary's life, matter-of-fact. A fundamental element, a given. How odd, I imagine, to hear me stammer to say aloud the simple word that relentlessly framed so much of her experience under segregation and Jim Crow.

Years later Mary would tell me via text: "We had already had a few summers together talking, but you were always cautious. That is why I said the eggshells thing." Mary's sage advice that night would chasten and guide me for decades. Even today, I try not to walk on eggshells around issues of race and class. I often fall short, but I do understand, from Mary, that tiptoeing around racial issues endangers relationship. Call this tiptoe-tendency WASP politeness, call it arrogance, call it "white fragility," a term coined in 2016 by white sociologist Robin DiAngelo. DiAngelo argues that white-skinned privilege can take shape as a paralyzing fear of making mistakes, based on the illusion that any human being could always be right.[1]

In warning me away from my sudden, self-centered awkwardness around race, Mary chose not to play safe, not to back off. She delivered both wise advice and an urgent personal request. *"Don't do that,"* I hear Mary saying. *"Don't make it impossible for*

---

[1] Robin DiAngelo, *White Fragility*. A white academic, DiAngelo writes and teaches about "what it means to be white in a society that proclaims race meaningless, yet remains deeply divided by race." DiAngelo urges white people to develop "racial stamina" so that we can acknowledge and take open feedback about our racism. "Racism is the norm rather than an aberration," she writes. "Feedback is key to our ability to recognize and repair our inevitable and often unaware collusion." Meanwhile, we cling to the belief that only "bad" people are racist, and we believe that no one can be both "good" and "racist" at the same time.

me to continue the conversation we've started." With this warning and plea, Mary transformed our relationship.

I've reflected for many years on Mary's and my exchange about Anne Moody's book. As Mary put it many decades later, "You had never asked me anything before on how I was raised or how my childhood was." In reading about Moody's reality, I'd received a vivid education about Mary's life, without her having to spell everything out. I began to appreciate that, in order to enter my family's beachside house, Mary had to keep silent about many things: fears and dangers that my family could not even imagine. She kept to herself the heart-in-throat alarm that she felt, back home, when a white man strode out of a neighbor's woods. *Perhaps he's a hunter, but hunting season is over. Surely, he brings no good.* She put aside the confederate flags that proliferated back home in protest of each overdue move towards justice—*Brown v. Board of Education* in 1954, school integration, the Voting Rights Act in 1965. If Mary felt frightened in the isolated beach house when my parents went out for the evening—if the sea breeze wobbled a chair on the deck or flapped a window shade in an unlit bedroom—and if these sudden sounds took Mary to the dangers back home, Mary reminded herself that these alarms were hazards of the job. She rose above them.

Entering my family's house, Mary was required to adopt the persona of a silent and never-angry Black person. She must limit herself to a small back bedroom where she couldn't go two feet without bumping into the ironing board and the basket of laundry just in from the outdoor clothesline. Mary took pride in doing an exemplary job for my mother. Part of excelling at this job was sharing, or seeming to share, my mother's perspective about what was important: peace and quiet, a full ice bucket, meals served on a schedule, tiptoeing around my father's moods, and loving me. In this job, what worked best for Mary was silence.

Then, one night, I came to Mary's door, bearing *Coming of Age in Mississippi* and a passel of contradictions. I was rebelling against my parents' perspective on almost everything, while Mary's job involved forwarding their goals. I was friendly and kind, also sheltered and clueless. I was not Mary's boss, but I was her boss's daughter. Out in that isolated hamlet, I was the friendliest person around. As we entered midlife, I was developing a feminist and more egalitarian spirit. Our conversations about work, children, single parenting, if not as mutual as I assumed at the time, were different from Mary's exchanges with the domestic employers who mined her life for juicy tidbits. Still, I had no idea about microaggressions—and committed them rampantly. I did not realize, for example, how much fortitude I asked of Mary the times I refused to let her wait on me, when this was her job.

After twenty years, Mary knew all about me, and I knew almost nothing about her. Even as I groped to understand a wider reality than the one I'd been taught, I was still a golden child with every privilege of affluence and skin color, education and ease. I assumed that I offered Mary authentic friendship. I had a long way to go. Mary's candor was the most precious gift of the summer. Despite the rule of silence in that divided household, she trusted me with a useful and usable truth.

I wish I could end the story of that summer with Mary's historic warning, but we stumbled, later that week, over my parents' drinking.

One night Matthew and I went out to dinner with my parents at a nearby hotel, while Mary stayed home. Service at the stately harborside restaurant was slow. In the long wait for our meals, my father ordered one cocktail after another. Joining the Al-Anon program would teach me one day not to count drinks, but that night I counted. When Dad ordered a fourth cocktail for himself and my mother, I remembered the letter I'd written him that spring, warning that I'd absent myself if he went beyond two or three. I left the restaurant and walked home, leaving Matthew with his grandparents. This was an extreme lapse in judgment. After dinner, Matthew would get into the car with my drunken parents, who would drive him dangerously back to me. He did reach home safely that night, though he had every reason to feel sorely shaken by his mother's thoughtless desertion.

Arriving alone back at the beach house, I went directly to Mary's room. Today, I note my willful and self-serving stance in her doorway, my demand for attention, my assumption that Mary would not mind being interrupted by my needs. "Dad drank so much that I left the restaurant," I announced, expecting sympathy.

Mary frowned. "Did he get mad with you?"

I told her that I'd left too quickly to find out.

Mary looked thoughtful. "Seems like Mrs. C. and I do everything we can think of to make things the way your dad wants them. Sometimes it seems we haven't tried hard enough."

Slowly, between the lines, a meaning. Even when Mary and my mother tiptoed around my father, still he raged. "I had to do something, Mary. If no one ever tells him . . ."

"I'm sure you did what you thought was right."

"You think he'll take it out on Mom?"

All Mary did was look at me, and I knew that my father would attack my mother for my sudden departure.

"Don't you hate filling and refilling the ice bucket," I asked, "when you know they're getting bombed?" Stung, I had lashed out at Mary, the last person who deserved it.

Mary flinched. "It's my job," she said.

Of course, filling the ice bucket was Mary's job. I was cruel to insinuate that she played any role in my parents' drunkenness. I apologized immediately for my accusing barb, but my aggression stood.

Mary and I would find ourselves in this difficult territory again. Each of us would have to find a workable path through my parents' addiction and boozy, dangerous decline. The paths we found rarely put us side by side.

To become an emotionally dependable person in Mary's life, I would have to unwind the invisible threads linking alcoholism and white supremacy in my own. First, the thread of denial. We talked in my home about keeping the ice bucket full, and Dad being "tired"—not about his violence, not about my parents' dependence on the daily drug. We kept a similar silence about race and class, the boundaries kept so carefully in that beach cottage, the histories behind us all. I think of the phrase "the elephant in the living room." Twin elephants crowded the cottage during those summers: my parents' increasing alcoholism, and stark divides of race and class. That year—awkwardly, crudely—I made a first attempt to acknowledge both.

There was also a thread of rage. Anger boiled beneath my father's stately exterior, ready to burst through and scald us at any provocation. This had made me afraid of and careful around anger—any anger. But the more I learned about racism in the writing that so drew me that year and in all the years afterward, the more I have become aware of Black people's righteous reasons for rage. Being afraid of righteous rage is not a useful response.

Finally, there was a thread of caution. We all walked on eggshells after Dad got drunk. Though he almost never raged directly at Mary, her job seemed to include walking on eggshells *and* cleaning up the mess. I tiptoed around Dad with the rest of them. I feared making the mistake that would make him erupt. Similarly, that week in Mary's doorway, I felt the stranglehold of caution. I feared making the mistake that would turn Mary away. *"If you walk on eggshells, I won't be able to talk to you the way I do."* To fit myself to be any kind of friend with Mary, I had to drop the self-conscious carefulness I'd honed—in my alcoholic family, in my bubble of whiteness. A lifelong relationship was at stake.

ten

Sister Outsider

FALLING IN LOVE WITH A WOMAN PROPELLED ME OUTSIDE MY extremely narrow world. It's not that Polly Attwood was so different from anyone in my family—I fell in love with a WASP like me—but desire between women was so transgressive back then, so counter to what I'd been taught was right and natural, that, for the first time in my life, I found myself a rule-breaker, literally outside the law.

In the fall of 1979, Matthew was home in Cambridge living with me; I was a full-time mother again. At that phase of my self-discovery, I longed to be swept away so dramatically by love —or lust, I wouldn't have minded lust—that I'd know for sure I was lesbian. No Princess Charming appeared that autumn to sweep me away, but—ironically, aptly—attending a lecture on white racism by noted poet and white lesbian-feminist icon Adrienne Rich brought me the clarity I needed.

That a winner of the prestigious National Book Award for Poetry would address the public about racism, not poetry, signaled a vital emergence in second-wave feminism. Rich was one of the first white literary figures publicly to interrogate her own role, as a white woman and a feminist, in compounding racism.

She joined the stellar Audre Lorde, a Caribbean-American poet, lesbian, and social visionary, in a published series of dialogues spotlighting the complex intersections of sexism and racism. These dialogues helped to launch multiracial feminism. Reading them, I felt drawn to the vision of an inclusive, multiracial women's movement.

Rich chose the Boston area for her speech that November evening because twelve African American women had been murdered that year in Roxbury, a primarily Black residential area of a very segregated Boston. Blaming the violence on its victims by claiming that they were prostitutes, the Boston police had taken little action. The women of the Combahee Collective, the activist group of Black lesbian feminists in Boston, mobilized around the need, in the words of member Barbara Smith, to "look at these murders as both racist and sexist crimes." As a committed white ally, Rich wanted to urge Boston-area white women to join the effort. The Cambridge YWCA, with its primary mission of eliminating racism, stepped up to host her.

After getting Matthew settled with homework and a promise of TV, I reached the Y just in time for Rich's talk. Beneath raised basketball hoops in the dusty gym, I found an expectant audience that included many of the lesbians I'd admired from a distance at political gatherings and women's concerts. In a motley mix of clothing, from long hippy skirts to work shirts and vests, the women laughed comfortably and called to each other across the gym. I dropped as unobtrusively as I could into a seat by the door. I never knew where to look in a crowd like this. Where was the woman who would usher me across the threshold, take me to bed and deliver me at last into a lesbian identity? I looked for this woman, and away from her, in every face.

The revered poet moved towards the podium. I stood with

the others and clapped so hard that my palms stung. As a white, middle-class woman, Rich began, she had grown up comfortably situated in the country's structures of power and privilege. In leaving her marriage and coming out as lesbian in her forties, she stepped outside the protection of those structures. Family, friends, colleagues, and strangers castigated and even hated her for her choice of sexual partner. Experiencing this homophobia opened a window in her political analysis. As she came to understand the deadly impact of gay oppression, she saw her own role, as a white person, in oppressing people of color. She saw that she benefited from the very system that oppressed them.

I admired how coming out as a lesbian and loving Michelle Cliff, a biracial Jamaican-American woman, awakened Rich to her role in white racial dominance, how being an outsider sharpened her critical edge. She said that honest relationships between white women and Black women could forward the hard work of racial healing. Love between women could fuel that hard work. Rich offered me a perspective on the shift in Mary's and my relationship, a vocabulary for the limits and the possibilities between us, a sense of the rightness of the direction we were moving in, and a caution about the work ahead.

All around me, women leaned earnestly forward, as I did, to hear Rich's every word. So many lesbians. In a moment of quiet recognition, I thought to myself, "I am a lesbian, too." No fireworks. I had the same long legs in corduroy jeans I'd always had, the same sandy hair and snaggletooth, the same Matthew at home in his Red Sox jacket sneaking in a little extra TV—only, I was a lesbian. In that moment, after years of uncertainty, I felt settled, and grateful. I had thought only a Princess Charming could carry me over this edge. I made the shift through community, not between the sheets.

The political and the personal, so intertwined in that time of ferment and change, merged for me that night at the Y. In the same moment that I understood myself to be a lesbian, I also grasped the possibility of becoming more informed, more proactive, more accountable as a white person in a society where my people receive privileges that damage others. I am indebted to the wave of multiracial feminism that brought me out that night to listen to urgent wisdom from a poet-leader.

Weeks after I came out to myself at the Y, a young friend came to visit Matthew and me in Cambridge. Polly was a spirited, athletic young woman we'd met seven years earlier, in 1974, at an inter-denominational religious conference where she was a teen participant and I served as a "women's liberation" resource. An intensely questioning person, Polly at fifteen was feeling that she had to leave her parents' Episcopal church because the male God and male clergy no longer spoke to her. I was leaving the church for similar reasons, and we were each thrilled to find a kindred spirit. Each summer for the next several years, we returned to the conference. Polly pitched whiffle balls to little Matthew—and then, as the summers went by, baseballs—while she and I talked and talked. I became her feminist mentor. There was no clue that we'd ever be lovers—even when, during her first year in college, she and I came out to ourselves and to each other.

When Polly came to visit Matthew and me at my single-mother apartment in Cambridge in late 1979, she was a college senior just returning from two years of teaching English in Taiwan. She declared right away that she wanted to leave the roles of mentor and mentee behind us—to be, simply, friends. I accepted. Polly was twenty-two, no longer a girl. She'd had a woman lover in Taiwan. In that respect, she was miles ahead of me. As we walked together through the Cambridge streets, she took my hand. I snuck glances ahead of us, behind us, across the street. No one seemed to be watching. I let my fingers lace loosely with hers. As we drifted, chastely clothed, into a friendly afternoon nap, I felt every inch of her leg stretched out along mine. Her neck cradled comfortably in my open palm. That night, we became lovers.

Being lesbian catapulted me outside social spheres where I'd once felt an easy belonging. I remember a sparkling Saturday in the summer of 1980, when Polly and I went with friends to Crane Beach, in Ipswich, Massachusetts. We arrived to a cloudless blue sky, a lilting breeze, and the lap of waves along a clean, sandy shore. Perfection. Two days earlier, however, the Republicans had nominated Ronald Reagan for president in what felt to me like an orgy of right-wing enthusiasm. As we threaded our way through the families with their toddlers and teenagers, beach blankets and umbrellas, balls and thermoses, they all seemed like Republicans to me, all straight. Polly reached for my hand. I didn't want to ruffle anyone's prejudices on this sunny Saturday, so I pulled away. Later during that same beach excursion, my long-time friend Judy, who is straight, reached out to link arms with me. I flinched. "You always walk arm and arm with me," Judy protested. "You always hug me." In a sea of nuclear families, I was afraid to touch Judy, even in friendly affection. Like many people damaged by our dominant culture's hatred and fear of homosexuals, I carried homophobia inside myself.

At a women's bar with Polly that night, I studied the other women. Many held themselves stiffly. There was a tightness in their knees as they stood, a bluff rigidity in their torsos on the dance floor. I had always thought of this stiffness as a "natural" attribute of lesbian physique—maybe an affected masculinity. But Judy had felt me tighten away from her that day. Maybe, I thought that evening, a new reserve, a kind of body armor, was settling into place in me.

To use a ringing term from Adrienne Rich, in loving Polly I became "disloyal to civilization." Loving a woman set me outside the norms I'd once easily fit, with my blond hair and blue eyes, my heterosexuality, my education, and my checkbook. Buffered as I would still be by most of these "assets," I was no longer safe from the hatred and violence faced by openly queer people all the time. Loving Polly opened me to a sweet, passionate, hungry vulnerability—to her, to my own sexual needs. Loving Polly also opened me to risks that I had not known in my sheltered life.

The work of Audre Lorde, a towering figure in the creation of multiracial feminism, invited me to let my new experience as an "outsider" open my mind and heart to people I'd always thought of as "other." Whenever Lorde introduced herself in public, she made a point of claiming her many identities—Black, woman, lesbian, poet, mother. She lived across many differences. She bore her son and daughter with a white man, and raised them with a white woman partner. She took the Black community to task about homophobia and confronted white lesbians about racism. In a 1978 essay called "Scratching the Surface," later published in *Sister Outsider,* Lorde recognized "the notion of difference as a dynamic human force, one which is enriching rather than threatening to the defined self, when there are shared goals." Lorde considered the many oppressions she faced

to be complex and interlocking. This ground-breaking consciousness helped give rise to the concept of "intersectionality," a
term established by Black scholar Kimberlé Crenshaw a decade
later in a key evolution of political and feminist theory.

I thrilled to Lorde's brilliant theorizing and to her sense of
herself as a "sister outsider." She urged "outsiders" to join and
support each other, despite the efforts by mainstream white society to divide us. She appealed to "those of us who stand outside the circle of this society's definition of acceptable women;
those of us who have been forged in the crucibles of difference—
those of us who are poor, who are lesbians, who are Black, who
are older." By becoming lovers with Polly, I entered a single one
of Lorde's categories of difference: lesbian. "As outsiders," Lorde
urged, "we need each other for support and connection and all
the other necessities of living on the borders." I felt that Audre
Lorde was calling me in.

Not so easy, not so fast. When I re-entered my parents' upper-
class beachside life the following summer, the political tide that
lifted me in Cambridge ebbed abruptly and, with it, my fledgling sense of being a sister outsider. I was an outsider, yes, as a
lesbian in my conservative family. Whether I could truly connect
with Mary, the other outsider in the household, was less certain.
Rules of domestic service stood in the way, and so, I was soon to
learn, did my own internalized homophobia.

Mary worked for my parents again that August of 1980. She
had recently divorced her second husband. He had turned out to
be a violently abusive person, and the marriage had been brief.
When I arrived for my usual two-week visit, I was eager to dis-
cover how Mary was doing with the breakup. As we hugged each

other in greeting at the cottage, I paused with my arms around her, trying to sense how she was, but unable to read her signs. My mother's goal for Mary's annual return was to keep life at the beach house forever the same. An implicit part of Mary's job performance was to stay the same, herself. "The same wonderful Mary," my mother would say happily, another lesson in my family's curriculum of affluence. Until Mary and I walked the beach, or found another way to talk openly, I would get no chance to find out how she was really doing.

Perhaps I couldn't read Mary's signs that summer because I was distracted by my own romantic drama. Polly, Polly, Polly. Where was she, what was she doing, when would we talk?

Polly was due to visit my family on Nantucket in a few days. We knew the plan was risky—with Polly under the same roof, my parents might suspect that we were lovers. And yet, what my parents knew of gayness seemed limited to the inane cocktail-hour jokes they told about "fags" and "fairies" in the interior decorating business. Maybe, I told myself, they didn't even know about lesbians. Polly was thirteen years younger than I, so we planned to pose her as a family friend of Matthew's and mine. A male colleague would call at the cottage, pretending to be her love interest. How easily the lying came to us. Polly and I may not have had a prayer of hiding our searing vulnerability and blossoming lust from my parents, but we were determined to try.

On the morning of Polly's arrival, Mary emptied the ancient clothes washer and took a wicker basket of wet linens out to the yard. I followed. Standing at the rope that ran between two poles across the rough seaside grass, we fixed the corners of the first sheet with wooden clothespins.

"Tell me about your friend Polly," Mary said. "You seem happy that she's coming."

All Mary's and my summer nights of soda crackers and jam at the kitchen table came to me then. If a boy kissed me on the sandy walk home during my teenage years, Mary had been the first and only one to know. Here was my chance to tell her about Polly. I looked quickly back at the house, where my parents were getting ready for their daily golf game. The wide-open windows, with their shadowy screens, were like ears ready to snatch my secret. I didn't dare speak. Finally, Mary wedged a weathered clothespin onto the towel she was hanging and looked away. She seemed to take my hesitation as a rebuff.

Fear caused me to hold back the big blushing gush of love story. Mary and I had begun to tell each other more of the truth, but I was scared. My "Our Bodies" friends welcomed Polly as my lover. They were happy for me, to be sure, and there was another factor: having a lesbian in the group—until then we had all been straight—seemed to swell our stature as feminists. But, beyond the bubble of Cambridge, Massachusetts, gay bashing ruled. Bullies harassed suspected and out lesbians and gay men on the job, threatened them on the streets, kicked them out of families, murdered those who crossed gender lines, and drove gay youth to suicide. As Audre Lorde wrote at the time, "Lesbians and gay men . . . are threatened with castration, imprisonment and death in the streets."

My father, born in the rural South, was deeply traditional, and my mother lived within reach of his explosive rage. Mom might be able to handle having a lesbian daughter, I thought. In a drunken outburst, however, she might spill the news to my father, then bear the brunt of his fury. Even though I believed that Mary wouldn't reveal my secret, I reasoned that telling her would bring the dangerous truth one step closer to my parents. And, the part I most hate to admit: I was afraid that Mary might disapprove, that she might turn away from me. This is ironic, given that Mary is the most thoroughly non-homophobic person I know, but, when I am honest with myself, I see that I didn't trust Mary with my news.

Recalling this exchange forty years later, Mary would say, "I guess you forgot—I worked with women at the women's prison for ten years before I transferred to the men's unit. We had lesbians there." Mary lived in a wider world than I did. I could have trusted her from the start.

Keeping my tone matter of fact as we unfurled wet pillowcases into the fresh breeze, I informed Mary that Polly was a college senior who had spent two years in Taiwan with Volunteers in Asia. She was an athlete, a mountain climber. She took me hiking in the mountains. She and Matthew shot hoops at the local Y. I kept my gaze down in order to hide any eager light that might shine in my eyes as I talked about Polly.

I may have missed Mary's signs that summer, but she read mine with ease. Years later, Mary laughed about this. "Polly was all you talked about that summer! Polly this, Polly that. Polly took you camping, Polly went with you to Quaker meeting. Every chance you had to mention her, there was Polly. Of course, I knew."

I lied to Mary out by the clothesline that day, if only by omission. Perhaps because of this, our talk dwindled. We emptied the basket, and there was nothing left to do. We ducked under the laden rope to head back to our separate places in the divided household. Had I spoken more openly, we might have taken another step towards each other. Mary might also have warned me. Keenly observant, she understood that my parents did, in fact, know about lesbians. They were alert, and prepared to be alarmed. Forty years later, Mary remembers her sense of danger. "I was so scared for you that they might find out. I thought, 'Oh God, I hope she doesn't let them know . . .' Just that year, a person in your dad's office had said something to him about you maybe being a lesbian, and I heard your dad hollering at your mother about it. He really upset her. Back in the kitchen, she cried and said to me, 'He's such a mean, mean man.' And then when Polly got there, you could tell she was in such admiration of you, I knew your dad would pick up on that. I was so afraid he'd see it."

Mary was an ally from the start.

On the first morning of her visit, Polly and I went out to the sunny deck with bowls we had piled high with yogurt, granola, and summer peaches. My father banged out through the screen door and sat down several feet away from us with the *Times*. I tried to think of friendly, casual topics to talk about with Polly in his presence. Nothing too intimate or free.

After watching us eat for a few minutes, Dad said, "What kind of God-awful concoction is that? Ho Chi Minh stew?" The twinkle in his eye told me that he thought he was being funny, linking our breakfast to the country's recent arch-enemy.

Polly stopped her spoon in midair. "It's yogurt," she said, choosing to take his jibe as a request for information. "Plain, low-fat yogurt, with homemade granola, which we make from oats, oil, honey, sunflower seeds. Then we . . ."

The "we" worried me. "I like some fruit in it, myself," I said, trying to sound uncoupled, unilateral.

"Whatever became of good old bacon and eggs?" Dad said with a frown as he returned to the sports page. "It's a lost generation," he muttered into the paper, "a lost generation."

Polly was chewing with her mouth open. As if looking through the window of a front-loading washing machine, I caught glimpses of oats, nuts and peaches churning in white liquid. Alarmed that my father might see this display, I clamped my own mouth tight as if to shut hers. I cringed, too, at Polly's unshaven legs. All along her calves, the hairs curled in the sunshine, springy and brown. Polly—in shorts, eating her breakfast—was comfortable being herself. She acted as relaxed and natural with my family as she would with her own. With my parents, this ease was a mistake. Looking at Polly through my father's elitist gaze, assailed by all my childhood lessons in "good taste," I felt embarrassed. I wanted breakfast to be over.

Finally, we finished and stood to go. Dad looked up at us, shielding his eyes from the sun with his left hand in a mock military salute. He sat straight-backed, at attention, as we traipsed by with our empty bowls. "Tell me something, will you girls?" We turned to find him scowling at us, thick eyebrows looming together above intense hazel eyes. "When are you two going to join the human race?"

We reached the sudden dimness of the living room before Dad could say anything more. *Not too bad*, I thought. I turned to Polly in conspiratorial relief, but the lips I had surreptitiously kissed that morning were set in a straight, sober line. No sign of the flecks of green I loved in her brown eyes. In eight months as lovers, I hadn't seen Polly angry like this. She stood stiffly, knees locked. Her athletic shoulders were dense with muscle. "No adult has ever talked to me like that," she said.

"Dad? What he said out there was nothing compared to . . ." I stopped. Polly was studying my face. "Really. Compared to the things he sometimes says, it was mild out there. He was mostly being funny."

No smile.

My breakfast settled in a lump. I felt hot with digestion. "You're a guest," I said. "I'm sorry."

"No, I'm sorry," she said, still staring at me.

"You?"

She touched my cheek. "I'm sorry you had to live like that."

In my romantic notion of lesbians back then, women lovers slipped into intimacy like peas in a pod, like a cliché. In this romance, my having "lived like that" would create no threat to Polly's and my chances as a couple. I know now that any two people learning to love each other stumble over exactly "that"—how they lived, what they learned, or didn't, in their families. The family whom Polly met on her first visit to Nantucket had shaped me in ways that would, for years to come, undermine my efforts to live up to the love and admiration I felt for her.

Even my mother fired a warning signal. I drove alone into town for some errands, leaving Polly at the cottage. When I returned, Polly told me she'd had a great time doing the jigsaw puzzle.

"Where?" I asked quickly.

"On the card table in the living room," she said, as in, *Where else would a person do a jigsaw puzzle?*

"Was my mother there?"

Polly thought for a moment. "She was reading for a while."

When my mother was enjoying "a little peace and quiet," the mere presence of another human being caused her major irritation—my father folding the paper too noisily, my brother chasing a ball into the room, Polly talking to herself over a puzzle. I felt no surprise later that day, when my mother found me in the hall and whispered urgently, "You'll be sure to take Polly with you next time, won't you?"

Polly had taken my parents at their word that she was welcome.

One evening later that week, after Polly had gone home, Mary and I headed out to walk. A gusty wind buffeted the beach, so that making our way across the sand was tougher than usual.

"So, you and your husband separated," I said.

A shrug in the falling light.

"I'm sorry it didn't work out."

Mary pulled her jacket tighter against the wind. She did not seem eager to talk about the end of her marriage. "I like Polly," she said after a while. "She's a nice girl."

I do, too! I wanted to say. *I love her!* By now, however, I had conjured an airtight rationale for secrecy: Asking Mary to keep a secret from my mother would put Mary into an uncomfortable—and therefore unfair—position. I was not aware, until encountering Judith Rollins's work years later, that domestic workers become skilled at keeping secrets. When I decided to shield Mary from news she couldn't tell my mother, I imagined I was protecting Mary. I was actually trying to protect myself from my own anxious illusions.

Mary turned away from the head-on wind and started back towards the cottage.

"Such a short walk," I said.

"The wind makes me feel a little chilly," Mary said.

I reached out to walk arm in arm with Mary, as we often did on our beach walks. Then I let my hand drop. Touching a woman had a new meaning for me now. I didn't want Mary to think I was coming on to her or flirting with her. I didn't want to send the wrong signal by taking Mary's arm.

I felt desperate for the flow of conversation that seemed to have dried up between us, but couldn't think of anything fresh to say. The wind pushed at us from behind. Waves rushed the shore.

"Is there anything new at the correction center?" I finally asked, falling back on an old topic. "How are you doing with the guys you work with?"

Mary slowed down, wind at her back, and looked me in the eye. "There's a new guard," she said. "Another woman, finally. She's okay. Comes to work on her motorcycle. Wants to give me a ride."

A motorcycle? My heart jumped. This was a lesbian stereotype, whether Mary knew it or not. (She did.) We were getting dangerously close to the topic I had vowed to avoid. "Is this new guard good at the work?" I asked. "Do you like her?"

"She is good at the work, and yes, I do like her. She and her . . . friend . . . came to my Fourth of July barbecue."

Her friend. Was I wrong, or did Mary pause for emphasis before she said these words?

"On the . . . motorcycle?" I asked.

"Yes," Mary said, as in, *Of course.*

Mary used a lesbian trope to send me a message. She knew, and liked, a lesbian. I could talk to her freely. Still hiding behind my faulty rationale of (self) protection, I kept mum.

Then we were back at the splintery wooden stairway that would take us up to the cottage. Beams from my parents' headlights might come bumping down the driveway any minute, announcing their fraught and woozy return from dinner. Mary and I climbed back up the rickety steps, each as solitary as when we had begun.

Mary and I both kept secrets that night. I was in love, and didn't tell her. Mary didn't talk about freeing herself from an abusive and dangerous man. When she knew all too well that I was keeping a secret from her, why would she trust me with her painful story? The setting, too, constrained our truth telling. We were interacting in Mary's workplace and my uneasy parental environment.

Mary and I would go on in future years to tell each other more of our truths. But, that evening on the beach, our secrets settled a net over our fledgling conversation, trapping us in stale topics while the wind flung stinging sand at our ankles. Our dual silences kept us separate, and lonely. As Audre Lorde famously wrote, in "The Transformation of Silence into Language and Action" (1977), "It is not difference which immobilizes us, but silence. And there are so many silences to be broken."

eleven

Sanctuary

MARY WAS THE FIRST TO GIVE SUSTAINED AND DEDICATED time to the possibility of a more robust friendship, the first to venture across a bridge that we were constructing between us. I had stopped by her home in Trenton a few times when visiting my parents in New Jersey, but never to stay over. In the winter of 1986, Mary made time in her packed correction center and moonlighting schedules to come north for a weekend in Cambridge.

I was eager for two full days together. I wanted to pamper Mary, persuade her to take it easy, take her out to dinner, browse together at New Words Bookstore, and gift her any books that she might choose from their curated, progressive offerings. I wanted to start making up for all the years Mary had tended to me. The morning of her arrival, however, found me edgy and distracted. I yanked the vacuum cleaner through the third-floor walk-up where Polly had joined me five years earlier, after graduating from college. Clouds of hair from our two cats wafted along the wooden floor. The machine caught on corners and toppled wastebaskets with its lurching weight.

I felt peevish. Polly usually vacuumed; I cooked. She took out the trash; I balanced the checkbook. We had settled into roles that worked for us—until the previous September, when Polly started teaching a hundred ninth graders. In time, she would become a skilled and sought-after teacher with a pedagogy that encouraged critical thinking and fostered a vigorously respectful learning community in the classroom. In her first year, however, she woke daily before dawn, feeling like a failure already. Evenings and weekends, she muttered to herself at her desk. Nights, she tossed and worried on her side of the bed.

Now the vacuum wheezed and whined while the nozzle pushed dust around. The bag was stuffed. No fresh bags waited tidily on the closet shelf the way they had before Polly started teaching. I jammed the machine into the hall closet, knocking jackets off hooks, resentful of the unheralded work, feeling like a housewife. The irony of my petulance: I was cleaning house to prepare for Mary, who cleaned for white families from the age of eleven; her mother and grandmother cleaned white people's houses for a living, for a lifetime.

I re-hung the jackets and leaned against their soft bulk in the dim closet. Mary had planned to visit us a year earlier, but my mother had scheduled a last-minute dinner party and asked Mary to help out. Immediately, Mary had canceled the trip. I'd blamed my mother's selfish dependence on Mary's help for disrupting the visit I had so eagerly anticipated.

Had I been paying more attention to Mary's life, I might have grasped the economic pressures that spurred her to moonlight for my mother and other white women in Princeton. We were in the midst of the conservative Reagan Era, which brought drastic cuts in the social safety net, under the pretense of supply-side economics that profits for the wealthy would "trickle down" to poor and working people. I opposed Reaganomics on principle, but did not feel the impact on my own pocketbook. I also lacked a sense of history: Reagan's greed on behalf of the upper classes was only the latest crime in a country built on the unpaid or poorly paid labor of African Americans. A living wage, never part of Mary's employment in corrections or domestic service, can do a lot to free a person to go away for the weekend when they want to.

And yet, now that Mary was finally free to visit us, something was wrong in my household. Polly and I had become lovers in 1979, seven years earlier. Good years, I thought. Polly's immersion in her new teaching job, however, had turned me into a solitary, restless housewife. Matthew had left three years earlier for prep school at his dad's alma mater and spent most of his vacations with his dad's new family. Long before most of my friends would face the "empty nest" as their children moved away for college or work, my role as a mother had shrunk to nearly nothing. I had a job I liked, as a campus minister at a local commuter college. I was blessed to have friends like the women of *Our Bodies, Ourselves* in my life. But Matthew's absence left me feeling as empty as his unoccupied bedroom, and Polly's new absorption in work felt like another loss.

Today, I look for my part in the vexation that awaited Mary in our household. I think of my father's mantra: "In this family, we don't like changes." The changes of that particular time—Matthew's absence, Polly's new job—asked me for a flexibility, and perhaps a kindness, that I did not learn in my childhood home.

I'd recently begun to distract myself by developing a crush. J. was a woman in my writing group whose poetry was intensely personal and smartly (I thought) political. She had a passionate, self-confident, and somewhat mysterious persona that intrigued me, and she was decidedly flirtatious. I started fretting over what to wear to meetings, and went out for coffee with J. afterwards, just the two of us. Returning home to Polly, I'd stroke my arm where the poet had put her hand, and spin out scenarios in my head. *We run into each other by chance. We have so much to talk about. We touch, we kiss, we fall into bed. (Several trite scenarios for this.)* To this day, I don't know what J. had in mind as she flirted with me. That's the thing about crushes: what the other person thinks or wants, who the other person might actually be, is irrelevant. The poet I conjured, and the crush I nurtured, were in my head.

I was eleven when my mother took me to a film called *The Seven Year Itch*, the kind of sexist romantic comedy that taught me ways of being female I'd later spend years undoing. In the film, maybe most known for its iconic shot of Marilyn Monroe's white skirt lifting in a subway updraft, a white male publishing executive has been married for seven years. While his wife and son are away on vacation, Marilyn Monroe's character moves in upstairs, and every manner of sexually charged comedy ensues. *Seven-year itch* drifted into my lexicon as a humorous term— until J. If this was the seven-year itch, I chafed at being so predictable.

Mary moved gracefully through the gate at Boston's Logan Airport, looking elegant in a tailored tan pantsuit and high heels. I persisted in distrusting the stylish beauty that had never protected my mother, and wore my usual corduroy pants and practical walking shoes. Beaming and waving, Mary strode towards me in heels so high I could only have wobbled. Passengers streamed around us—two women on the other side of forty—as we threw our arms around each other and held on.

Today, recalling our airport reunion, longing sweeps over me. By now, Mary and I have reached our seventies. Disabling arthritis keeps Mary close to home. I travel to visit her every year. How I long for Mary to come through an arrival gate once again and to stride towards me in high heels and an elegant pantsuit.

As we pulled up to the four-story brick apartment building where Polly and I lived, I wondered suddenly whether Mary would be comfortable in my mostly white life. At home, Mary moved in and out of white and mixed settings daily, but how would she feel in a building where all the residents were white? I had turned away from many aspects of my parents' upper-class existence—the big house, the wooded acres, the fur coats and Mercedes Benzes—but I got up every day, just as they did, in a white neighborhood and traveled in a mostly white world.

Mary showed no signs of discomfort. Once upstairs, she plopped down on the bed in Matthew's old bedroom, with its white walls and navy-blue trim, its posters of boats under full sail. She gave the mattress a celebratory pat. "I made it," she said.

"At last," I said. I felt so happy to have Mary in our home that, for a moment, I forgot the tension that had taken up residence with Polly's new job—moved in with us like an unwanted roommate.

That night, Polly and I took Mary to dinner at Legal Sea Foods. In racially segregated Boston, Legal's clientele was more racially mixed than that of other restaurants we knew, and I thought this might make Mary feel comfortable. Once we were seated, I watched a Black couple dining at a nearby table and hoped that she noticed their presence. I wonder now at my racist tokenizing, and my hope that the presence of a token Black couple would make a difference to Mary. She, for her part, was already instructing the waiter. "Bring us a bottle of the Pouilly-Fuissé, nice and chilled." She winked at me. "My treat," she said.

Mary slips quietly into my parents' Princeton dining room with a chilled green bottle of Pouilly-Fuissé folded carefully into a linen napkin. Expertly, she pours a quarter-inch of the pale gold liquid into my father's glass. My mother watches him lift the glass to his lips, smiles as he swallows and nods. Mary tops his glass off and pours generously for my mother. Not a drop lost.

The waiter arrived with the wine and poured a half-inch for Mary to taste. "Yes!" she said. "This is delicious," and gestured for the waiter to pour full glasses for each of us.

"I wanted to spoil you while you're here," I said to Mary. "Here you are, spoiling us."

"Just about the only thing my second husband left me with is a taste for fine wines," Mary said. "Oh my, did he wine and dine me at first. There was nothing good he wouldn't do for me." She shook her head, as if to shake him off and good riddance.

With a mischievous light in her eye, Mary looked from me to Polly, and back again. "Does Polly know how long you took to tell me about her?" Lifting her wine glass to her red lips, she took an appreciative sip. "Remember that night in Nantucket, what was it, six years ago already? It was the second summer Polly came to visit. You were still pretending to be just friends. One night after Polly left, you and I walked miles up the beach, and it looked like you were still not going to tell me." Mary chuckled, waiting for me to join in.

I couldn't feel less like telling our love story. "Maybe I was trying to get up my courage," I mumbled.

Mary laughed as if I were right on cue. "And I was about to go lame!" She turned to Polly. "We trudged on and on."

Mary looked back at me expectantly, and so I took up the story—how I'd asked Mary at the farthest point of our beach walk whether she'd feel burdened by knowing a secret she'd have to keep from my mother. Mary reassured me, and I finally confessed to her that Polly and I were in love.

Mary set her wine glass down, laughing. "I told you that I'd known all along. You were so shocked!"

I darted my eyes quickly to Polly's, and away again.

Mary's smile took us both in. "Remember how I'd carried on the year before about the new correctional officer who motorcycled to work, how she and her girlfriend came over for a barbeque? I wanted you to hear that I knew women like you." Then she grew serious. "After you told me that you were lovers, and we were walking back along the beach, you asked whether I thought you two had done a good job of pretending to be friends."

I remembered Mary trudging along thoughtfully after I asked her that, remembered the whispery scrunch of her Keds on the sand. At last, she'd said, and I had never heard her so sharply cautionary, "Tell Polly not to look at you like that."

Mary turned to Polly now, as the waiter set down large oval plates with our meals—swordfish, sole and tuna. "You looked at Wendy so adoringly," Mary said to Polly. "You just couldn't help it."

We hadn't looked at each other "like that" in months. Polly's new job claimed all she had. My resentment lurked and festered.

J. comes into Legal Sea Foods and strides across the restaurant in her assured, confident way, heading for me. She flashes her blue

eyes and kisses one cheek, then the other—almost formal, eyelashes
down. I thrill to her touch.

"Earth to Wendy," Polly said. I yanked myself back from the
fantasy. "The waiter asked if we want dessert."

"I'm fine," I said, with a fake smile. "And you?" I turned to
Mary.

"Mary already answered," Polly said.

I'd been lost in my inner soap opera.

I had friends who said crushes could be fun. You enjoy the
rush of sexual feelings, and then bring the excitement back to
your partner. Do you, though?

Saturday morning, while Mary slept down the hall, I woke early.
Next to me, Polly stared up at the ceiling as though she had
been stewing for hours. My thoughts snuck to the edge of my
sleepy consciousness, ready to slip out to J., but I laid my head
purposefully on Polly's bare shoulder, pulled the blankets
around us, and put a hand on her small breast. "Is my hand too
cold?" I asked.

"Nice," she said.

We lay there.

For seven years, Polly and I had moved across each other's
bodies with purpose and desire. That morning, my assessing
fingers felt only a small, inert mound. I marvel at how inert two
bodies can be, side by side, when there is dishonesty or squir-
reled-away anger.

"If I get up now," Polly said, "maybe I can grade enough ninth-
grade Africa maps to join you and Mary at the play tonight."

I took my hand from her breast and asked resentfully,
meanly—as though I had been feeling sexually interested,

which I had not—"You mean we have to choose between sex now and sociability later?"

"I'm sorry," Polly said, sounding more worn down than sorry. "It's a big deal, having Mary here. I thought you'd want me with you tonight. If I don't grade forty maps, I'll go crazy tomorrow."

"You working the whole weekend, then?"

Polly sat up with her back to me. "Guess I'm a lousy teacher and a lousy partner, both."

"Wait," I said. "I'm just whining."

She turned to study my face. "What is this really about?"

"I don't know," I said, which was, and wasn't, true.

If you are rooting for Polly to break up with me and move out, I don't blame you. Here she was, still in her twenties, working to be a success in a new job, living with a cranky, critical, mean, and distracted girlfriend.

The word "itch" seems too small.

Down the hall, I put my ear up against a faded Spiderman sticker on Matthew's old door, and listened to the silence of deep rest. I wanted Mary to sleep in.

Mary emerged an hour later. Seized by a yawn that took over her whole body, she leaned against the doorframe in a long white bathrobe. "Goodness, I'm a lazy bum. Did you want to go out? Have I ruined your morning?"

"No way you've ruined the morning," I protested. Her hint of deference bothered me. She was our guest. I wanted her to leave behind her long-established practice of deference to my family. In my script for the weekend, Mary's role was to do and be as she liked—and yet here I was finding fault with her attitude.

We headed towards the living room, down a long hall that

led us away from the small, crowded study where Polly was already at work grading Africa maps. Winter sunshine bathed the living room through a bay window that faced southeast. Sunlight pooled around a large, upholstered chair that I'd brought up from my parents' home in Princeton. As with many hand-me-downs, the chair had a complex history. This was the seat I'd perched on, as a girl, to field my father's quizzes on current events; my front-row seat at cocktail hour; the seat I sank into for shelter from my parents' marital sniping; the seat from which I watched my mother retreat with her wounded feelings to the den, to her favorite TV shows, to her tall scotch-and-sodas.

As a servant, Mary had not been welcome to sit in any chair in my parents' living room—to rest, to take her ease. Watching her settle into the chair now, in the sunlight that streamed in through the bay window, made me feel less ambivalent about preserving this loaded vestige of my childhood.

Mary winced as she sat, though, and gingerly straightened out her right knee. "Look at me, all these aches and pains," she said. "I'm an old woman already."

"Forty-six? If you're old, I'm old," I said.

"You are not," Mary countered, revealing a difference between us that could not be argued. Mary had aged more quickly than I, and one weekend's pampering wouldn't change the reasons why. I pictured Mary at eleven, kneeling each Saturday on a white family's floor, inhaling chemicals from the cleansers and polishes, straining her young knees as she scrubbed and perfected the shine. What Mary called her "aches and pains" reflected decades of sustained labor and persisting stress—the worries of poverty, the dangers of white violence, the Jim Crow South that defined her childhood, uncertainty about her children's safety and her own on the streets of a northern city, dogged opposition from white male officers at the correction center, and the more polite but no less entitled manipulations of the white women who paid her to work in their homes. The outcomes of the aggressions of racism, sexism, and economic injustice were taking a toll on her body.

Mary lay her head back. "Can't believe I'm so tired today. And this knee aches something terrible. I really do think it's arthritis." Then she sat upright. "At least I've been promoted to lieutenant," she added. "I'm a shift commander, at last. Been qualified to do that work for years."

"Sounds like you had to fight for the promotion."

Her face clouded. "There's a new warden who gets riled that so many people in the town know me. Whenever someone on the outside wants information they can count on, they call for Mary. Some folks . . ." Her smile crept back. "I've heard that some folks on the outside think I'm the warden." She bent over in a half laugh, half cough, then sat back up with a serious look. "Just last month he switched me from my night shift to payroll and scheduling. I think he hoped the numbers would confuse me, but I have the shifts and back-ups organized better than ever. Watch him switch me again, just to make my life miserable. Used to be, evenings when I wasn't due at your mother's or some other lady's, or my department store security job, I'd stay at the correction center way past quitting time. I loved my job. Now I can't get out of there soon enough."

I sat up abruptly. "Department store? How many jobs are you working, anyway?" In my affluent family, people worked one job or, like my mother, none. Never two, three, or four jobs. I thought Mary must be a workaholic to work so much. I was wrong. Like most people, Mary worked for the life she wanted.

"The extra jobs are nothing," Mary said. "When I'm sitting

at a security desk, or cooking a little dinner, that's where I relax. With the new warden in charge, believe me, I need to unwind."

"But you're exhausted!" I said, chewing at the same old bone.

"When I got free from my second husband, he predicted I'd never have my own house. I showed him. Bought that house you came to see me in last time. I've got to keep it in good shape, repair the roof, insulate the attic. Need something put aside in case the boiler blows. So, I sit guard at Strawberry department store and do dinner parties for a few ladies in Princeton. The work is easy." She paused, thought. "No, inside is where I'm tired," she said slowly. "I'm divorced again. All this work, and my life doesn't seem to mean anything. Maybe it's loneliness makes a person tired."

I lay my head on the armrest of the chair, pressing my cheek into the rich, brocade upholstery. Away from the set roles and required silences of my parents' home, Mary was speaking more openly and freely to me, as a trusting friend would do. I wish now that I had opened myself more fully to this precious opportunity. Instead, even as Mary spoke of her loneliness, as I kneeled at her feet looking up at her weary and sad expression, my thoughts veered off. *Where was J, when would I see her again?* The addictive, distracting force of a crush thrust me out of the precious moment.

Mary must have noticed my drifting attention. Quickly, she shut down any glimpse of her own feelings and switched the topic to my life, not hers. "You seemed on edge with Polly last night," she said. "If it's okay my saying so."

I got up and closed the living room door. Whispering, I told Mary about Polly's disappearance into her work, how I missed her, even (embarrassing to this day) how I felt like a housewife. I want to pinpoint this moment, my failed attention and Mary's shift in focus from her life to mine. Decades later, activists would coin a term for my behavior: centering whiteness.

I talked about the poet, her smoldering eyes and political verse, how I couldn't get her out of my mind.

Mary looked embarrassed. "Did you . . .?" she began.

I knew she was asking about sex. "Only kisses on the cheek hello and goodbye."

"Oh," Mary said, as in *Oh, that's not so bad.*

"In my imagination, though, it's a different story."

Voices and laughter filled the local theater, where Mary, Polly, and I had come to see a new play by Boston's Underground Railway Theater. *Sanctuary: The Spirit of Harriet Tubman* promised to draw connections between Tubman's anti-slavery crusade and present-day struggles of refugees fleeing Central American death squads. Progressive faith communities across the United States at that time were creating a "sanctuary" movement to harbor refugees dubbed "illegal aliens" by the U.S. government, which supported the oppressive regimes that caused the refugees to seek safe haven. Polly and I were getting involved in this movement through our Quaker meeting.

Underground Railway's growing reputation for socially relevant theater had brought out a modestly multiracial crowd of socialists and feminists, Quakers and anti-racist activists, Central America activists, lesbians and gay men. This was Polly's and my community. I wondered what Mary would think of them all. Dressed for the evening's excursion in a shapely wool skirt, stockings, and high-heels, Mary was no flannel-shirted activist. Her style was closer to my mother's than to mine. She reached over and squeezed my arm. "I'm excited," she said. I kissed her cheek.

We settled in to read our playbills. The cover featured a grim photograph of metal shackles attached to thick, rusted snakes of chain. I stole a look at Mary. We had never directly talked about slavery. She turned to an inner page, where another photograph shouted out: a murdered Black man, hanging from a tree, a crowd of white people enjoying the spectacle. I worried suddenly. What if the play was too painful for us to handle? Too truth-telling? What if it stirred Mary's righteous anger against white people? Would she focus that anger on me? These were self-centered questions based in my own discomfort, and, although I didn't see it as such at the time, a measure of how much more informed and robust I had to become around racial issues if Mary and I were truly to be friends.

Before the lights went down, I looked around the theater once more and found myself checking who might be noticing us. Difficult as this is to admit today, I was proud to be seen with Mary. I wanted people to know I had a Black friend. Somehow, I thought of this as a credential. Years later, the work of white sociologist Robin DiAngelo would help me unpack this desire. Amplifying her theory on white people's "fragility" around race, DiAngelo suggests that we want to insulate ourselves from the terrible knowledge that we participate in racism. Having friends of color, we believe, proves that we are "not racist," as though not being racist is even possible for a white person in a context of white supremacy. Counting our friends of color helps us to avoid self-reflection and, ironically, to keep racism in place. With Mary sitting next to me in a community of my peers, I was eager for everyone to see that I was one of the "good" white people.

Only a few years before Mary's visit, an iconic work by a local poet had warned me against such tokenism. Kate Rushin was a well-known figure in the Cambridge women's community, tall and graceful, smart and wryly funny, a member of the women's collective that founded and ran New Words feminist bookstore. More than once, I'd thrilled to hear Kate Rushin deliver "The Bridge Poem," which appeared in a break-through 1981 work called *This Bridge Called My Back: Writings by Radical Women of Color.* "I've had enough," Rushin wrote, of her experience as a Black woman called on to bridge many estranged communities. "I explain my mother to my father / my father to my little sister / My little sister to my brother / my brother to the white feminists / The white feminists to the Black church folks . . . / I do more translating / Than the Gawdamn U.N." Rushin became "sick of being the sole Black friend to thirty-four individual white people," "sick of being the damn bridge for everybody." Rushin had pointed advice for people like me: "Find another connection to the rest of the world / Find something else to make you legitimate / Find some other way to be political and hip . . ." In a line that stirs me to this day, Rushin went further: "I will not be the bridge to your . . . humanness."

I recently learned that Rushin collaborated on writing the script for *Sanctuary*. There's every chance that she was in the audience that night as I hoped to be noticed with my Black friend. Had I truly heeded Rushin's warning, I might have understood the ways I was asking Mary to serve as a bridge to my humanness.

The gripping first half of *Sanctuary* took us from an antebellum Southern plantation to a modern-day workplace, from the Big Dipper constellation's lifesaving guidance to a mid-1950s civil rights sit-in. As we stood to stretch at intermission, Mary said,

"This play stirs old memories. It's a very emotional experience."

Just then, I spotted J a few rows below us in the theater. She stood, turned, and began making her way towards us, splendid in a shimmering green silk shirt. I watched, electrified, as she came close, shook Mary's hand, and Polly's, and offered her cheek to me.

For the second time that day, I ignored a heartfelt revelation from Mary, let her pregnant words drop, unheard, between us. Southern white antiracist activist Mab Segrest suggests that white people have for centuries willfully distracted ourselves from looking at the pain of enslavement and systemic racism— we use alcohol and other mood-altering drugs, we go shopping, we watch TV. I would add that we also escape into crushes.

Sunday morning, Polly and I walked stiffly towards the Friends Meeting a mile away, while Mary slept in. Polly and I went to worship most Sundays. Even if we arrived at the meetinghouse depleted or disconnected, the quiet gathering of Friends' worship and the sense of shared spiritual seeking often drew us together. That morning, I wondered whether prayer could stop me from thinking obsessively about J.

As I drove Mary to the airport later that afternoon for her to leave us, I learned that praying had not worked the way I'd hoped. Even during our precious last minutes together, I asked Mary what she'd thought of J.

"Oh, her," Mary said.

I pictured the woman, trimly erect in black slacks and green shimmery shirt, turning her bright, assertive gaze on Mary, shaking her hand, chatting her up. "What was your impression?" I asked.

187

"I had an uneasy feeling from her," Mary answered promptly. "I think she might be a little in love with herself."

I bristled. "She is self-confident, if that's what you mean. Self-confidence is what Polly lacks so utterly these days. Couldn't you see it? Polly doesn't know how to be tough with her students, she feels like a failure as a teacher, she tiptoes around me." Behind us, a car honked. I accelerated sharply. Mary clutched her seatbelt.

Mary's cheek against mine at curbside marked the end of our visit. I held on, willing my hug to make up for my weekend of distraction. She pulled back, checked the ticket tucked inside the novel she'd brought for the flight, and fixed her eyes on mine. "You have a jewel in Polly," Mary said. "A treasure. Why would you give her up?"

Thanks to Mary's wake-up call, I did wrestle myself free of the crush, and started the deliberate work of adjusting to Polly's whole-hearted commitment to her teaching career and to the power shifts between us. I began learning to be a kinder and more mature lover.

Last summer, in 2019, thirty years after we saw *Sanctuary* together, I asked Mary whether she remembered the woman in the jade-green silk shirt. She chuckled.

"I certainly do. She was a self-centered person. It was all about her. It wouldn't have lasted. You made the right choice."

Then Mary grew thoughtful. "I enjoyed the play. I'd never been to one before. But there I was with a whole roomful of Caucasians who were seeing for the first time what I was living.

To them it was just a play. It was entertainment to them. I came later to understand that maybe some were really there for learning."

In the second act of *Sanctuary,* a hard-working white waitress in a Chicago restaurant plans to report an undocumented young Latino busboy to Immigration, believing that his slow work pace affects her tips. When a compassionate cook tells her the boy's harrowing story of escape from Guatemala, she changes her mind about him, and persuades her church to take him into sanctuary. At the play's end, a choir sings a powerful 1977 anthem by Walter Robinson about Harriet Tubman and the Underground Railroad: "Come on up, I've got a lifeline. Come on up, to this train of mine." A giant puppet of Harriet Tubman rises in the back and glides forward, transforming in aspect until she is also a Central American refugee. Sanctuary stretches across centuries.

Mary was a safe haven to me in my family's tense household whenever we were there at the same time, a sane and loving presence. She gave me sanctuary from the start. She says that, especially during those early summers on the isolated beach, I provided a bit of the same.

2020 update. On the phone these days Mary and I ramble through talk of siblings and children, her health and mine, weather and politics. "Now that I'm elderly," Mary says, "we get on the phone and talk about everything." We bemoan our aging bodies and slipping memories, protest the latest right-wing outrage. We touch the horrors—murder after murder of Black people by whites, in churches and on city streets. For a few weeks in the spring of 2020, as the Covid-19 pandemic took hold, we spoke every day. Mary says, "You were such a comfort to me when I was stressing that I'd caught the virus. You were like a support system for me when the virus broke out and I wasn't being around anyone." Our calls comforted me just as much. Due to the pandemic, we are still unable to see each other in person. I hope that we will be able to do so in this life. Meanwhile there is the phone, there is texting. In a companionable, elderly kind of way, Mary and I seek to be safe havens for each other, still.

twelve

Good Daughter

IN THE TWO YEARS AFTER MARY ADVISED ME TO STICK WITH Polly (I did), gravity seemed to pull my mother down. By the summer of 1988, Mom was weary, weighted, stuck to her chair. Her belly ballooned out, pressing against her bathing suits and bright silk cocktail dresses. I read what I could find about late-stage alcoholism and thought I saw signs of advancing liver cirrhosis.

When a person drinks too much alcohol for their body over too many years, liver tissues that were once flexible and robust begin to thicken and scar. Scarring slows the flow of blood and other fluids through the liver, hampering the ways a healthy liver strains out toxins, transfers nutrients, cleanses. Blocked from flowing easily, the fluids build up pressure and begin to push forcefully out into thousands of liver capillaries. The thin membranes of these tiny blood vessels give way, and fluid seeps into the abdomen. My mother's belly began to look like a beach ball.

Mom's doctor advised her to stop drinking. She switched from bourbon and gin to half-gallon bottles of Chablis. I tried telling her that wine would damage her liver, too, and she bristled. "I've already given up all the drinks I love," she said. "You try living with your father without something nice to help you bear it." My father—both cause and excuse.

By the fall of 1988, weakened and dazed, Mom retired to bed in the Princeton house. The seepage from her liver robbed her of nutrients, and the fluid's escalating pressure on her stomach killed her appetite. She began to starve. Having fancied himself a chef since retirement, my dad whipped up gourmet creations to tempt her to eat. When my mother could not, or would not, eat, Dad's late-blooming instinct to nurture bled into rage. Lost and furious, he lurched around the house. He drank alone.

Mary immediately altered her work schedule to meet my mother's new needs. For years, Mary had come to Princeton from Trenton one evening a week to iron my father's shirts and, while Dad snored on the living room sofa, to talk with my lonely mother. Now Mary switched to coming every afternoon. By starting at the correction center two hours earlier each morning, she could slip through my parents' back doorway by three, bearing groceries and whatever else she thought the household needed. Mary tended to my mother, cooked the dinner, and tackled jobs she thought the weekly cleaning person should have completed. Mary replaced worn out light bulbs, restocked paper goods, called in repair people, tacked down rugs where she thought my mother might trip. In a household that would have fallen apart without her, Mary became, in essence, not only my mother's daily caregiver but also the de facto house manager. Years later, Mary would look back and say she wondered how she found the stamina and strength for the pace she kept during those months, how she got by on three hours of sleep night after night. My mother paid Mary for the extra hours but, despite this spike in responsibilities, I believe she thoughtlessly continued paying Mary at the usual hourly rate.

What Mary provided was, in fact, priceless. Her role as an employee blurred rapidly into that of a central—though unacknowledged—member of the family.

Like many children of alcoholics, I wavered between faithfulness and self-protection. I ached to go to my mother's side, but dreaded Dad's rages. Because Mary went so dependably, I could stay home in Massachusetts and call in.

I called on Labor Day afternoon to find my mother still in bed despite the late hour. She was feeling puzzled and worn down, and she blamed my father. "This is all brought on by stress and pressure," she said, "and we know where *that* comes from."

Then she cried suddenly, gratefully, "Here's Mary, come to give me a bath!" Hearing the relief in my mother's voice, I felt a stab of guilt. Mary, not I, was arriving to care for her. I swatted away a mental picture of Mary tendering my ungainly mother into the tub, soaping and gently rinsing her distended belly, helping her rise dripping from the bath, folding her into a towel. I knew I was being irrational to wish for such intimacy with my mother. We didn't have that kind of relationship. My father's presence meant I didn't feel safe in that house. I took advantage of Mary's willing service in order to stay away, and yet the thought of Mary bathing my mother stirred a sudden, perverse envy.

I picture Mary as she climbed the stairs towards my mother. Mary was a year shy of fifty. Her left shoulder ached her painfully, there was a nagging complaint in her knee, and she was bone-tired. Her work day at the correction center had begun before dawn. The plush carpeted stairway and the quiet of her employers' suburban house marked a stark difference between her two workplaces. All day she'd walked the hard floors and bare corridors of the jail. All day, she shielded her ears from gates slamming shut and from the accosting shouts, jibes, and protests of men doing time. All day, she kept alert to danger, knowing that resentful fellow officers presented as much hazard as any inmate.

Mary's work in Princeton was demanding in a different way. Mary knew my mother intimately, and my mother depended on her utterly. Each day, my mother saved up all her discomforts and needs for Mary to address. My father had to be managed, too. Beside himself with grief about my mother's decline, he drank heavily each evening, then bullied her. He was a volatile mix of misery, contradiction, and danger.

As she climbed the stairs to my mother, Mary joined many generations of Black women drawn into white people's scenes of sickness. For three hundred years, enslaved women had no choice but to caretake white enslavers in childbirth, in infirmity, in death. Today, most home health care and hospice support workers are low-paid Black women and immigrant women of color. There is a persisting racist expectation that white patients' needs will supersede the needs and wellbeing of their caregivers. Just that spring, Mom had reported to me that Mary had "woman" problems: "Mary is having a lot of bleeding you-know-where," my mother had said. "She is awfully tired. I'm worried about her. She needs a hysterectomy. I don't know how I'll manage."

I'd recoiled. "How *you'll* manage? What about Mary? How will *she* manage?" My mother's self-centeredness made me cringe. I didn't want to see myself in her.

"Mary needs this job," my mother had huffed defensively. "We pay a healthy sum for her services. She knows that your father and I couldn't do without her. She's a very loyal, loving friend."

Here, in a nutshell of illogic, was Mom's rationale for all she asked of Mary: Mary needed the work, my parents needed her services, and Mary was a "friend." My mother did not treat Mary like her other friends. Still, there was a bond between my mother and Mary, woven of money and caring, need and diligence, dependence and income-based decision making. As my mother grew more ill, the bond between the two women showed no sign of fraying.

Between Women, the book by sociologist Judith Rollins that offers me critical insight into what Mary may have experienced in my family, cites overwork as a primary job hazard in domestic service. Most employers in her study, including those she cleaned house for as part of her research, assigned more tasks, than could reasonably be done in the allotted time. I recognize my mother here. In her dying months, she was willing to absorb whatever time and energy Mary had to give. And, as I have come to admit, so was I.

I have thought a great deal about Mary's above-and-beyond service as my mother grew sicker. I remember one summer in Nantucket, some years earlier, when Mary seemed especially weary after a grueling year with the dreadful new warden at the correction center.

"Next year you'll take a real vacation, right?" I remember saying. "You won't pile the Nantucket job on top of your regular work?"

After the briefest pause, Mary turned to me. "Have you ever tried to say no to your mother?"

"All the time," I said quickly, but, as I spoke, the privilege of refusing my mother dawned on me. "You don't get to say no to her, do you?" I asked.

Mary's silence was my answer.

Long after both my parents died, Mary would tell me of my mother's request. "Back when Mrs. C. was doing fine, she asked me if I would be there for her in her time of need—you know, if she got very sick."

"No matter what was going on in your own life, your own family?" I'd ask.

Mary would look at me steadily, soberly. "I told her I would be there."

Judith Rollins writes that many female employers manipulate with kindness. My mother spoke gently to Mary and expressed sincere gratitude for her work. She loaned money when Mary asked and gave her new gifts, not hand-me-downs. As Mary once said to me, "She used to give us both the same thing for Christmas. What she gave you, she gave me—the sweater, the cozy bathrobe, down to the oranges."

My mother loved Mary and would have been shocked by the suggestion that she was manipulating her. But my mother expected a great deal in return for her "kindness." *"Have you ever tried to say no to your mother?"* In asking for Mary's promise to tend her on her deathbed, my mother was demanding payback. Looking back on this "deal" my mother made, I understand that I, too, made such a deal. I was "kind" to Mary—and I, too, benefitted from her unfailing service. In this, I was more like my mother than I so self-righteously thought.

Working every available hour had long been Mary's strategy for survival and success, but I don't think she went to my mother's bedside primarily for the pay. Mary had made a promise. As my mother surely knew when she extracted that promise, Mary keeps her word.

In the affluent WASP circles in which I grew up, we paid

other people to do hands-on caring. We hid from the intimacy of bodies, the messiness of wounds, blood, stool, the sounds and cries of pain. During my mother's last months, I entered her sickroom only when she was what we euphemistically called "ready"—after Mary or a nurse had cleaned her, dressed her, and tucked her into crisp, white sheets. In extracting Mary's promise to be there for her "in her time of need," my mother orchestrated, for herself, a well-tended, upper-class death.

As I learn more about Mary's home community, I realize that she inherited a deep ethic about caring for dying relatives. Jacqueline Woodson's powerful memoir in verse, *Brown Girl Dreaming*, works as a touchstone here. In a beautiful poem, Woodson recalls visiting her dying grandfather as he lies under blankets in his bed at home. He has lost much weight. She brings him a bowl of chicken soup. Perching on the bed beside him, she coaxes him to take tiny swallows. He says he feels too weary to be hungry.

In Mary's home community, as in Woodson's poem, hands-on caring for sick and dying family members happens at home. There is no money to pay for outside care, and horror stories spotlight the mistreatment of poor and Black neighbors with the bad luck to land in local nursing homes. The work of caring for the sick is grueling, especially on top of full-time jobs, but—in a melding of obligation, faith, and love—family members care for loved ones at home.

As a child, through long Sunday hours on the hand-hewn pews of Oak Grove Methodist, and through fellowship hour and picnics, fundraisers, and funerals, Mary learned at the knee of faithful church people. At any one time, several adults in the church—mostly women—would be caring for ill family members at home. Each Sunday, the congregation raised prayers for the sick or dying. They entrusted their ailing family members to God's hands, understanding that God's hands were, indeed, their own.

From the Find a Grave website, I've learned that Mary had early and direct family experience of such caring. "At the end of his life," the record reads, Reece Cox (Mary's great-grandfather) lived in the home of his daughter, Verna Cox Phipps, "and her family." He died there in 1941. Dailey Phipps, who was Verna Phipps's husband and Mary's grandfather, died at home just three years later. Born in 1940, Mary lived those same years with her Mamaw, under the same roof as both men.

I mentioned this fact to Mary recently. "I was intrigued," she said, "when you told me my great-grandfather was there in the house I was born in." She called family members for confirmation, was surprised that she hadn't known.

Mary was too young when they died to remember her great-grandfather and her grandfather, but Find a Grave shows a grainy 1942 photograph of Mr. Phipps, just two years before his death. Wearing a jacket with no tie, he sits informally, relaxed, not posing. Perched on his lap is a little girl dressed all in white: his first granddaughter, two-year-old Mary.

As a small child, therefore, Mary lived in the presence of her grandmother's fierce diligence in tending her father and husband as they died. Years later, when Verna Phipps was dying, one of her daughters cared for her at home until her death. For as many generations as Mary can remember, her kin have lived their last years at home, in the care of family members. These generations of faithful care would converge, for Mary, into a determined pride that would impel her to devote ten years of her late middle age to caring for her mother, Alice, and then her stepfather, George Johnson.

Before Mary served her own aging parents, she served mine. Beyond the paycheck, beyond even keeping a promise, this was simply what people in Mary's community did for close and beloved family members. Mary tended to my mother like a member of her own family. In a later chapter in our lives, Mary would tell me how deeply she loved my mother, how she felt, during those months of Mom's dying, like she was losing her own mother. Mary tended to my mother out of love.

With her swollen, heavy belly and flagging strength, my mother at last agreed in September of 1988 to see a doctor. The diagnosis: advanced liver cirrhosis. Her liver was too damaged to do its work. Mom stopped drinking, cold turkey. Both my father and Mary seemed to cling to hope that this step would save her. For them, the next four months would be a see-saw of hope and disappointment. Mary would tell me years later that she hadn't realized that the booze was actually killing my mother, and I suspect my father believed the same. After all, most people back then thought that only bums and "skid-row" drunks died of drink. Denial, which is such a big part of this "family disease," would also have operated powerfully to prevent both Mary and my father from connecting Mom's drinking to her decline. In my own form of defense against the inevitable, I figured my mother didn't have a chance.

The medical visit itself created a crisis. Apparently, my mother shut the door firmly behind her as she entered her doctor's office, leaving my father in the waiting room. She would soon pay for treating Dad like a hazard, not a help, for seizing this moment of safe haven. Fury at being shut out leaked into my father's genuine anguish over her illness, forming a toxic mix. I don't know the specifics of how he vented his rage, but by nine that night, he made a desperate call to my brother. Mom had locked herself into her bedroom and would not come out. Copey decided to head to Princeton to "sort things out," and I jumped at the chance to enjoy the protection his presence would offer me with Dad.

Copey eased the rental car off the New Jersey Turnpike into the stop-and-go traffic of Route 1 as we headed from the Newark airport to Princeton. We had taken the first flight from Boston that morning. "Dad has to get on board with Mom's recovery," Copey said. "He can cut down on the cocktails, if only to make it less tempting for Mom."

"Not to mention how badly he treats her after a few drinks," I added.

"Jesus H Christ," Copey shouted, as the car in front of us slowed down for a yellow light. I clutched my seatbelt as he swerved angrily around the offending car and gunned across the intersection.

The flash of road rage was a warning. Any talk of Dad's violence bothered Copey. He had never been physically afraid of Dad, as I was. Most people back then thought a man should be the boss in "his" household, forgave men for all but the deadliest ways of asserting dominance, and even blamed women for "deserving" what we got.

As Copey swung into a familiar shortcut through the manicured grounds of Princeton University, he softened. "Look," he said, "I won't be able to handle it if Mom looks too bad, if she's throwing up or bleeding or anything. I figure I'll do Dad. You do Mom. Divide and conquer."

We pulled up to the Princeton house: two stories of white clapboards and whitewashed brick, cushioned in beds of pachysandra. The surrounding pines had grown tall and dense since our youth; shade now dominated sunshine. At the large, black front door with the brass knocker, our father stood with his head down, hands at his sides, feet squarely beneath him like he might topple. His shoulders moved spasmodically up and down: he was weeping. "I'm sorry," he mumbled enigmatically as we came closer. He shook his lowered head back and forth, seeming older than his seventy-three years. I imagine he felt overwhelmed by Mom's collapse, by being on his own, by our presence, even by the possibility of our help.

We trooped out to the screened porch, where Dad sank into his usual chair and Copey settled in near him, loosening his tie as a gesture of arrival. I fled upstairs to see my mother.

Shortly after I married in 1964, Mom had started sleeping in my old bedroom. She changed nothing in the room, perhaps out of nostalgia. I found her in my old bed, lying quite still. A soft, rose-colored blanket draped the swell of what could have been a nine-month pregnancy. Beneath her limp, white hair, her face was gaunt and sallow.

"How was your trip?" she asked, in a voice as dry as her cracked lips. The effort of speaking made her cough, and she lay patiently, without expression, until the cough subsided. She tried awkwardly to puff the pillow behind her head. I leaned forward to help, holding my breath, as I always did, against the cloying odor of yesterday's alcohol. I kissed her rough, dry cheek—which had always, before, been so soft—and breathed in, despite myself. No smell of booze, only a trace of lotion on an old woman's skin.

"I thought I was being so good, giving up all the drinks I loved," she said. Her earnest, confiding look made her seem more girl than grown woman. "Dr. Clark says even the wine was killing me. You tried to tell me that."

"I did," I said. I'd always wanted her to stop drinking, in good time—to save her own life. Now, everything had changed: I just wanted to hug her, to hold close the child she seemed to be in this illness. She seemed too fragile to hug.

Copey's instructions arose, unwelcome, in my thoughts. We'd barely arrived, my suitcase wasn't even in the guestroom yet. I didn't want to tackle my assignment so soon.

My mother must have seen me frown. "What is it?" she asked, pulling with trembling fingers at the blanket's silky edge.

I told her that Copey and I had been thinking about her visits with Dr. Clark. I felt her legs flex along the length of the bed next to me, as though she were preparing to kick, or to run.

"*What* have you been thinking?" Her words were like sandbags between us.

"I know you don't want Dad in on those appointments, but . . ."

She erupted into a long coughing fit, turning her head from side to side on the pillow. Finally, she whispered, so quietly that I leaned over to hear, "I'm afraid he won't behave."

"He's going to make life miserable for you if you don't let him in."

"That will be nothing new," she said. Then her eyes widened. "I have to get to the john," she gasped.

I leaped up to help, but she said, "Go down to your father like a good girl. I have plenty of handholds along the way. Just ask Mary to come up when she gets here."

I was no longer a child to be so easily shooed away. I could have insisted on staying to help my mother lift her big, heavy belly out of bed, limp across my childhood rug, raise her baby blue nightgown and lower herself onto the commode. But a curtain hung between us—white voile with eyelet flowers laced along the border, almost but never quite transparent—a legacy of our upper-class heritage. I couldn't bring myself to fling this curtain aside. Mary was on the way, after all. Mary was not my mother's daughter. She did not enjoy the benefits that my brother and I did. And yet, she played the role that a daughter in a different family might play: helper, confidante, comforter, cheerleader, errand-doer, and dependable presence. Because Mary was so faithfully present, I did not have to lift the curtain, and I never would.

I left my mother to her bathroom scramble and went to face my father.

Dad sat staring fixedly at the flagstone floor of the porch. I sat down in what I realized, too late, was my mother's customary chair. A bead of condensation slid down my father's martini glass, pooling on the table between us.

Doctors were all goddamn purists, he announced to Copey and me. "No fat, no sugar, no booze. Next they'll be saying no meat." He shot me a dirty look. "Hasn't anyone heard of a little healthy moderation?" Before I could respond, he fired again. "You children think all the problems in the world are caused by alcohol. Your mother has fallen prey to some mysterious, systemic assailant—a virus, or her blood pressure gone out of control."

I gaped at him, aghast at this denial. Dad picked up his martini. Swinging around to his left, he took a long gulp that his right shoulder blocked from my view, then swung back and set the glass carefully on the table between us, like a treasure. "I've known some complete falling apart was coming, but your mother would confess nothing. I am the enemy as far as she is concerned."

"Look, Dad," Copey said affably, man-to-man. I envied his matter-of-fact tone. "Let's face it. Mom may need some extra TLC right now."

At this suggestion, no matter how affably Copey said it, Dad reached so abruptly for his martini that he knocked it over. Gin and ice slid off the table. Dad lurched to his feet and nearly toppled. Copey leaped up to steady him, while I snatched the glass before it rolled off and shattered on the flagstone floor.

Mary appeared in the doorway just then, freshly arrived from her job at the correction center. As she surveyed the scene, my father slumped back into his chair and lifted the glass I'd rescued. "I'll have one teeny martini, Mary, if you don't mind," he said, like a child wheedling for sweets. Mary hugged Copey, hugged me, brought the drink, then headed upstairs to my mother.

My family was falling apart, and Mary responded with a sturdy, level-headed competence. The needs were concrete in this job; she could make a palpable, visible difference. Mary clearly felt grounded in her competence, her ability to bring a modicum of peaceful order. For a long time, she may have believed these would be enough to save my mother.

Later that evening, while Mary prepared my mother for the night, I went through the kitchen into the room that my family called the "maid's room" and plugged in the iron. Mary was the only one my mother trusted to iron my father's expensive, made-in-London shirts. Having shirts pressed at home was a marker of upper-class life, as were the shirts themselves, with their labels from London's elite Saville Row. I picked up one of the shirts, feeling almost peaceful. Mary would soon be free to talk with me, and here was one shirt I'd iron so she wouldn't have to.

I looked around me at the "maid's room." Green linoleum underfoot, like the kitchen. An unpainted pine bureau, a single bed with no headboard, an ancient black-and-white TV, a bookshelf with a few toppled paperbacks. There was nothing of Mary in this room besides the half-empty green packet of Salems on the bookshelf and the corrections uniform hanging on the door—blue trousers, a jacket with gold roping, five gold buttons, and a shiny lieutenant's badge. Mary had led the way for women to rise in Mercer County corrections, but, in my parents' home, she was relegated to this bare room. This was the only room in the house where she could feel free to sit down.

As I lifted my handiwork up for inspection, Mary appeared in the doorway. I followed her eyes to a pesky crease that I had ironed into the front panel.

"You could take a rest after this shirt," Mary said with a smile. She lit a cigarette and sat down straight-backed on the edge of the bed like a guest.

"I butchered it, didn't I?"

"You've had a long day."

I pointed to the uniform hanging on the closet door. "You've had longer."

"Grab that spray starch."

"Ah-ha. A secret ingredient."

Mary began to talk about her day job. Still jealous of Mary's competence, the new warden continued to obstruct her work. Mary had created an innovative program for inmates to volun-

205

teer in the community, but he still kept switching her jobs around.

"He's got me in a back office this month with no assignment at all. We're on civil service, so he can't fire me, but he seems fixed on wearing me down through sheer boredom." A grim smile. "I wouldn't give him the satisfaction."

There was a loud clatter in the kitchen, followed by a curse, then my father's voice, sounding pitiful. "Are you out there, Mary?"

Mary went to him.

"How is Mrs. C.?" I heard him ask. "Did you put her to bed already?"

I pictured the two of them in the yellow kitchen, my father's shoulders bony and stooped in his sports jacket, Mary keeping an expected distance, standing a few feet away. I heard Mary offer to check on Mom. "If she's awake," Mary said, "you can peek your head in and say something sweet to her."

When Mary came back from tending to Mom, I told her she was brave, telling Dad to say something sweet.

"Sometimes he just needs to be reminded."

I asked if he ever blew up at Mary the way he did at Mom and me. Mary said no. Mom and I triggered Dad's resentments, I reflect now, but Mary called out his desire to be comforted.

"Your mother comes back here, crying mad, when he's said something to hurt her," Mary began as she sat back down on the bed. She looked towards the ceiling as if she could see into my old bedroom above us. "She and I talk about everything. Love. Marriage. My job. I'll iron, and we'll talk. She always knows what I should do next in my life."

I felt a surge of rivalry with the dying woman upstairs. I wanted Mary to prefer me over my mother. I wanted to be the good one—the true friend, the one who listened and didn't presume to give advice (though I did). I got so busy jockeying inwardly with my mother that I missed the feeling in Mary's voice. *"She always knows what I should do next."* Had I listened as well as I prided myself on doing, I might have heard Mary's grief.

With a sigh, Mary sank her elbows to her thighs, leaned forward, and rested her head on her hands. When she let her posture of bright efficiency lapse, weariness seemed to flood in everywhere.

"Aren't you upset with Mom for drinking herself into such a mess?" I asked. Al-anon meetings were beginning to teach me not to blame alcoholics for their disease, but I asked Mary this question.

As though I had physically jabbed her, Mary breathed in sharply and sat up. "How could you think that?" she shot back. Mary had chosen to respond to my mother's crisis with positivity and optimism. I had not. She checked the battered Timex on her wrist and said: "Go on up and remind her to take her nighttime pills. It'll cheer her to see you." Our visit was over.

I touched the door to my old bedroom with a finger, ghosting it open. "Took my pills already, darling," my mother said into the dark. The brilliant red numbers of her digital clock switched from 10:03 to 10:04. I had missed my chance.

I picked up a small jar of night cream and held it up to the dim light from the doorway. My mother touched her cheek as if to say yes. Sitting beside her on the bed, I smoothed cream over her rough, flaky skin.

"You keep getting better Mom, okay?"

She drew her head back into the pillow and eyed me warily. "Don't ask for more than I can do," she said.

≈

I hurried downstairs to hug Mary goodnight. She would be leaving for home soon, and this gave me a hollow feeling. I felt safer with Mary present. I believe my parents did, too.

I found the back door standing open, Mary's purse on a nearby chair. Soon Mary trudged purposefully up the path from the driveway, her arms flattened against a large cardboard carton. I knew that she went out of her way to keep my parents stocked with groceries, and realized I hadn't thanked her for this. I opened the door, and she lugged the box to the counter.

"Oof!" she said, as she let her burden down with a thud.

In the open box were no groceries, but bottles of booze—Scotch, bourbon, gin—and two half-gallons of Chablis.

"What are you doing?" I asked Mary, horrified. I wanted to take the heavy steam iron from the back room and ram it through each bottle, watch the poisons puddle uselessly on the linoleum floor.

Mary reported that she passed a discount liquor store on her way to Princeton every day. Keeping my parents stocked was easy for her. They paid her back, and she saved them money.

I wanted to shout, "How could you do that? This stuff is killing them!" But I had never yelled at Mary. In a burst of aversion and cruelty, I turned away abruptly, didn't say goodnight, left the liquor box standing between us.

That night instead of sleeping I stewed. Whenever Mom called, Mary dropped what she was doing. She showed up when Mom needed her, gave up time with her own family, sacrificed her own health. She helped my mother live. And yet, here she was, bringing alcohol into the house. *Mary has been helping my mother kill herself.*

The wildness of the accusation shocked me. How could I blame Mary? She was just doing her job.

The box of booze made me feel angry with Mary for the first time in our lives. I still regret the hostile way I expressed this anger, how I turned my back on Mary and went off in a huff. When a loved person is dying, grieving family members often vent their distress by turning on each other—and we know so well how to hurt each other. That I did this, even once, to Mary —the person who with such love and hard work was keeping my family going—feels both very human and starkly entitled.

Later in the fall of 1988, Mary stood watching for me just inside the doors of the Princeton Hospital as I arrived from Boston. Her eyes, usually bright even after strings of eighteen-hour days, had dimmed to a kind of flatness. Her rich, chestnut skin seemed gray, almost dusty. Despite the chill, early dark of the November afternoon, Mary urged me to walk with her. We set off around the block, her grip tight on my arm.

Steady starvation had so weakened my mother that she finally agreed to enter the hospital. Fearing needles, hating every kind of intervention, Mom begged to be spared the IV. Her doctor agreed: no IV, as long as she ate enough food on her own. The hospital staff would track every morsel.

As we walked, Mary told me that, after the first hospital meal, Mom slipped her a little napkin-wrapped bundle. "Just take this home, Mary, and throw it in the trash for me." When Mary got home and opened the bundle, she found my mother's dinner, untouched. Aghast that she had helped my mother trick the doctors, perhaps even harmed her chances at getting better, Mary cried all night. The second evening, she dreaded going in. Sure enough, my mother fumbled under the covers again for the tell-tale bundle, and asked Mary for "another little favor." That time, Mary forced herself to say no.

"I told her I was so sorry, but that if she didn't eat she might get worse. She was crying and coughing, she was so upset with me." Mary shook her head with the anguish of this refusal. She put her hand up to her cheek. I covered her hand with mine. "Here she was, so sick, and all she was asking me to do was to take a little package. I had to say no, didn't I?"

Struck by the integrity and caring that moved Mary to refuse my mother, possibly for the first time in her life, I told her I thought she made the loving choice.

I found Mom looking dazed and defeated in the hospital room, her gaunt face turned away from the IV tube's steady drip, a purpling bruise forming already along her emaciated arm.

Election day in November 1988 came and went, most notable for a last-minute Republican TV spot that played on white voter racism. Out of prison on a weekend furlough program approved by Democratic candidate and then-Massachusetts Governor Dukakis, a Black man named Willie Horton raped and murdered a woman. Then, as now, many voters were wary of going "soft" on crime, and too many white people ignorantly lumped all Black men together as criminals. Horton's mugshot worked as a scare tactic, and the racial fear-mongering tanked Dukakis's campaign.

But none of us talked politics that year, as the family circled inwards around death. My father and brother were happy with the election results, and I was not. Like me, Mary was scandalized by the Republicans' manipulation of the Willie Horton story, but, given our roles in the family hierarchy, I would have had to broach the topic first, and I didn't. Twenty years later, she and I would quote favorite liberal news sources to each other, weep with joy over Barack Obama's win, and cheer for the star power of First Lady Michelle Obama. We'd deplore the racist hatred and violence unleashed by Donald Trump's campaign for President—and then, to our dismay, by his presidency. In 1988, however, as my mother lay dying, unspoken racial and class barriers blocked us from discovering our passionately similar views.

By late autumn, the doctors could do no more for my mother, and she came home. In the losing battle to save her from starving, Mary and my father became the front line, with food as their primary ammunition. When I was down from Boston one weekend, my father grilled Mom a lamb chop and stuffed a baked potato, his specialty. In the living room, I found my mother sitting mutely in her wheelchair, with the untouched plate in her lap. "Your mother doesn't like her lunch," Dad announced bitterly, and took a noisy gulp from his martini. Her rigid back and razor shoulders, poking from the rose-colored blanket, expressed a profound loneliness in his presence.

And, truly, my father was beside himself. He made himself such a string of cocktails that night that I skipped dinner to avoid him. Later in the evening, I skulked around the kitchen trying to make myself something to eat without drawing his attention. He lurched drunkenly into the kitchen and stood, swaying a bit, impaling me with his intense hazel eyes. I hunched over my plate of fried egg and toast on the counter, trying to keep my motions small.

"You disappoint me," he intoned. "You disappoint me beyond belief."

Afraid of what he might do next, I picked up my plate and began to edge towards the door.

"Your mother is *dying*," he said. "I haven't the slightest idea how you want to respond."

Finally, he'd said it: his wife was dying. From decades away, I ache to comfort him. In the moment, however, he loomed, drunk and menacing, in my childhood kitchen. "Good topic, Dad," I said, backing away further. "Let's tackle it in the morning."

"You little prick!" he shouted at me, spittle flying. He wheeled around and strode from the room. "Fucking little prick!" The curse resounded through the house.

Tiptoeing upstairs with my dinner, I ducked into my brother's old bedroom and locked the door. Copey's room: same yellow walls, sports trophies, abandoned yearbooks. I paced the square rug. The plate sat unattended on the bureau, egg congealing on soggy toast.

Footsteps on the staircase. A shadow of shoes through the crack at the bottom of the door. The sound of Dad's ragged breathing. I wasn't alone in the house with my father—by that time, there were round-the-clock nurses downstairs in the guestroom, where we had moved my mother—but my heart pounded in my chest as though I had no protection at all. Dad loomed outside the locked door for what seemed forever. Finally, he muttered more mildly this time, "You little prick," and headed off to bed. I slept with my brother's light on.

At breakfast the next day, as though he hadn't lost it the

night before, my father was groggy but affable. I broached difficult topics—funeral homes, power of attorney. He was decent,
thoughtful, teary. What were her wishes on burial? Cremation,
he said.

I planned to head home—ostensibly for work, really for Polly,
for the nourishment of my daily life. That, and a break from
Dad.

The day nurse didn't want me to leave. "Your mother does
better when you're here," the nurse said, holding me in her gaze.
"She told me that her protector is leaving tomorrow."

Mary didn't pressure me to stay. She said she didn't understand Dad's attitude towards me. "He complains when you don't
come, but, when you do, he treats you terribly. I truly understand
why you stay away."

"You don't think I'm a bad daughter?"

"I don't think I could take how he treats you," Mary said.

On my last visit, just after the year turned to 1989, Mom told me
she wanted to write Mary a check. "You don't have to do that,"
Mary said, but I fished around in Mom's purse for one of the
loose checks she stashed everywhere, cranked up the head of the
bed, and moved the rolling table into position.

"I owe you for the past two weeks, don't I?" my mother said
weakly to Mary. The pen slipped from her fingers, bounced off
her swollen belly and slid to the floor. I held the pen out to Mom
again, and she looked up at me with pleading eyes. "Five thousand dollars," she whispered, as I wrote the check.

Mary gasped at the amount. Five thousand dollars in early
1989 would be worth about twice that today. Far less than what
my mother owed Mary for years of selfless service, though clearly

more than Mary expected. I steadied my mother's hand at the wrist, and she angled her name shakily across the signature line.

It was the last check my mother wrote, a parting "gift". Love and money, woven together to the end.

The next night, Mary and I brought her meal and sat with her. Mom ate nothing. Then she, Mary, and I watched my father enter the room. Shuffling forward with rounded shoulders, his unbuttoned cashmere cardigan hanging askew, Dad stood over his wife.

"Can't we get you to eat a little something?" he said, in the wheedling, cajoling tone he'd use for a resistant child. He fumbled in his pocket and pulled out a green sourball, held the hard, round candy between his thumb and forefinger, thrust the sourball close to her face.

Glaring at him, she pulled her head back into the pillow. "Someone is going to get hit in a minute," she hissed.

"Oh, and hard," he mocked, pushing the sourball at her.

Shooting him a look of pure hatred, she opened her cracked lips and took the candy with her large, yellowed front teeth, like a mare.

A silver-framed photograph on a nearby bureau showed my just-married parents bursting exuberantly from a Park Avenue church. Looking like movie stars, they radiated sensuality and hope. Maybe everyone with a dying parent looks down the hallway of history: I search for what became of their bright hope, and find a hard green sourball.

Mary recalls the sourball incident to this day. "Your mother pulled the covers all the way up to her chin," Mary says. "Her eyes were just fire."

I am grateful that Mary and I witnessed this searing exchange together, this final impasse. We confirm the memory for each other. The love and battle, collusion and heat of that complicated couple shaped my childhood and gave rise to many of my adult weaknesses and strengths. Their struggles affected Mary, too, from age fifteen on, setting the particular challenges of her work with them over forty years—and more than work. Mary loved my parents, as I did. We bore their battles and their unrelenting self-destruction.

Moments after the sourball episode, Mary and I stood in the kitchen together, cleaning up the tiny meal my mother had not touched.

"The time has really come," I said to Mary, expecting that we would hug, even cry together. "Mom is dying for real now. All we can do is love her, and pray."

"Don't you ever say that!" Mary shouted. Eyes flaring, she threw down the dish towel. Her lips trembled as she tried to get control of herself. "I'll buy fresh shrimp for her dinner tomorrow," she said, as though stabbing me with each word. "She just needs to eat."

Mary had never glared at me, never yelled. In this moment, her grief broke through. As she said many years later, "I was mad with you because I didn't want her to die. I was really, really attached to her." She clung as fiercely as any grieving daughter to the belief that Mom would not die.

This moment, too, we remember.

❧

The next day, my mother wanted to be alone. Through a baby monitor, we heard her fidget, sigh, yawn, turn, tap her thickened yellowed fingernails on the bed's metal bar. Mary arrived after work and headed straight for Mom. When the nurse on duty tried to stop her, claiming officiously that Mom didn't want visitors, Mary countered fiercely. "You go in there," she commanded the nurse, "and tell her Mary's here."

"She called me right in to her," Mary reported later. The nurses got on Mary's nerves; they didn't appreciate her role in the family. That Mom asked for her was a triumph over rivals.

Mary persuaded Mom to see the rest of us, and we trooped in to deliver kisses. Her face in a grimace of grief, Mom whispered, "Take care of Daddy." Copey and I promised. Stroking her cheek, I told her she didn't have to stick around for us. She could let herself slip away.

"I'm *trying* to," she said, almost irritated. After an awkward silence, she grumbled, "You can't just sit here all night acting like you're at a wake."

Dad leaned stiffly over to plant a kiss on her forehead. "Thank Mary for coming," I heard her say. I looked around. Mary had slipped out of the room.

The night nurse guessed that Mom had a day or two left, and advised us all to sleep. Mary left for home, and the rest of us went to bed. At four in the morning, the same nurse was at my bedside; my mother was going. Flustered that this stranger, and not I, had been with Mom during her last night, I rushed downstairs to hold Mom's hand. No one held her other hand. A fateful choreography landed us where we were at that moment—my father stumbling into the dimly lit room to stop, stooped and uncertain, at the foot of the bed, my brother coming up stalwartly next to him, Mary an hour's drive away.

"Here's Dad!" I said, and thought I saw a change in my mother's face. I will never know whether she took Dad's arrival as permission to let go or chose to close him out one last time.

Thirty miles away, Mary woke abruptly from a heavy sleep. "I knew," she told me later. "I knew the exact moment."

Dad shambled off towards the living room. Copey and I sat by our mother's body for a while in awed silence, but soon called the undertaker. That's what our people did—call the undertaker.

Because the night nurse advised us all to get some sleep and because neither my father nor I thought to ask Mary to stay the night, Mary missed being physically present with Mom as she died. If I'd thought of Mary soon enough, strongly enough, and called her immediately, she could at least have driven up Route 1 in the dawn light to sit with Mom's cooling body. In the deep practice of a community that tends to dying family members at home, Mary would have bathed Mom's body tenderly before any stranger came close. She would have dressed my mother in the softest, silkiest nightgown and robe. Even at the last, my mother would have left the house looking her best. My failure to call soon enough robbed Mary, and my mother, of these priceless ministrations. By the time Mary arrived, the long, black undertaker's vehicle had pulled out of our driveway.

Update 2020. I confessed to Mary a year or two after Mom's death that jealousy, not distraction, may have kept me from calling her on time. In the moment of farewell to Mom's physical body, I managed to be the only daughter in the house. Just recently, twenty years later, I asked via text what she remembered feeling back then. Mary responded: "Seems as if we both were feeling the same thing towards each other. I also felt jealous."

Mary had never before spoken to me about feeling jealous. Even today, we still expand the truths we tell each other.

Mary also described more fully in this recent text what Mom's death stirred in her. "I felt a terrible sense of loss. I did feel hurt that I was not there for her at the end, and then on the other hand it hits you that she's not your mother but your employer. That did not stop the tears or feeling of emptiness." I take her words to mean that, in the cruel confusion of love baffled by racial and class inequities, Mary wrestled with dichotomies— mother, employer, servant, daughter—that troubled and compounded her grief. Ironically, I had access to a daughter's whole and socially sanctioned grief while Mary did not, even as she had been the faithful, dependable, hands-on daughter I chose not to be.

Today, in 2020, a time of crucial debate about reparations to African Americans for centuries of white exploitation, a friend posed a question I'd never before considered. Did I and my family ever recognize Mary's central, daughterly role by including her as an equal in the estate that passed from my mother to my father to my brother and me? The short answer is no. The longer answer, which, to be transparent, also ends in no, is the stuff of the following chapter.

thirteen

Equity

MY MOTHER DIED IN 1989. A YEAR OR TWO LATER, DAD LEFT New Jersey behind and moved to their upscale condo in Delray Beach, Florida. There, he joined a set of wealthy white friends who, like him, could afford to spend the last years of their lives viewing the Atlantic Ocean through their own picture windows. Having been a two-pack-a-day smoker before cancer surgery, Dad lost breath too fast, at seventy-six, to enjoy the resort pleasures of golf or swimming. Although he would have denied the connection, he hobbled along with the slow, shuffling gait of long-time drunks.

After trying for several months to cope on his own, Dad asked Mary to relocate from New Jersey to Florida to help him. When he made this request, Mary was still working in the New Jersey corrections system, five months from official retirement. With the warden from hell in charge at the correction center—the man who so resented her reputation that he confined her to clerical work in a tiny back room—the only thing that tied her to the job was her determination to get the full retirement package. When Mary discovered a state regulation by which she could buy out the last five months, my father offered to pay for the buy-out, and Mary accepted. Her husband, Fred, had long ago retired from his career in the U.S. Army. Abruptly, Mary and Fred sold their house in suburban New Jersey and made the move.

Shortly after that, in the winter of 1992, I flew to Florida for a weekend. As I maneuvered a small rental car through the hurtle of traffic speeding south on Florida's I-95, I did not expect the theme of my trip to be equity—as in property value, fairness, and honest dealing.

Palm trees in the glaring sunlight, hibiscus blooms as large as fists. The scenery was as strange to me as Mary's sudden move south to help my father. I resented Dad for asking Mary to leave the comfortable suburban home that she and Fred had purchased when they married. I thought Dad shouldn't have asked Mary to move so far from her grandchildren, from her aging mother and stepfather in Virginia. I wondered whether Mary had felt free to say no to Dad, even if she wanted to. Seizing my favorite culprit, I figured he wouldn't have been desperate for Mary's help if he weren't drinking so heavily. I didn't know which bothered me more—that Dad would ask or that Mary would (I imagined) drop everything to do what he wanted. I chafed at the idea that, despite a government pension, Mary had chosen to become a servant again.

So many gaps of ignorance in these opinions. I'd never had to worry about money and assumed that a government pension would be enough for a person to live on. I hadn't reached retirement age myself and had no idea that a retiree might be eager to stay busy, to be of use. And there was another missing piece. Many years later, Mary would tell me of a deathbed promise she'd made to my mother. When Dad got sick and needed Mary's help, my dying mother had asked, would she be there for him? As estranged and mutually lonely as they had grown by the end, my parents united in a sense of utter and unquestioning entitlement with respect to Mary's time, even in the future. Mary had said yes, and Mary kept her word.

As I approached the exit for Mary's new house, which would be my first stop, I puzzled over a new book Mary and I had shared that year—civil rights activist Barbara Neely's mystery novel, *Blanche on the Lam*. Neely's unlikely sleuth is a dark-skinned Black woman named Blanche White, who does domestic work for a white family. A dead body is found, and Blanche—camouflaged within the structured invisibility of servanthood—nabs the killer.

Unlike most every Black domestic worker in books by white writers, Blanche is no mere foil or source of humor. She is proud and independent, she speaks her mind, and she hones an especially witty, incisive critique of her white employers. What gets on this fictive domestic worker's last nerve is when Black domestic workers "love" their white employers and believe themselves loved in return. Dubbing this condition "Darkies' Disease," she wonders "how you convinced yourself that you were actually loved by people who . . . never offered . . . their cottage by the lake, or even their swimming pool; who gave you handkerchiefs and sachets for holiday gifts and gave their children stocks and bonds." To Blanche, in order to look at your customers through love-tinted glasses, "you had to pretend that obvious facts—facts that were like fences around your relationship—were not true."

I read *Blanche on the Lam* in one sitting and mailed the slim book to Mary. In our next phone call, she wondered aloud whether she herself had Darkies' Disease. I didn't know what to say. Blanche's sharp critique spoke to my political mind. In my heart, however, I felt that I loved Mary, and I hoped that she loved me. I wanted this loving to be okay. When Mary asked if I thought she had Darkies' Disease, I said I didn't know. Mary seemed to have relocated to Florida because of loyalty and love for my father. Neely's sleuth might well detect pathology in the precipitous move.

Picturing my father with Mary as his full-time Florida caretaker galled me. She'd climb the stucco staircase outside his Florida condo, lugging heavy bags of groceries, laundry detergent, bottled water. She'd keep the condo in fresh flowers and coach him to entertain his women friends for dinner. She'd cook fresh lemon sole and parslied potatoes, lay out his London-tailored clothes, and adjust his tie for the guest's arrival. I'd once seen Mary brush flakes of dandruff from the shoulders of Dad's navy-blue blazer as he stood before her, arms down like a docile child. Remembering the intimate gesture made me cringe. I careened onto the exit ramp towards Mary's new neighborhood, fleeing another disturbing thought: My father would eat up Mary's pampering. He'd take her TLC as his due.

I felt implicated in Dad's urgency that Mary transplant herself. Shortly after he moved to Florida, he called me about upcoming cataract surgery. He asked me to fly down and help him out.

We were actually in a good period when he asked. He had softened towards me since Mom's death. Three times, he had reached out. In a condolence letter to Polly when her mother died, he wrote, "It was good to see you and Wendy recently. As ever, Roy." Not a full embrace of our relationship, but closer than he'd ever come. In a later letter to me, he returned to a point I had argued back in the 1970s, when he had bemoaned the "Negro problem in American education." Bristling, knowing he was one hundred percent wrong, I'd countered that until Emancipation, teaching enslaved people to read and write had been a crime. Now, twenty years later, he wrote, "Brief and superficial research by me indicates that the laws in slave states commonly made it illegal to teach slaves to read or write. So, I concede your point." For someone as entrenched as my father was in his own opinions, this was progress. In a third letter, he even broached the rage that stalked my childhood. "That ugly temper of mine has surfaced only to your mother and you," he wrote. "Perhaps that says something—if only that it was with respect to you two only that I could conjure a hurt that justified my actions to me, if not to anyone else." This was not an apology, but the admission mattered to me.

In this mood of détente, I considered helping Dad out after the cataract surgery. Soon, however, dread invaded my sleep. If I went to Florida to help Dad, I'd be alone with him in the evenings, something I'd wisely avoided for decades. Would he expect me to make his cocktails? Would I make them? What if he turned into the seething man who hit my mother, the angry, grieving, drunken father who muttered "you fucking prick" at me through a locked door? I wouldn't be able to escape.

Here I was, nearly fifty years old, physically strong, a respected campus minister at a Boston commuter college, and afraid of my father. Someone asked me recently why I still feared him, even as an adult. I thought maybe my inquirer had never had reason to fear her own father. In response, I told her a story. When a stroke in his seventies left Dad unable to stand on his own, I'd felt a surge of relief that he could no longer climb the stairs to the third-floor walk-up apartment where Polly and I lived. The relief was irrational—he hadn't visited our home in years. But he'd hit my mother and verbally assaulted her when I was a child; his rage loomed over my childhood. That Dad could no longer physically climb stairs became a living metaphor for protection.

To be honest, as I debated whether to help Dad after his surgery, I was angry as well as wary. After how he mistreated my mother, I felt I owed him nothing.

I wrote to Dad that I couldn't go. He fired back that he wasn't surprised. Détente was over.

Just recently, in 2020, Mary revealed that, after both my brother and I begged off helping Dad with his cataract surgery, he asked her to fly down from New Jersey to care for him. To do so, Mary stretched her vacation time from the correction center so thin that a colleague had to jump in and cover for her, and still she nearly lost her job. Mary says she is glad she went: during her ministrations after the surgery, Dad told her he felt like he had a second daughter.

"How do you like my new house?" Mary asked, pressing a glass of ice water to one temple, then the other, as we sat together on the glassed-in porch of her new Florida home. After I arrived from the airport, we had toured every room. Despite the air conditioning, the insistent Florida heat weighed on us. She folded a paper napkin and wiped at the small puddle of condensation on the glass top of the patio table beside her. She settled back in her T-shirt and shorts, letting her plastic sandals drop to the floor.

"Sit," Mary had said, as we came onto the sun porch. She pointed to the wrought-iron chaise with bright floral cushions. "Stretch out there. You had a long trip."

In the hallway by the bedrooms, I had seen Mary lean against the wall to catch her breath, pressing her hand on top of a low bookshelf for support. Her back was hurting, I could tell. I wanted the years of Mary focusing on my comfort to be over. I passed by the chaise, plopped myself on an upright chair, and crossed my legs definitively. Mary let herself slowly down onto the chaise, which was clearly where she always sat—her book and glasses on the glass-topped table, her cigarettes, a toppling pile of envelopes and papers. I'd lounged moodily on that chaise on my parents' flagstone porch in New Jersey during humid summer afternoons in the 1950s. Now, the seat was Mary's.

All over Mary's new home, I'd noticed items she and Fred had rescued from my parents' house. Not the expensive antiques that my brother and I claimed when our father moved south— tall grandfather clock, cherry wood sideboard—but a great deal else. There were end tables, vases, paintings, and one of the pair of cream-colored brocade armchairs I'd perched on in the living room as a girl, skinny legs tucked under me. Mary's guest room held the bedroom set Dad's mother had given me for my tenth birthday, expertly repainted. Mom's china figurines adorned every polished surface—ducks, pelicans, elephants.

I shouldn't be surprised, I told myself, as I *ooh*-and-*ah*-ed my way through the house. Mary had promised Dad that she would clear out everything that he didn't need and Copey and I didn't want. She and Fred had restored the furniture expertly; every piece looked better than it had in years. That all this now graced Mary's home was a satisfaction to me. Still, the tour left me lightheaded with a mix of envy, regret, and an unsettling sense of contradiction: Mary, not I, had chosen to recreate the ambience of my mother's house.

I must have grimaced at the complex feelings, because Mary sat up in the chaise. "You don't like the house?" she asked.

"It's beautiful. Mom would be proud."

"Oh!" she exhaled in a high voice. "You had me worried."

"A place like this in Boston would cost an arm and a leg," I said. My mother's phrase: *an arm and a leg.*

Mary glanced quickly at the cascade of envelopes and letters on the table next to her and pressed her head back into the cushion of the chaise. She reached over as if to straighten the papers, but wearily dropped a hand on top. "I moved down here so fast, before my retirement details got sorted out. I guess the benefits never seem as much, when they come, as all those years you were looking forward to them." She lifted her hand, let it fall again. "And then, you see, we sold the house in New Jersey in a hurry so we could get down here to your dad. I've got the final figures here somewhere. We didn't get what we paid for it."

I did not understand the weight of the quick sale that Mary lamented on her new sun porch. Only after learning about twentieth-century housing discrimination against Black people and racism in bank lending and federal policy can I begin to appreciate the economic significance of Mary's rush to my father's side. I credit "A Case for Reparations," a 2014 piece in *The Atlantic,* with pointing me to information that I had not known, or perhaps selectively ignored. Polly and I first heard of this essay by Ta-Nehisi Coates when two Quaker friends reported reading the article aloud to each other on a long car ride. Soon, we did the same. This was a perfect way to encounter, interpret, and discuss Coates's stunning analysis. "A Case for Reparations" taught me the historical and ethical context for the abrupt sale of Mary's suburban New Jersey home. If you already know that context better than I did, feel free to skip the next few paragraphs.

When the U.S. fighting forces returned from Europe and the Pacific in 1945, Congress passed the G.I. Bill to support them in rebuilding their lives. On paper, the G.I. Bill allowed a returning soldier to buy a house with little or no down payment and a low-interest mortgage insured by the Federal Housing Authority, an agency founded in 1934 as part of the New Deal. My father, a lieutenant in the U.S. Army who spent much of the war in London assisting top brass in planning D-Day, may not have thought of himself as a G.I. He may have lumped enlisted soldiers into a G.I. identity that, being an elitist, he didn't claim. I don't know if he took a G.I. Bill mortgage for our spacious and well-appointed home in Princeton, New Jersey, but he could have done so by walking in and shaking hands with the local banker.

Not so for Mary's uncles and stepfather. Like other Black veterans, they returned from war to find themselves excluded from the G.I. Bill's generous housing plan. As Coates writes, "Though ostensibly color-blind, Title III of the [G.I.] bill, which aimed to give veterans access to low-interest home loans, left black veterans to tangle with white officials at their local Veterans Administration as well as with the same banks that had, for years, refused to grant mortgages to blacks." Inexpensive new suburban housing developments, available to white GIs at low prices and generous borrowing terms, rejected one Black applicant after another. In rural southwestern Virginia, where Mary was four years old and living with her grandmother, white-owned banks continued to disqualify people from mortgages just because they were Black. Mary's stepfather George Johnson was able to build a house in Elk Creek only because a white man in town had "taken a liking to him," Mary says, and vouched for him at the bank.

I was shocked to find that federal policy supported these disqualifications and rejections. From its beginnings, the Federal Housing Authority had adopted a system of maps that rated neighborhoods according to what Coates refers to as their "perceived stability." White neighborhoods were considered excellent prospects for FHA-backed mortgages. Neighborhoods where Black people and people of color lived were marked in red on the FHA maps—hence the term "redlining"—and were deemed ineligible for FHA backing. This mortgage discrimination was written into federal policy for decades, until banned by the Fair Housing Act in 1968. By then, the extraordinary terms specified in the G.I. Bill had fueled a huge post-war housing boom for white people; a generation of white families had built up equity in the homes the G.I. Bill enabled them to purchase.

Equity: the value of property once debts are paid. Millions of white families borrowed on their rising equity to send their children to college and, by eventually downsizing, secured a nest-egg for retirement. This is how federal policy robbed Black citizens of what has been called the "greatest mass-based opportunity for wealth accumulation in American history." The result has been an immense wealth gap between races, a gap that ignorant critics wrongly take to prove that Black people "don't work hard enough."

For decades, I failed to register or analyze the wealth gap between Mary and me. I accepted as a given that most Black people lived in tired wooden homes like the ones along my mother's Witherspoon Street shortcut. This is one of the ways that white supremacy works. I, an "educated" person, remained ignorant of all the ways the class difference between Mary and me had been socially constructed over three hundred years, from enslavement to sharecropping, from Jim Crow to restrictive housing policies.

Mary's success in buying her first house was no easy step, no done deal. Free from her brutal second marriage and absolutely determined to own a house for herself and her son, Mary was able to purchase a home in Trenton, New Jersey, through a military foreclosure program that she discovered. There was no "family money" to call on; she was on her own. Because she made the purchase in the late 1970s, only a few short years after the Fair Housing Act became law, she was able to secure financing. Through her own tenacity and vision, Mary owned a house of her own.

Still, the deck was stacked against Mary's success. Despite the new fair housing law, banks continued to refuse people of color loans for housing in white neighborhoods, and charged higher interest on loans made for areas considered "unstable." Mary's description of seeking a mortgage at that time conveys the discrimination vividly: "You were always struggling to fill out the papers to get a mortgage in the neighborhood you could afford. And then you wouldn't be approved for it." Banks considered urban Trenton a "high risk" investment, at a time when "urban" was fast becoming a code word for Black people living in poverty.

As a result, even once Mary secured a mortgage, her payments were higher than those her white colleagues paid for equivalent homes in white neighborhoods. She worked three or four jobs in order to meet payments on a mortgage set at a higher rate because she was Black.

When I learned, in my thirties, that Mary was moonlighting in several extra jobs, I worried that she was a workaholic. She was wearing herself to the bone, I said to her. No wonder her joints ached; she was working too hard. Oblivious to the cumulative burdens and limits laid on Black people by white-run institutions—oblivious, that is, to the mechanisms of white supremacy in Mary's life—I actually encouraged her to quit her night job as a security officer at a Trenton department store. Or, I said blithely, she could stop doing dinner parties for my mother and her Princeton friends.

This is how clueless I was about Mary's realities. Should her boiler burst or her roof leak, there was no comfortable cushion of savings to cover a large and sudden expense; if she borrowed money for the repair, interest rates would be exorbitant. As she puts it now, "There were so many setbacks. You had to have a mindset of 'I am going to make it.' You had to have a purpose, and keep your purpose up front in your mind, work on that. Otherwise, you wouldn't make it." I wonder now what Mary made of my unsolicited advice over all those years. Stop this job, stop that job, your back hurts, take better care of yourself. I bristle when friends proffer me advice I haven't sought. Mary had every reason to bristle with me. Even today, I still offer bright ideas for what Mary should do—urgent advice (don't drive all that way by yourself!) that may be as off the mark as ever.

Wondering what kind of balance my mix of caring and ignorance has struck in Mary's heart, I would finally ask her in 2020. "Back then," she responded, "I never felt that you could even relate to the things I had been going through, because everything would have been entirely different from what you had gone through. When I was working so many jobs, you couldn't relate to that, but that's what a person had to do. You probably have a better understanding of it now. You weren't being mean, wishing I didn't have to work that hard, but you could be very insistent. If you remember, I never had much to say in response, but I was thinking, 'Does she think I'm doing this for the fun of it?' I didn't want to hurt your feelings. I surely did walk on eggshells with you, too."

∾

Had any aspect of my elite schooling touched on housing discrimination against Black families, I might have understood what was at stake in Mary's abrupt move to Florida. She had sold her Trenton home in the 1980s when she and Fred married. Her Trenton neighborhood, in the continuing squeeze of economic discrimination, had "gone downhill" in the eyes of potential buyers and lenders. This decline in value eliminated any increased equity in Mary's Trenton home and deprived her of any profit she might have reaped from the sale of a home she had owned and kept in excellent shape for more than a decade. Mary and Fred pooled their resources for a move to suburban Willingboro, where they could reasonably expect their property value to rise over time. Mary had a real opportunity to build equity for the first time in her life. Then came my father's commanding desire to be rescued. The abrupt sale of the suburban ranch house, for less than Mary and Fred paid for it, robbed them of precious equity.

I've carried a mortgage only once. My wealthy husband paid outright for the Cambridge house where I cooked elaborate Julia Child meals. When we separated, I moved with Matthew into a rental apartment. When I later purchased that apartment as a condo, I had a mortgage, yes, but one that a monthly check from my mother quickly helped to pay off. Thirty years later, I bought the condo where I now live by selling that first one, which had increased more than ten times in value. Equity. I have equity. I have, essentially, lived without debt. As I seek to construct a bridge of understanding from my narrow world of affluence to Mary's experience, I need dependable spans built of learning and compassion. Ta-Nehisi Coates, in "A Case for Reparations," provides history, clarity, help.

I believe now that undoing white supremacy requires equity as an exacting and indispensable guide.

fourteen

Class Secret

LYING BACK INTO THE CHAISE ON HER FLORIDA SUNPORCH after we toured her new home, Mary took a weary breath. Closing costs and legal fees were high, she said. "I shouldn't have been so sure I could afford this house, nice as it is," she added, fixing her gaze on the shiny leaves of a grapefruit tree outside the sliding screen door. "Each month, I don't know if I'm going to make the mortgage."

I protested the fix my father had put her into. "Dad shouldn't have asked you to relocate if the move was going to cost more than you could pay."

Mary told me then that Dad, not a bank, held the mortgage. He claimed to her that he could beat any bank's interest rate. So far, he had accepted none of her payments. "Every time I bring my checkbook over," Mary said, "he says it's not a convenient moment. I'm afraid that by the time he gets around to it"—she began rubbing her temples in small circles—"I'll owe him more than I can pay." She was putting money aside from her paycheck to cover the mortgage payments, she said, but any unexpected event—a health crisis, a car maintenance bill, air conditioning in her new Florida home on the fritz—could wipe out her savings.

"Dad couldn't mean . . ." I stopped. I didn't know my father well enough to know what he meant. With my mother's estate and savings from his work as a corporate lawyer, he was a wealthy man. I could imagine Dad buying Mary's house out of impatience for her to get to Florida. He had the money; he wanted what he wanted when he wanted it. As I tried to put myself in his shoes, I could also imagine him in a practical mindset, wanting to give Mary the best possible interest rate, or even in a competitive frame, priding himself on being able to do better for Mary than the bank. Or, maybe his desire to reduce Mary's burden arose from gratitude. For forty years, she had been a kind, steady and hard-working presence. Putting myself in my father's shoes, however, was never easy. I couldn't fathom why he hadn't started taking Mary's payments.

Mary reached for a half-empty pack of Salems on the table beside her, but didn't light up. Fred was turning the garage into a woodworking shop as fast as he could, she said. He hoped to get orders for bookshelves, TV tables. They would handle the mortgage somehow. She was perspiring copiously, breathing as though her lungs couldn't get all the air she needed.

"You seem exhausted," I said.

"Guess I am, a little," Mary responded, but soon she swung her legs over the side of the chaise and started to pull herself up. "It'll be your Dad's lunchtime soon."

I jumped up. "I'm going over there now," I said. "I'll make his lunch."

That Mary sank back down was a sign of how tired she felt.

"When's your day off?" I asked.

She studied her sea-green plastic sandals. "Days I don't go over there, his bed doesn't get made. I don't think that's right. The room needs airing. The sheets need changing. He's not going to do that."

"You *don't* take a day off."

"This is hardly work at all. You know that. Now, hold on. I'm going over and fix you both lunch."

As I rushed through the house to stop Mary from going, she called out behind me that I'd find a freshly-baked Virginia ham in the fridge. Washed lettuce in the crisper. White Pepperidge Farm bread, remove the crusts. "Love you," she called.

I peered back through the dining room with its formal drapes, past the kitchen's modern cooking island, out into the slatted light of the enclosed porch where Mary lay back against the cushion. "Love *you*," I repeated. This is the first time I remember our saying these words to each other.

To get to Dad's, I drove east past stunted strip-mall palm trees towards the inland waterway that ran along much of Florida's east coast. Mary's route to work, I thought. I headed over a bridge to the towering palms and mansions of a plush strip of oceanfront that local people called "the gold coast." I wondered how many times a day Mary made this drive to the gold coast from her modest neighborhood. Remembering Mary's deep weariness back on the sun porch, I thought of all the routes that she had taken to work over fifty years: the country roads she walked at eleven years old to tackle a white family's Saturday wash; at fifteen, hundreds of miles by bus and boat to become my mother's summer helper; the commute across Mercer County to the correction center every workday for twenty-five years, or to the mall for evening security work; the drive up Route 1 from Trenton to Princeton to clean houses and staff dinner parties in white homes; and now, in Florida, A-1-A along the gold coast, not five, but seven days a week.

I couldn't get Mary's worry out of my head. *"I'm afraid that*

by the time he gets around to it, I'll owe him more than I can pay."
Dad was scaring Mary by not taking her checks.

Today, looking back on the dynamic of debt between Mary
and my father—how worried she was about owing more than
she could pay—I think of sharecropping. In that vicious post-
Reconstruction institution, as Anne Moody's autobiography made
so vivid, sharecropping families lived in shacks on poor land
"provided" by white landowners in return for the whole family's
labor in the landowner's fields. Landowners charged tenants a
yearly rent and kept track of seed, food, and clothing provided
on credit. After the harvest, landowners calculated whether each
family had earned back what they "owed" or fallen further into
debt. Sharecroppers were excluded from the calculations, and
dishonest accounting increased plantation profits. Morality was
no factor; despite legal emancipation, most white landowners
did not see Black farmers as whole human beings deserving of
human decency. By keeping sharecropping families in debt,
landowners ensured themselves an ongoing source of cheap labor. After a year of back-breaking physical work, sharecropping
families had every reason to fear that they would still be in debt.

By not being straightforward about Mary's mortgage, Dad
was creating an eerily similar uncertainty for Mary.

Arriving at Dad's oceanfront building of condos in Delray
Beach, I looked up at the sunlit stucco walls of his unit with less
anxiety than I'd felt on previous visits. I would not be alone with
him for long. By dropping everything to move to Florida, Mary
had improved my life as well as my father's.

Dad had changed nothing in the Florida condo since my
mother's death. In the airy living room where I found him, my

mother's colors were everywhere: creamy lemon yellow, delphinium blue, spring green. The walls held the same watercolors and oils that my parents had purchased at the pricey galleries of Palm Beach over the years: ocean waves, sailboats, a profusion of flowers. A large porcelain pelican still digested its catch on the coffee table. With the Princeton house emptied and sold, this was a place where I could still feel my mother's hand. Not her presence, however. She seemed resoundingly gone.

My father sat stiffly at his corner of the sofa. Pressed madras shorts, knobby knees and skinny legs, thinning hair combed carefully across his scalp. The *Times* crossword puzzle lay on the coffee table in front of him, completed in pen. He lifted his smoothly shaven cheek for my kiss. "I'm not getting up," he said, indicating the cane on the sofa beside him. Dad suffered from a mobility problem called peripheral neuropathy; he couldn't feel his feet, so he shuffled rather than walked. The doctors he favored blamed a deficiency of Vitamin B; I tended to blame drinking and was probably correct. Ever the citizen researcher, I read up on peripheral neuropathy. Excessive alcohol use was a common cause. While addiction to alcohol is an illness and not a moral failing, I felt plenty judgmental as I headed for the kitchen to make lunch for a man who, in my opinion, should be able—and willing—to cook for himself.

Dad was in a state about my brother, who had just separated from his wife of twenty-five years. "I lie there half the bloody night stewing about him," he said, pushing aside the second half of his ham sandwich and glowering as though I were somehow responsible. "Why did he never *tell* us he was unhappy? Is there a floozy in the picture?"

Floozy. Such an odd word, so old-fashioned. I had nothing to report that could ease my father's distress. Copey had been the

impressive one, with his four bright, well-dressed children (all furious at their father at the moment, which I did not tell Dad), his
lucrative work in banking and venture capital, his mansion on the
outskirts of Brookline. Everything was now split in two.

After lunch, Dad wanted me to take him shopping. As he
buckled himself stiffly into the passenger seat of my rental car,
being on an excursion seemed to lift his mood. He reported
cheerfully that several lady friends in Delray seemed glad of his
company. "Your mother's old friend Margaret is a lovely girl. Too
goddamned preoccupied with a plethora of children and grandchildren if you ask me, but I pry her away from time to time for
Mary to cook us dinner."

I recoiled at the satisfied ease in my father's voice. To him,
Mary's presence in Florida was already part of things as they
"should" be, her skilled and ready service a reflection of the uni-
versal right order of things. I remembered leaving Mary exhausted
on the chaise, her hand on a pile of bills. "Mary seems terribly
worried about money, Dad."

"Well, she shouldn't be."

"Says she bought the house before she. . . ." I stopped, not
wanting to reveal anything Mary might want to keep secret.

Dad stared out at the passing scenery for several moments,
fingering the rim of his golf hat. "I bought Mary's house," he announced finally. "I hold the mortgage. I do not intend to accept
her payments. At my death, I will instruct you and Copey to forgive the debt, and I imagine you will oblige."

Dad was giving Mary the house. She didn't have to worry.

"Wow!" I cried. "That's so wonderful!" I reached out to
grasp his shoulder in awkward gratitude, and found it so bony
and reduced that I felt a surge of tenderness. "Oh, Dad," I said. "I
can't wait to tell her."

He stiffened. "I will thank you to keep this conversation to yourself," he said.

I gaped over at him, with his clean shave and white golf hat, his reddening neck. "You're not going to tell her?"

"Goddamned husband of hers retired from the army years ago. Hasn't even looked for a job, as far as I can tell. Mary's been supporting him since day one. Fred knows a good thing when he sees it. If he finds out she's going to get the house, he'll never pull his own weight."

"But she worries so much," I said as I turned into the Walgreens parking lot. "Could you just let her know?"

"Absolutely not," he declared. As if to end an intolerable exchange, he thrust his door open despite the fact that the car was still moving. I hit the brakes as Dad sat, stolid against his seatbelt. Then he fumbled the belt open and got out of the car, using his cane to heave himself up.

As Dad shambled across the parking lot, I vowed to tackle the mortgage issue with him again. As only a wealthy and hugely entitled person could have done, he'd accelerated Mary's arrival by buying her a house and assuming the mortgage. A mortgage is a legal instrument, a formal declaration. A mortgage is all about repayment with interest. A mortgage signifies a massive debt, a roof over your head, your very safety. By not telling her he planned to forgive the mortgage and by not accepting her payments, Dad exerted control over Mary to indulge a petty, racist whim against her husband. Dad took charge of Mary's financial standing, her level of indebtedness, and her shelter. He withheld the honesty that Mary deserved. He ratcheted up the stress in her life—though he would have said he cared about her. Sharecropping's shadow.

❧

That evening, Mary stood at the edge of the living room rug while Dad glared at her from the sofa. A fresh cocktail glistened on the table before him. "Didn't I tell you that I would recommend a tax advisor for you, Mary? Apparently, you paid no attention whatsoever."

"You'd been so helpful already." Her voice trembled. "I didn't want to bother you. When Mr. Hamilton offered me a name, I took it."

A recent arrival to my father's circle of friends, Chris Hamilton was an effusively friendly man, slick, almost smarmy. My mother would have called him a glad-hander. I gathered from the tense exchange between Dad and Mary that Mary needed a local lawyer and had sought Chris Hamilton's recommendation.

"Why you would listen to that moron stuns me, Mary," Dad said, shaking his head in exaggerated disappointment. "It absolutely stuns me."

I'd never heard Dad talk to Mary in this jarring, attacking way—to me and to my mother, yes, but never to Mary. I moved up behind Mary and touched her arm, hoping to reassure her. Startled by my touch, she jumped back, and we collided. "Wendy! I didn't see you! Did I hurt you?" She reached out a shaking hand to steady us both.

The rest of the evening found us stuck in our separate places: Dad irascible in the living room as he drank a series of cocktails; Mary hard at work on the other side of the kitchen door; me hovering in the kitchen, being no help.

"Wendy!" Dad barked from the living room. "Your father is alone with his cocktail."

Mary pushed at me. "Go."

I went into the living room and sat down gingerly near the kitchen door. "Don't know what to make of your brother's divorce situation," Dad began ponderously.

As I rummaged in my mind for a way to avoid triggering his anger, the phone rang. My father liked Mary to answer, to say, "Coppedge residence" in her soft voice. But the dinner hour was close, and I knew Mary was juggling different pots and cook times. I jumped up and called through the closed door, "I'll get it."

Dad threw up a hand like a traffic cop. "I pay Mary, do I not?" he said. "Mary!" he bellowed. "The telephone!"

Mary made it on the fourth ring. Wrong number.

Dad was in a bad state emotionally. Perhaps my brother's divorce set him loose from familiar moorings. I believe, too, that the new arrangement with Mary unsettled Dad. In the learned helplessness of the wealthy, and the advancing dependence of alcoholic old age, Dad had called desperately for Mary to save him. There was now a new intimacy to Mary and Dad's relationship, with his medical needs and his increasing dependency on her care. Dad also intended to make a larger gift to Mary than he'd ever made to anyone—maybe this unsettled him, too. But Mary was on edge, as well. She had made a high-stakes move in order to care for Dad. For the first time in their forty years of dealings with each other, she owed Dad more money than she might be able to repay. Shaken by these changes, Dad bullied and fumed, while Mary, as always, did her best.

After dinner, Dad dropped off to sleep on the sofa, Mary took a cigarette to the back stoop, and I joined her. "Has Dad been this irritable and pissy ever since you moved down here?" I whispered.

Mary shook her head. "Some days, no."

"Other days?"

She frowned. "I'm just letting it get to me more than usual." She looked out at the flickering lights of the cars that inched north and south along the coast road. Took a drag on her cigarette, blew the smoke out in a long thin line. "I think I understand why your mother drank," she said.

I had never heard Mary speak so candidly. *"I think I understand why your mother drank."* With these blunt words, Mary invoked my father's bad behavior, my mother's drinking and death, and Mary's predicament as the one left coping with Dad. She spoke the truth of her experience in a way she had never before done with me.

With a rush of tender appreciation for the veil she had lifted between us, I hugged her. Mary held her cigarette away and, with her free arm, hugged me back.

Then I remembered the mortgage. *Don't worry*, I wanted to whisper into Mary's ear as we hugged. *Dad's giving you the house.*

I have asked myself repeatedly why I didn't speak the single sentence that might have eased Mary's burden. The simple answer is that I couldn't predict what Dad would do. I was afraid of screwing things up and landing Mary in a worse situation. If I told Mary that Dad planned to give her the house and Dad found out, he might change his mind about forgiving the mortgage. Today, with what my mother used to call "20–20 hindsight," I don't think Dad ever would have reneged on his plan to give Mary the house. *"In our family, we do not like changes."* But, every day, twice a day, he drank enough to get brutally volatile. I could not predict for sure what he would and wouldn't do. Still, I turned down a chance to stand with Mary, to make a real difference in her life. Sitting out there on the stairway in the night, Mary had revealed her feelings to me more honestly than ever before. This could have been a new turning point in our friendship. In keeping my father's secret, in holding on to information that Mary needed, I missed a chance to help Mary and once again stalled the growth of truth-telling between us.

My father did leave the house to Mary when he died three years later. Dad's bequest might have surprised Blanche White, Barbara Neely's independent-minded sleuth; he passed on more than the usual token "handkerchiefs and sachets" that she complained about. I figure that Mary's three-bedroom ranch house in Florida may have cost about $100,000 in 1992 when Dad purchased it. In my very rough calculations, this $100,000 may have represented about three percent of his total estate at the time. In the language of a critical debate in the twenty-first century, three percent of my dad's estate was a minuscule installment in the rightful repayment of white wealth built over centuries by unpaid and poorly paid Black people, among them Mary's ancestors and Mary herself. Though Dad would not have thought in this way, and though his act arose from a highly human mix of selfish urgency and rightful gratitude, he could be seen as making a tiny step towards reparation. He poisoned the act utterly by not telling Mary what he planned to do.

I ask myself why Dad kept the plan secret, and remember his complaint: "That goddamned husband of hers hasn't even looked for a job." He bought into a racist trope about lazy, shiftless Black men. In Dad's century, the lack of jobs available to Black men fed stereotypes of indolence; further back in time, white people developed the myth of lazy Black men to hide the truth of enslaved men's grueling work and to justify the brutal methods by which enslavers sought to extract more work. Dad's peculiar stridency about Fred not getting another job after the military said far more about Dad and about racist mythology than about Mary's husband. After all, Dad, too, had retired after decades of work. How did he have the gall to resent Fred's similar step? My father's scornful dismissal of Fred reflects the kind of white supremacy that does damage without anyone marching in white KKK robes. When Black activists speak of a deep hatred of Blackness endemic to white people, I think of my father's take on Fred.

And this happened in the face of all that Fred gave my dad. Fred moved abruptly to Florida for Mary's job, giving up an established woodworking workshop and New Jersey clientele. He lugged heavy baskets of groceries and other supplies up the steps to Dad's condo and made every repair for Dad that Mary pointed out to him. He woke to phone calls and commotion in the night, like the time when Dad the insomniac called at 2 a.m. to ask Mary to drive around looking for the *New York Times*. I didn't know Fred well—he had been in Mary's life only a few years at this point. Confronted with my father's demanding, dependent behavior and dismissive attitude, Fred seemed to summon immense patience in order to do what Mary wanted. Fred was devoted to Mary, and she was determined that they both serve Dad.

En route from Dad's to the airport two days later, going home to Boston, I stopped by Mary's to hug her goodbye. I pulled up to her new home to find her backing her car out of the driveway. She stopped when she saw me. Behind big dark glasses, she watched me running towards her across the neatly mown grass. At the open window, I felt the acrid humidity of anxious perspiration filling the car. Mary's blouse had large sweat blotches under the arms.

"Where are you going?" I demanded, as if I had a right to

know everything about Mary. "This is supposed to be your time off." I pulled a tissue from my pocket and reached in to blot her forehead, her temples.

Mary took the tissue from me, kept blotting. "Promise you won't be mad?" She took her sunglasses off but didn't meet my eye. "I've taken another little job."

"No," I exclaimed, still unable to look beyond my own easy affluence to Mary's financial realities.

"Once a week I will clean for your dad's friend Mrs. Lyman."

"It's the mortgage, isn't it?"

She shifted her car into reverse.

This was another chance to reveal Dad's plan for the house, to reassure Mary that she didn't have to take on extra work. But I didn't trust Dad and didn't know how to play God. I planted a kiss on Mary's moist cheek through the open window. As though thirty-pound weights anchored my feet, I stood, rooted, as she backed out of the drive and accelerated once again towards the gold coast.

I wish I had defied my father and told Mary. Until Dad died, Mary would worry each month that she couldn't pay what she owed him. Stress causes illness. Stress kills. Dad's secrecy—and my collusion—taxed Mary in ways we were too ignorant or oblivious to imagine.

I've returned to old journals to explore more deeply what fueled my obedience to the caprice of a self-centered old man. When I was debating whether to help Dad after cataract surgery, I wrote that "I hold back from honesty with him because of the money that I hope he will leave me. He has such a rage in him that he might, were I to cross him by not coming down for his surgery, change his will. Fear of this keeps me unchallenging. I want to inherit the money he plans to will to me. Frankly, this has been a factor." I didn't want to risk my assurance of future financial comfort.

When I refused Dad's request for help, I learned that the father I feared might disown me was not the real Roy Coppedge. For one, Dad was a traditionalist. I would have had to do far worse for him to consider the untraditional act of disowning his child. He was an angry, crotchety, controlling man, but he would not disown me. That I conjured a disinheriting bogeyman to fear says less about him than about me. I was scared to risk my class privilege.

My dependence on family wealth is profound. I count on having ample food, shelter, and health care, a new car when the old one wears out, even vacation travel. Like many people coddled by affluence, I don't trust that I could survive without that cushion. Never having had to test my own resourcefulness, I doubt my ability to support myself on my own. This fear is part of being upper class—fear of not having the cushion we count on, fear of not being capable. The fear makes us condone shady behaviors, makes us obedient.

Obedience to my father in keeping his secret about Mary's house was a kind of insurance, my own assurance of future ease —and a humbling example of classism and white supremacy at work within me.

Dad died two years later, in 1995. Mary sold the Florida house and used the proceeds for a gracious ranch house next to a golf course in a leafy New Jersey town near her grandchildren. When I visited her there, Mary and I sat together in yet another new sun porch, this one surrounded by hollies and lilacs rather than grapefruit trees. I confessed to Mary that I had known about the mortgage.

A long silence. Finally, Mary said, as if musing to herself, "If he had told me, I wouldn't have had to sell our house in New Jersey so fast and lose that money."

"And the extra job you took," I said. "I should have told you."

Mary shook her head. "You were as scared of him as I was. With your dad, we didn't do things we weren't supposed to do."

I had seen Mary stretch many times to give my parents the benefit of the doubt. Now, she did the same for me.

2020 update. On a recent phone call, Mary and I reflected again on the mortgage secret, how I had not told Mary what I knew. We tallied the worry and stress that this knowledge could have saved Mary. I apologized again. This time around, Mary did not let me off the hook. She did not say, "We didn't do things we weren't supposed to do." She did not include herself in the story of my silence. She said, simply, as though this explained everything: "You were obedient!" With my new understanding of obedience in the context of class, I believe that Mary spoke a complex and accurate truth.

A last thought on reparations. Real reparations will require more of wealthy white Americans than what seemed generous to me in the 1990s, when Dad forgave the mortgage. Even though my brother and I do honor Mary's care for our parents, and our love for her, by sending her money regularly, when you add it all up, we have not given anything close to an amount that would reflect my father's recognition, at the time of his eye surgery, that he felt he had a second daughter.

fifteen

Heirlooms

GIVEN HOW MY PARENTS' DRAMAS AND LIMITS HAD influenced and circumscribed us—all they had given, all they had taken—there was no pre-ordained path for Mary and me after they died. In the summer of 1996, Mary took a generous step towards our friendship by visiting the New Hampshire lake cottage that my father had paid for. There, our reckoning with their legacy lurched forward. I say *lurched*: certain memories of that visit still make me flinch.

LEGACY #1: HOUSE

My mother had left Dad her whole estate when she died in 1989. Dad's getting everything in this old-fashioned way felt strange to me, given how they fought, how he abused her. Though my brother never voiced the same discomfort, he soon surprised me with a proposal. "I've sounded Dad out on this money thing," Copey said. "I have more than I need. He has more than he needs. He's afraid if he gives you cash outright you'll donate it to some left-wing cause of yours." When I huffed, he said, "Wait, wait. Don't protest. I think he'd be open to a request for help with something tangible, like a little vacation house."

I wasn't sure I wanted to owe Dad anything, including gratitude. But I was touched by Copey's idea—and, to be honest, eager to benefit from my mother's estate—so I risked asking Dad for this large and unusual gift. To my surprise, he agreed readily. Polly and I built a small, year-round cottage next door to friends on one of New Hampshire's myriad lakes. I would not have this vacation house without my father's funding. In the file I keep of our letters back then, I find the record of Dad's payments to the builder—every one of them on time. His gift turned out to be a high point between us. After decades marred by his bullying and my fear, Dad was the "good guy" in giving us money to build the house, and I a truly grateful daughter. Polly and I welcomed him to the lake for a visit. He wasn't physically able to walk with me in the woods, but he and I solved the Sunday *Times* crossword on the sofa, side by side.

The gift of a house, even a small one, revealed my class standing. Having a second home boldly announced my place in the owning class.

LEGACY #2: EGGSHELLS

On the July morning that Mary and her husband Fred were due to arrive in New Hampshire in their RV, I woke before birdsong. Stars shone, though dimly, over the quiet lake. Beside me, Polly still slept.

Six years had passed since Mary's first and only visit to the lake. Dad had been alive then, still in Princeton after Mom's death, and the lake house was brand new. For that first visit, in the fall of 1991, Mary had wrested three days free from her corrections work and Dad's needs. She flew to Boston, and we drove to the lake, just the two of us. We traipsed through the woods, marveled at the brilliant autumn colors, stood arm in arm watching brisk fall winds ripple the lake's surface. We no longer needed the cover of darkness to walk together, as we had on the Nantucket beach. Mary was fifty-one that year, and I was forty-seven. I remembered feeling that this, finally, was different from Mary's domestic work, her summers in Nantucket. We were on a new path, we two, as grownups. We were finding ways to share our lives. After we'd walked, and talked, and rested, Mary let me cook for her.

Now, at the dawn of Mary's second lake visit, I began to worry. I didn't know Fred well, and he and Polly had met only once. Among the four of us, Mary and I had the bond. I wasn't sure how our partners would manage. And New Hampshire was one of the ten whitest states in the United States. During their stay at the lake, Fred and Mary might not see a single person of color other than each other. Mary had worked in many lily-white settings but, rightly or wrongly, I worried that Fred would be uncomfortable. And, finally, Fred had never been in our home, never seen Polly's and my double bed, never had to confront our being lesbians. As with any guest I didn't know well, I couldn't be sure how Fred felt about gay people. The uncertainty made me worry. Fred had always been cordial to me. I, for my part, was so eager for him to like me that I tended to become awkwardly hyper-friendly—the eggshells issue again. I couldn't picture addressing head-on with Fred either lesbian relationships or the whiteness of New Hampshire. But Fred was Mary's husband. I wanted him to feel welcome, to have a decent time, to be glad he made the trip.

Light seeped into the bedroom, revealing cobwebs under the skylight and a splat of bird poop on the window. The lakeside house was six years older than when Mary first exclaimed over its beauty. Steady use had scratched the pine floors and teal countertops. Remembering how devotedly Mary took care of everything in her own home, I wanted mine to be perfect.

As soon as Polly woke up, I cajoled her into going up the tallest ladder we could borrow. She climbed high to sweep the cobwebs from the bedroom and living room skylights. After we lugged the heavy ladder back to our neighbor's basement, I noticed another filament high up the sloped cathedral ceiling in the living room, wafting in the lake breeze. "Damn," I said. I looked from the renegade cobweb to my lover in her shorts and tank top, her feet bare, a novel in her hand.

Polly shook her head definitively. "I'm not going for the ladder again, if that's what you have in mind." But I couldn't stop thinking how spotlessly Mary kept her own house. The gleam of antiques, expertly refinished. The lemony smell of polish. Everything in its place. "Mary is not coming to check on our housekeeping," Polly said as she poured herself a mug of tea. "I wish you could relax. You've been wanting her to come back here for years."

"*I've* been wanting her? Don't *you*?"

Polly frowned and started to speak, seemed to think better of it, and nudged the screen door open with her elbow.

"Sorry," I said to Polly's back as she headed down to the short stretch of beach in front of our cottage. "I should have started cleaning sooner."

"I don't think this is about cleaning," she said.

Polly was correct, of course. I was so eager for Mary to come, so eager for her visit to go well, that I over-worried. Mary had warned me not to walk on eggshells around her. I should relax, I told myself, and just welcome my friend. Besides, in imagining that Mary might hyper-focus on our housekeeping,

I'd pigeonholed her into the domestic role she had played for my mother—my own version of racial profiling. In the little guesthouse across the street that we shared with several neighbors, I made up the double bed with fresh sheets, hoping Mary and Fred would kick back, enjoy, watch sunset and moonrise, maybe even sleep in. In other words, have a vacation.

LEGACY #3: BODIES

That afternoon, Fred hopped down from behind the wheel of a spotless white RV. Seven years younger than Mary, Fred was a large, tall, solid man, efficiently built and muscular, with deep chestnut skin. As he stood at the road's edge to shake my hand, and then Polly's, he held his back upright, military posture. He seemed at once friendly and reserved.

Mary eased herself down painfully from the passenger seat. She took a limping step and stood a moment to look around at the trees and the lake, as though the beauty of the place might counter the pain in her swollen knees. As we hugged each other, the difference in our physical wellbeing struck me once again. Mary and I were only four years apart, but our histories divided us. Mary had labored since she was a young child. I had not labored, period, except perhaps in childbirth. At work, I might have colleagues who drove me crazy, but I never endured the harassment Mary experienced from male corrections officers who didn't want a woman on the team, and from white guards who resented having a Black woman as a boss. Mary had lived with the stresses—both chronic and acute—of racism and poverty. I had not. And I had benefited from all the medical and dental checkups that ward off future disability.

After five decades, our bodies (and our lives) told very different stories. Chronic health problems, unrelenting pains, increasing disability—these were Mary's legacy from a lifetime of hard physical work, insufficient financial resources, and inadequate health care. As I greeted Mary and Fred by the lake that day, I was flexible and strong, a picture of "good health." Twenty years would pass before age-related arthritis would make me stride less, walk less, take shorter paths through the New Hampshire woods—woods that already, as she eased herself out of the camper, Mary knew she would not be able to savor on this visit.

LEGACY #4: GRIEF

Dinner went well at first. Polly and Fred talked lawnmowers, baseball, home repair, and Tiger Woods. Woods had come into the public eye that April as the youngest golfer ever to win the prestigious Masters golf competition in Atlanta. In the swiftest ascent in golfing history, that summer Woods reached the number one spot in official world golf rankings. That Tiger Woods was biracial drew extra attention to his meteoric rise. Mary and Fred seemed to feel a fascination, a pride, an almost proprietary solicitude towards this biracial man who was dominating a sport that had been nearly one hundred percent white. Woods's devolution into a troubled figure—ruined by stardom, perhaps, as so many celebrities are—was years away. At the lake that evening, his already legendary skill provided at least ten minutes of affable conversation.

As I cleared the table, however, and set out the coconut cake that Mary had baked and brought with her in an ice chest, we stumbled against a new topic. "Your dad was so cute," Mary said as she sank a knife through the gooey white frosting. "He had to have those B-12 injections, remember? One morning I gave him his shot and he let out the most awful yell. I jumped back and cried out, 'Oh, my god, I've hurt you!' He burst out laughing. He'd been joking!" Mary chuckled merrily, passing me a big slice of cake. "That yell just about gave me a heart attack."

I watched Fred lift a soda to his lips, his neutral expression unbroken. Polly studied her placemat. My father's "joke" was appalling. He'd been playing with Mary's earnest anxiety about doing a good job, and his own power as her employer. Of the four of us at that table, only Mary had ever thought my father was cute. I imagined that Fred, at best, had tolerated Mary's willingness to put everything aside to serve a man whose surface civility barely concealed ugly racial stereotypes. I didn't think Mary's going on about Dad's cuteness was going to help Fred enjoy New Hampshire. Mary missed my father, she loved my father, she grieved him. To the rest of us, she voiced an unsettling, even embarrassing commitment to someone we'd each had our own reasons to stay away from. In the presence of her mourning, the rest of us chafed.

Mary had described Dad's death to me shortly after he died in the spring of 1995. Soon after I returned home from what would be my last visit, Mary was with Dad in his Florida bedroom. He asked Mary to turn on the six o'clock news, and she went to the TV. She turned back to find him sliding out of bed towards the floor in a final stroke. She caught him as best she could and called 911. Dad died in her arms. I've always felt that this was just right, since she missed Mom's death.

The EMTs who rushed into Dad's room soon afterwards seemed shocked, Mary told me, to find "a Black woman sobbing over the body of a dead old white man." Although EMTs must encounter many kinds of unpredictable situations, they may only rarely encounter a domestic worker sobbing over an employer's death. I think now that Mary's sense of bereavement traveled with her to the lakeside dinner table. Its form had changed from keening to doting nostalgia. The rest of us were no readier than the EMTs to encounter or process the unexpected, discordant truth of Mary's grief.

LEGACY #5. SERVICE

Mary's vitamin B-12 story brought an abrupt and muted end to the evening. Soon, I walked Mary and Fred across the narrow road to the guesthouse. I hoped they would have, at least, a comfortable night's sleep.

At six the next morning, I spotted the flicker of TV through the guesthouse window, Fred's solid profile outlined in the dim light. So much for romance, I thought to myself. So much for a double bed overlooking the lake. I'd been like a hostess who cooks an elaborate meal for guests without asking what they like to eat. What Polly and I had to offer may not look like romance to Mary and Fred, may not even look like vacation.

When a second cup of coffee marked the end of breakfast that day, Mary looked around her with an air of appraisal and expectancy. "So," she said brightly, "what needs fixing?"

Nothing, I told her. She and Fred should relax and enjoy themselves.

"Give us something to do," she insisted.

Soon, every repair that Polly and I could conjure became a purpose for the day. The guesthouse bannister needed securing. Great! The swinging door in front of the propane tanks had come loose. Perfect. The yard-sale kitchen table I'd purchased as a writing surface needed its wooden legs cut back by two or three inches. Just why they'd brought Fred's circular saw. Mary and Fred went to work. Or, should I say, Mary chose the tasks and monitored Fred as he carried them out. As he pulled tools, brackets, tape measures, and other supplies from the van, Polly and I began trying to help. Mary sent us away to our books and papers, to the beach and the lake.

LEGACY #6. HEIRLOOMS

Fred returned to the guesthouse after lunch, while Mary, Polly and I settled on the sofa in the small, lakeside living room. Almost immediately, Mary turned from the view to frown at a glass-fronted cabinet in the corner, its shelves stacked haphazardly with china I'd inherited from my family. Polly and I rarely used the china. Once in a while, we'd be inspired to pull two heirloom plates from the cabinet, pile them with tofu and vegetables for dinner, wash them by hand, return them to the cabinet, and feel like we were playing house. Storing expensive heirloom plates in a jumble is, in a way, a sign of class privilege.

"You're not showing all that china off near to advantage," Mary announced. She stood slowly up from the sofa, favoring her knees, approached the cabinet, opened the glass doors and studied the array.

"Leave them," I said, but already she was carrying a small stack of soup bowls to the kitchen.

An hour later, Mary and I had washed and dried every dish in the cabinet. We placed each newly-sparkling piece on the dining table—my grandmother's green ice tea glasses, breakfast china I remembered from summers with my Granny, an ornate tea set from Tiffany's, all colorful flowers and lavish strokes of gold. Since 1837, Tiffany and Company had featured diamond jewelry and other items admired by New York's WASP elite. The elegant tea set—an engagement gift from my great aunt and uncle when I was twenty—fit a life that I had quickly abandoned. Today, when I want tea, I use a mug. I try to imagine giving the tea service to one of my three granddaughters, but with their iPads and iPhones, their Facebook pages and MP3s, I wonder who in their generation would want a Tiffany tea set.

"Can you see," Mary said, surveying the clusters of china on the dining table before us, "how you lost the effect by stacking everything up?" She ran a finger along the deep blue-purple rim of a delicate dessert plate that I remembered from Sunday lunch at my Granny's, every aspect of the memory a marker of my class —sponge cake freshly baked by a full-time cook, vanilla ice cream hand-cranked in an ancient wooden maker by Granny's kindly Irish handyman, who let little blond curly-haired me "help" him crank. "Your mother wanted you to get these dessert plates when she died, and you did!" Mary said. I pictured my mother confiding to Mary over this china, weaving Mary into an upper-class fantasy of elegant legacy, summoning Mary's enthusiasm for plates that I, not Mary, would receive.

Pausing over a stack of formal plates rimmed in gold, Mary started to laugh. "Your father was so funny about these plates. After your mother died, once in a while I'd use one for his dinner. 'Why, Mary,' he'd say. 'You're using the royal china again.'"

Mary laughed merrily, but the royal china anecdote shot Polly to her feet from where she'd been reading on the sofa. "Guess I'll leave you two to your project," Polly said, so carefully neutral that she didn't sound neutral at all. Mary and I watched her take her book into the bedroom and close the door.

Fred had vanished next door, and Polly had shut herself in the bedroom. What Mary and I were enacting with the heirloom china—a ritual, a charade, an anachronism—put them off, at the very least bored them. We were obsessing with a bunch of dishes passed down through generations of people who had more than they would ever need.

Mary stared at the closed door. "Polly thinks I'm wasting your time," she said in a flat voice. "We should stop."

"Not at all!" I cried. "Polly's a butch," I said, half joking, half grasping for an explanation that might soothe Mary's feelings. "She could care less about china." But the screen of Mary's face had gone blank. "Please let's keep going," I said, touching her arm. "I love doing this! Who else would get me to make that cabinet right?"

I didn't tell Mary the whole truth. I didn't "love" washing, drying, admiring and repositioning my family china, but Mary was visiting, I loved her, I wanted to do something with her, and she couldn't walk without pain. Also, Mary has a strong will; I would have had to be stubborn, even ungracious, to refuse her initiative. I sense that Mary welcomed a joint project that didn't require walking, and she wanted to be useful, maybe even to complete a mission for my mother. Here was a chance to pass on expertise that she had learned, and not just from my mother. From the start, Mary's grandmother, Verna Phipps, had taught Mary to care skillfully for her furnishings and decorative objects.

Actually, I minded the project less than I expected. Moonlighting at dinner parties for my parents over the years, Mary had washed and dried each piece of this china by hand, as we did that afternoon. Piece by delicate piece, Mary and I passed our complex history back and forth between us. Through plates and bowls that landed in our hands via radically different trajectories, we touched my parents' absence together. We felt our way towards what connection we could forge based on the past that we shared and perhaps only we understood.

When the china was ready to go back in the cabinet, Mary stuck her head out the back door. "Fred!" she yelled across the narrow road. "Get on over here."

"Maybe he's in the middle of a show," I said, coming up behind her.

Mary shook her head quickly. "He doesn't half watch the TV anyway." We stood together waiting, two barefoot women in shorts.

When Fred wasn't forthcoming, Mary huffed down the steps and across the street to bang loudly on the guesthouse door. Fred came out, shielding his eyes against the August sunshine.

"Come on over here," she ordered, all business. She took him inside to my grandmother's cabinet. "See if you can't cut me some grooves in these shelves."

Fred toted the heavy wooden shelves outside to the circular saw he'd brought in the van. Mary and I watched him puzzle out the angles, cut the grooves.

"Good," Mary said when he finished.

Immediately, I started blathering. "Wow, thank you, this is so great, you are so good at that, you are so kind," I rushed, as if a tumble of thanks could hide the shame that suddenly assailed me. Here I was, another Coppedge benefiting from Fred's skilled, generous, and uncompensated help. Over-thanking felt false, however, even as I indulged.

Fred looked at the ground until my stream of thanks ended, and then he looked up, catching Mary's eye. "I like a challenge," he said, to her as much as to me. "Glad to do it."

Back in the living room, Mary selected the plates to prop up for viewing, their rims secured by the new grooves. She placed the china according to pattern: green pheasants, blue-purple borders, multicolored nosegays, gold-leaf edging. When we were done, Polly took a photograph of Mary and me in front of our newly resplendent display. I half believed my mother would appear in the picture between us.

LEGACY #7. HIGH TASTE

As Mary and I stood before the cabinet admiring our work, she turned to me, clear-eyed and serious. "Your mother taught me everything," she said. "I can still walk into a specialty store and select the best caviar and the perfect champagne to go with it. She taught me that." Her smile faded. She looked towards the trees on the far shore of the lake. "She taught me all the high tastes. Then she left me alone with them."

I didn't know what to say in the presence of this complex sorrow.

"There's not a man I meet who shares my tastes," Mary continued. "I think my appreciation for the finer things bothers them."

For Fred and Mary's wedding, my mother had lent Mary an expensive opal ring. I had no idea how Fred felt about this. He had certainly retreated from Mary's and my afternoon charade of elegance.

In my mother's jewelry box after she died, I'd found a sheet ripped from a steno pad, the message in pencil: "Make sure to give Mary the opal ring I promised her. She loves it so." I passed the opal ring along to Mary. Today, I reflect on my mother teaching Mary about fine china, jewelry, champagne, caviar— subjects I never wanted to study. From my mother, and from Mary's other employers in our affluent Princeton circle, Mary learned to speak a language of taste that keyed her to her employers' preferences and helped her excel at her job. But Mary and Mom connected around objects of beauty that my mother possessed and Mary only tended. What looked like kindness, then, had a double edge.

As she turned away from the now-completed task, I heard Mary say ruefully, as if musing to herself, "I feel like I am living in the wrong body." *Living in the wrong body*—a mix of protest and despair. Mary's words made me remember Pecola Breedlove, the character in Toni Morrison's *The Bluest Eye* whose plight first woke me to the intimate toll of racism. Oppressed by extreme poverty and family violence, considered "ugly" by all the community and even by herself, Pecola imagines vanishing, piece by piece, and harbors the desperate hope of waking up as a white girl with blue eyes. "I feel like I am living in the wrong body," Mary said. A protest and a lament.

Some call this internalized oppression. The "high tastes" that Mary studied in my mother seemed to make Mary feel that her own life, her own experience, her own body, were wrong. In a context of systemic oppression, my parents initiated Mary into a life that they would not support her to achieve, a life that went to the grave with them.

LEGACY #8. DAUGHTER

As we stood in the presence of my newly arrayed family china, Mary mused to herself once again with a kind of bemused regret. "I am the daughter who didn't leave home," she said.

I gasped. What Mary said had the ring of truth.

Through Mary's steady service—her diligent moonlighting—she'd given both my parents a comfortable, coddled death. She and I didn't yet know that, in her sixties, Mary would move "back to the hill" in rural Virginia to give the last healthy decade of her life to tending her mother and stepfather in the same way. Almost single-handedly, she would provide the care that kept them out of a nursing home. In the end—in her family, as in mine—Mary would be the daughter who didn't leave home.

Mary and I did not mention that afternoon that her presence, her work, had allowed me to be the daughter who did leave home. Her dependable presence enabled me to keep my distance while Mom was dying and while Dad sputtered through his last years. In this way, Mary eased and enhanced not only my parents' final years, but my own forties and fifties. Did Mary resent me for the life she freed me to live? With all that she and I talk about, I haven't dared to ask.

I do know that, by drinking herself to an early death, my mother broke Mary's heart as well as mine.

LEGACY #9. SISTER

Sunday morning, while Fred loaded the RV for a midday departure, Mary and I drove to a local antiques store in the aimlessly purposeful way of companions looking for something to do. Never an antiques buff, I hadn't set foot inside the store in local Georges Mills, but welcomed an outing that didn't involve our spouses. Mary and Fred were soon to head back to New Jersey, and I wanted her to myself.

Mary and I followed each other around the dusty barn, weaving through the jumble of wooden tables, hutches, sideboards, and linen chests from the previous century—all the things that white summer people fancied for lakeside vacation homes. We took turns pointing out the styles we liked, though the prices offended Mary. She and Fred had refinished enough old furniture, she said, to know what things should cost. Before we left, Mary bought me a bottle of orange-oil furniture polish. "You use this, now!" she said. Remembering my last-minute snit about cobwebs wafting from the skylights, I chuckled. If Mary did feel a responsibility to my mother to train me as a housekeeper, I silently wished her good luck.

I drove us back towards the lake house, acutely feeling the hollow of our impending goodbye. There was so much still to talk about. Quickly, I asked how things were going with Fred.

Mary shook her head as if to brush off the question. "We're fine. You know."

"He's so good looking," I said. No response. "He seems dependable and kind." She pursed her lips. "Fred was incredibly patient all those years when you put Dad first."

"He didn't have a choice," she said as though any fool would understand this.

I pressed on. "Is there something I don't know?"

In Mary's and my friendship, I tend to ask more nosy questions and offer more unsolicited advice. There is an ongoing exercise of power here: Mary may not feel as free to question and advise. Or maybe intrusive personal questions and opinions are not her style. Mary's advice has electrified me at key moments: her warning not to walk on eggshells; her warning, when I was infatuated with the poet in molten green, that I'd lose a treasure in Polly. But, due to a combination of privilege and personal style, I tend to be the one who interrogates. I pressed on about Fred.

Mary leaned towards her open window for a long breath of the piney New Hampshire air. Finally, she gave a small shrug. "Fred's happy if we stay home all the time. He likes it when I get fat."

Was she lonely, I asked, even in that beautiful house by the golf course? Perhaps Mary knew that her face radiated empty sadness, because she said, simply, "You and my mother are the only ones who know."

A friend had once confessed to me the shame she felt when her third marriage faltered, as though any woman who has run through two husbands and isn't happy with the third must be faulty, herself. I didn't want to stir that shame with Mary. I searched for something wise to say, but came up more cheerleader than confidante. "You and Fred are such a good team," I said. "On projects, I mean."

"We are that," Mary said, with some finality.

I had driven as slowly as I could, but now we pulled up to the cottage. Across the way, by the guesthouse, I could see bags piled above the rim of the RV's rear window. Fred was ready to go.

"Wish you could stay longer," I said. "As always."

"Me, too," Mary said. She fixed her eyes on the water ahead of us. "I like to pretend we're sisters," she said.

A motorboat whizzed by on the small lake, towing two white children in large, inflated inner tubes. Friends have to be earned, I thought, as the boat's wake sloshed ashore like miniature ocean surf. I wasn't sure I was doing a good job of earning Mary's friendship—not least because I tried too hard, the eggshells thing. A sister, though. Sisters were given. You got one, or you didn't.

"It's not pretend," I said.

Sinking into the emotion of the moment—the love that Mary and I were affirming—I gave no thought to a fuller picture. In terms of legacy and inheritance, for instance, I had not treated Mary like a sister, nor had my parents treated her like a daughter. I think of the two half-sisters in *Jubilee*, Margaret

Walker's sweeping novel of slavery, Civil War and Reconstruction. [1] Vyry, the main character, is the mixed-race daughter of an enslaved woman and the white plantation owner. Because her mother works in the house rather than the fields, Vyry and the plantation master's white daughter, Lillian, spend their first seven years together—living, playing, sleeping side by side, like sisters. When Vyry turns seven, in an abrupt and brutal switch, the white masters force her to become Lillian's servant, her possession. Because Vyry is light-skinned and beautiful, the picture image of little white Lillian, the plantation mistress grows increasingly cruel.

When I first read *Jubilee,* Vyry and Lillian's side-by-side childhood had a certain magnetism for me. The same father's blood flows in their veins, I said to myself. And yet, what first looks like sisterly play and connection disfigures into a mistress-slave relationship. Young Lillian may not be as outwardly cruel as her mother, yet she accepts her place in a merciless structure that gives her ownership of her childhood playmate.

"But they are sisters!" I protested uselessly. "How could a father separate his two daughters in this brutal and permanent way? Do they not love each other?" I needed four hundred pages of *Jubilee* to understand that, though Vyry and Lillian share the same father, they are not sisters, and that love as a concept, as a reality, as a relation, does not apply.

The barriers that divide the two not-sisters in *Jubilee* persist through their lifetimes, and so do those that divide Mary and me. Our life experiences are nearly as divergent as those of Vyry

---

[1] *Jubilee* is told from the point of view of its African American characters. Walker, an award-winning poet, based her 1966 novel on the life of her great-grandmother, Margaret Duggans Ware Brown. Brown was born enslaved, survived the Civil War, and lived her adult life amidst the grim segue to Reconstruction. Ten years of diligent research enabled Walker to portray, in vivid detail, the life and times of her protagonist, Vyry, a character she created in her great-grandmother's memory.

and Lillian. Mary and I shared my parents in certain ways, but this is no guarantee of sisterhood. Sisterhood between us is about action, or nothing.

LEGACY #10. CONTRADICTION

Mary's departure left me feeling unsettled and sad. Like many long-term partners who should know better, I tried to pin my discomfort on Polly.

"I worry that Mary felt your coolness," I said to Polly while we were cooking dinner. "Did you hug her goodbye?"

Polly shot me a look of irritation from the stove. "Of course, I hugged her goodbye."

"But you *are* cool to her. Like when she and I did the china, and you retreated to the bedroom."

Polly turned off the flame and set down the spatula as though she might burn something—or throw something. She stood squarely, facing the stove. Finally, she said, "Mary is so goddamned . . . servile with us. Here she has had a full career in corrections, the first woman—what?—lieutenant?—in the system. She did important work, damn it. But with us her life as a *maid* is what she goes back to. Her life with your family. It drives me nuts." Polly turned to face me, but stood in place, coming no closer. "My mother paid a woman to clean once a week. I can't say we didn't have help. But we didn't have a servant. You know what I mean? A servant!"

"You do care about Mary," I said, seeing her upper lip tremble.

"Of course, I do!" Polly was shouting now. "I just can't stand the contradictions!" She swiped the heel of her hand across her wet cheek. "I thought if I heard one more story about how cute your father was, I would . . . I mean, I have come a long way in forgiving him for the ways he hurt you, and I know you had some healing with him at the end, but, Wendy, your father was not 'cute.' And Fred! Here he is in lilywhite New Hampshire, and Mary's rearranging your goddamned heirloom china. It's like your family represented something to Mary, some dream of beauty, some never-never land."

Later that night, I stood in the living room, facing the cabinet. The blue, green and rose hues on the china were dim, now, in shadow. I couldn't argue against what Polly had said about Mary, the dream of beauty, the fantasy. The flowered plates in their grooves, the Tiffany tea set, all that Mary and I had washed and dried together, shrieked of my inherited class. And yet, that day, Mary and I had passed the objects between us as acts of love. I opened the glass-paned doors to our careful array and stood in the contradiction.

CODA: POLLY

Now, in 2020, I remember Polly's angry outburst as she stood at the stove that evening. At that time in our lives, she and I were continuing to inform ourselves about racism and class inequities—through books, courses, lectures, conferences, workshops. Polly strove to integrate race and class issues into her high school teaching, and I to incorporate them into women's health education. We both worked to re-examine our lives through these ideas. We were trying, in today's language, to "be woke" to our role in racism and classism. White people waking up to these evils feel many strong feelings, including shame, guilt, anger at the system, anger at our own complicity. I think that such feelings hit Polly that weekend. Mary's nostalgia about Dad, the china cabinet ritual, a heightened awareness of the whiteness of our lakeside locale—all these stirred an acute discomfort that Polly could not hide. Her awkwardness took an unexpected toll; for some years after that visit, despite my earnest reassurance, Mary suspected that Polly didn't like her.

Polly's and my class differences also surfaced that weekend. We grew up with similar privileges of white skin and advanced education, but I came from a pedigree of aristocracy that, according to the lopsided values of the upper-class WASP world, gave my family "higher" social status than hers. In our nearly forty years together, my internalized sense of superiority has more than once threatened our relationship (a topic for another book). What's more, "my" assets were now Polly's. My owning class status made Polly owning class as well. As Mary and I curated and tended the heirloom china, perhaps this confounding truth came home to Polly. The firmly closed bedroom door was a warning: Polly and I had our own work to do.

sixteen

Like One of the Family

TRENTON, NEW JERSEY, SUMMER, 1998. I STEPPED FROM the Northeast Regional train into the aggressive, humid heat I remembered from childhood. I'd come from Boston to visit Mary and Fred for the weekend. Mary waited on the platform in a flowing floral skirt and high-heeled sandals—even in retirement, she dressed with style. We ran towards each other, hugged long and hard despite the heat. As we headed for the exit, Mary caught me looking her up and down, fondly taking her in. She shook her head as if to shake off my fond gaze. "I'm a lazy bum these days. Just sit around and get fat," she said. 'And old," she added, like she was mad at someone.

"You are gorgeous as always," I said.

"Look at you," she countered, "skinny as ever."

We seemed to greet each other this way every time.

Mary commandeered my suitcase and wheeled it briskly towards the car. Trailing her, I scanned the parking area and surrounding sidewalk, with its discarded coffee cups, fast food containers strewn on the asphalt, and meager bushes desiccated by summer's heat. Since my childhood, the area around the Trenton train station had become what many white people call "bad"—a code word for a place where Black and brown people live. Thinking *bad,* thinking *high crime area,* I clutched my computer bag close to my side. White fear, my fear—unfounded as usual—and a pang of guilty awareness: The "goodness" of the neighborhood where Polly and I lived depended on the underfunding of neighborhoods like this one. A pang, too, of imagined retribution: As a relatively wealthy white person, I imagined myself a target, even suspected I might "deserve" to be mugged.

Had I reflected on what I actually knew, I could have spared myself the anxious paranoia. I knew, after all, that white fear of so-called "Black crime" is a projection of the founding white crimes of this country—mass killing of Indigenous peoples, three hundred years of chattel slavery, and a hundred years of Jim Crow. White slavers and overseers raped Black women as a means of control and source of profit, yet white people to this day portray Black men as "dangerous" to white women. I knew that the real crimes in so-called "bad" neighborhoods are housing discrimination, racist lending practices, underfunding of city schools, and financial starvation of other critical services. Crimes, that is, of the white majority—or, in Black and poor communities across the United States, of a white minority that holds doggedly on to control.

It was actually white people who had committed stunning acts of violence that year. In two different communities—Jonesboro, Arkansas, and Springfield, Oregon—white teenagers had opened fire on their teachers and classmates, one with a semiautomatic rifle. The white teens killed five people in one case, two in another, and injured more than thirty. Back then, in 1998, most Americans were shocked by these youthful massacres—though not enough, even then, to encourage passage of effective gun control laws. Then as now, most media covering massacres by white shooters portrayed the killers as personally deranged, never generalizing about violent tendencies among white youth. When individual Black people committed murder, however, the same media hyped violent tendencies in the entire Black community. As I clutched my belongings in the Trenton railway station parking lot, a lifetime of media distortions stoked my wariness.

Earlier that summer, three white men in Texas had dragged a Black hitchhiker named James Byrd, Jr., behind a pick-up truck, brutally dismembering and killing him. The Klan affiliations of two of Mr. Byrd's murderers were known by the time Mary picked me up at the station, though prosecution and sentencing were yet to come. She and I would not speak of this hate crime during my visit. Maybe I chose not to bring up such a jarring and painful reality; maybe Mary's silence arose from a similar hesitation. And yet, our visit would take place in the shadow of that savage murder.

White violence lay more heavily on Mary that summer than I knew at the time. On a spring night in Elk Creek in 1997, just a year earlier, white men had murdered Mary's cousin. Garnett P. Johnson, Jr., a slight, hundred-and-fifty-pound former Marine, had joined the men, relative newcomers to the area, for a night of heavy drinking. The two white men had checkered and difficult childhoods in other states, prison time in their twenties, could find only sporadic brief jobs in a depressed rural economy. Early in the morning, according to an eye witness, they attacked G.P. as he was sleeping, burned him alive, and decapitated him. From local news accounts of the killing, the crime was unplanned and drunkenly carried out—two white men woke from a drunken stupor into an eruption of race hatred and malice.

G.P. grew up two houses down the hill from Mary's parents in Elk Creek. He graduated from the local high school, and enlisted in the Marines. A few years later, he returned to a society no more supportive of his long-term success as a Black man than when he graduated high school and identified the military as the only dependable option for employment. News accounts of the crime quote G.P.'s father, Garnett Johnson, Sr. "He was a good boy," G.P.'s father said, like so many bereft and grieving parents in the ongoing onslaught of white violence against young Black men. "He never hurt anyone."

Local news sources speculated as to whether the U.S. Attorney General's office would prosecute G.P.'s killing as a hate crime. After the local trial resulted in a verdict of life imprisonment for the two killers—no parole for one killer, geriatric parole for the other—Attorney General Janet Reno's office declared itself satisfied that "justice was served." I wonder about the politics of the AG's decision, how many hate crimes seemed too insignificant or too expensive to prosecute federally, even under a Democratic presidency. I wonder whether, by officially calling G.P.'s murder a hate crime, the feds might have, in some small way, lessened the trauma for Mr. Johnson and all the family.

Hate crimes aim to instill terror, to scare people into staying small. As Mary put so vividly in 2020, more than two decades later, "Even now, when passing that area going to Independence, I think of G.P. and the terror he must have felt before dying." Activist lawyer Bryan Stevenson marks deadly white violence against Black people by calling it "racial terror lynching." Elk Creek, Virginia, is nestled at the edge of the stunningly green and picturesque Great Smoky Mountains National Park. White people—tourists and locals—flock there each season to hike and picnic. Mary recalls that her family rarely entered those woods, even for a brief Sunday outing. For Black families in predominantly white Elk Creek, danger lurks in both mountains and town—not from wild animals, but from white people. From the torture and murder of Emmett Till in 1955 to that of G.P. Johnson forty years later, Mary and I have been in each other's lives during what for her community has been a reign of terror.

Mary did not tell me about G.P.'s death until a few years after it took place. I try to learn from her silence. Mary, more than anyone, knew the safe and easy life I'd led inside the bubble that Ta-Nehisi Coates calls "the Dream." There was no guarantee that I would be of help to her, that I would do anything other than be helplessly horrified.

As Mary drove us out of central Trenton, her stepfather was on her mind. At the first stoplight, she handed me a brightly flowered card from the dashboard. "Look at what I got last week! See how Mr. George signed it?"

I opened the card and read the message aloud: "Happy Birthday and much love from Mommie and Daddy."

"He's never signed himself 'Daddy,'" Mary said. "It's always been 'George.'"

For as long as I'd known her, Mary had ached to belong to her mother's second family. Now her stepfather had called himself Daddy.

"He must have stayed on the phone half an hour talking yesterday. He never does that. Before we hung up—are you ready? —he said, 'I love you.' *Oh, my God*, I thought, *Mr. George said he loved me*. And now this." Mary took the card triumphantly from my hand and put it back on the dashboard. "I've wanted his attention for so long."

Hearing about Mr. George's "I love you," I knew I had Mary to thank for a similar moment with Dad. Just before I headed home from a Florida visit in the spring of 1995, not knowing that Dad would die before I saw him again, I stood transfixed in his bedroom as he said to me slowly, wresting each word from his stroke-stricken tongue, "I love you." I couldn't remember his ever saying that to me. I told him that I loved him, too, and there it was, healing that we both needed. Moments later, I told Mary what he'd said. Mary smiled triumphantly and said, "I've been telling and telling him to say he loves you!" Mary had coached my father into his humanity.

"That phone call is still in the very front of my mind," Mary continued as she drove us through Trenton traffic towards the suburbs. "How Mr. George stayed on, talking to me. I feel like I have a special secret."

We reached the township where Mary and Fred had settled after Dad died. Soon we drove along the neat lawns and ranch houses of Fairway Drive, with the rolling green of the community golf course just behind. Maybe because George Johnson had finally called himself "Daddy," I felt a sudden absence sucking at the air in the car. Mary had once told me that she never met her birth father. Heart pounding against my chest, I blurted out, "Do you . . . I mean . . . I was just thinking . . . do you ever wonder about your real dad, the one you never knew?" An awkward, out-of-the-blue question that surely took away from Mary's moment of celebration. I wished I could take it back.

Mary gave no answer. Instead, she swung the car sharply into her driveway and sat, staring blankly at the tidy house with its tended gardens and white trim, a profusion of pink from a hanging plant by the front door. When I'd first visited Mary in this home, shortly after she and Fred moved up from Florida, Mary had seemed upbeat and energetic, happy to be back near her grandchildren. She ushered me excitedly through the house. She and Fred had moved into every room already; pictures were up, boxes folded away. The house of her dreams, I had thought. Now, her look was almost one of weary appraisal. I wondered what had changed.

"You all right?" I asked. I'd upset her, I thought, by asking about her birth father.

She pulled a lace-edged handkerchief from her handbag and patted it along her perspiring forehead. "I'm okay," she said. She made a quick, rallying move to collect her things. Her voice came out high and breathless, as though she were reaching for enthusiasm. "Let me show you the new sunroom we built."

In the wood-paneled sunroom, vertical shades in the high windows slatted the intense summer sunshine to light the airy space without overheating. Mary dropped into the corner of a plush sofa and leaned back, set her shoeless feet on the coffee table. "I live in here now," she said, re-arranging small pillows behind her head. "I live in this room." She sank back and closed her eyes. "I'll get up in a minute and get us some nice, cool water."

"Let me!" I cried, and jumped up. Another time, Mary might have rushed to wait on me, but she stayed, eyes closed, where she had settled. Either Mary felt more relaxed with me than she used to, or she didn't feel well. Maybe some of both, I thought.

At Mary's spotless kitchen counter, the sound of ice cubes

dropping into tall glasses took me back to the built-in bar off the Rosedale Road kitchen, just thirty miles away in Princeton. The clink of ice, the glug of bourbon or scotch, the fizz of soda —sounds that Mary and I both knew well. Finally, our lives— and our relationship—no longer revolved around my parents' drinking.

When I returned to the sunroom, Mary yawned and stretched and thanked me.

I leaned over from behind the sofa to set her glass of iced water on the table beside her, my cheek brushing hers. "It's my pleasure," I said. "Thank *you.*"

Despite record heat the next day, Mary wanted to exercise, so she drove us to a local riverside park. In the parking area, the hot hand of the sun brushed away the meager shade and laid itself on the body of the car. A wet patch of perspiration darkened the back of Mary's T-shirt; my skirt stuck to my sweaty thighs. Resolutely, Mary opened her door into a blanket of hot humidity. "Let's walk!" she cried in a cheerleader voice, but she took so long to lift herself from the driver's seat that I was able to spring out of the car and reach her before she could rise.

I asked Mary—was she sure she wanted to exercise in this heat? "Walking is good for me," she countered. She ignored my offered hand and muscled herself up slowly to a standing position. "All I do in that house is sit around and eat."

The heat was muggy and oppressively humid. Since my arrival, Mary had seemed to be feeling under the weather. I chafed at her insistence on going out into the heat, putting herself in danger. "Don't blame me if you have a heart attack out here," I snapped, like an irritated spouse. Instantly, I regretted my outburst. Mary would never talk to me that way—caustic, angry, rude. "Sorry I spoke like that. It's just so hot," I said. "I don't want to lose you."

"So," Mary retorted, "walk with me."

We set out on the dusty riverside path. I could almost hear Mary's hips resist, her knees complain. After only a few minutes, she bent forward from the hips, hands on her knees, to catch her breath. A middle-aged Black couple in matching togs trotted briskly by, their arms pumping in unison.

"How much of the time do you feel this bad?" I asked.

"I don't know if I'm sick or if . . ." Mary sank down on a bench beside the path. "Some days I think I have a terrible illness and don't know it yet. Other days I think I'm just lazy."

We fell silent. A few sparrows pecked in the sandy soil at our feet. I tried to remember the last time Mary felt really well. She had been sick one way or another through most of our adult lives. Pleurisy the time she drove herself to the ER, thinking heart attack. High blood pressure. Lyme disease. Menstrual flooding and a hysterectomy. Arthritis burning in her knees and back. Stomach pains so fierce that, if I phoned while they were gripping her, she could barely say hello. I looked down at my narrow-boned body in my below-the-knee Quaker-lady skirt and sensible shoes. I had no pains raging around, making me drop down suddenly on a park bench.

A few years earlier, in 1992, a pioneering white research scientist named Arline Geronimus had proposed that repeated stresses "weather" the systems of the human body. For Black people in the United States, she argued, the chronic stress of encountering racism and poverty accumulates over time, making the body susceptible to infections, to diseases like diabetes and high blood pressure, and to critical health events like premature labor, and infant and maternal death. Chronic stress even causes cells to age faster than normal, which Geronimus refers to as "accelerated biological aging." The studies go beyond my level of scientific understanding, assessing telomeres and allostatic load, seeking to understand biologically and specifically how overexposure to stress hormones causes wear and tear on important body systems. The bottom line, for me, is that Mary has suffered far more illness and chronic conditions than I; she is four years older than I am, but she seems older by much more, and this may be biologically true.

Sitting on the bench side by side, Mary and I were living examples of the class disparities in health care, including life-long preventive care that I received and Mary did not. Mary retired from corrections at a time when the state of New Jersey still provided dependable health insurance benefits to retirees—benefits she had earned through hard work. These would make a difference in the health care she received for the rest of her life, but there is only so much that medical care can do. Mary was and is, in very real ways, unprotected by our society.

James Baldwin asserts in his essay "Notes of a Native Son" that rage at racism is like a lifelong illness, a fever in the blood. "Once this disease is contracted," he writes, "one can never really be carefree again, for the fever, without an instant's warning, can recur at any moment . . . There is not a Negro alive who does not have this rage in his blood—one has the choice, merely, of living with it consciously or surrendering to it." Battling white supremacy, Baldwin argues, gives rise to a rage that killed his father and will kill him, too, if he lets it. Continuing the metaphor of illness, Baldwin describes this hatred and rage as "some dread, chronic disease, the unfailing symptom of which is a kind of blind fever, a pounding in the skull and fire in the bowels . . . This fever has recurred in me, and does, and will until the day I die." Every time I read these words, I think of Mary's persisting, grueling and life-threatening health conditions and crises. Although her extremely strenuous work and lifetime lack of preventive care could fully account for her many painful health conditions, Baldwin lifts up the possibility of unexpressed rage.

In response to white supremacy, Mary chooses quiet, intentional actions of resistance. She still refuses, for example, to give business to the Independence, Virginia, drugstore that, decades ago, accepted her grandmother's money for prescriptions but barred her thirsty little granddaughter from the soda fountain. Privately, Mary vents anger as quickly as anyone, especially at family members who offend or disappoint her, but her choice has been, like Baldwin's, not to surrender to rage. She chooses to ground her life in the ethics of work and love, dependability and generosity, that she learned from her church and her extended family. Whether righteous rage seethes beneath—as Baldwin suggests for his father and himself—is not mine to speculate.

Mary rose slowly from the park bench, favoring her knees. I noted the white tendrils threading through her thick brown hair, marking her age. Mary has always straightened her hair. She never wore an Afro or a short buzz, always a smooth coif from a beauty salon that specializes in Black hair.

"If I could work again," she declared, "I'd get out of the house every day. There's an officer's job at the Trenton courthouse. You check people for weapons and get them to rise when the judges come in. I almost sent for an application, but the job is full time, and look at me." She took a deep breath and shook her head with a kind of bitter longing. "With that job," she said, "I'd have co-workers again. I'd have a reason to get up in the morning."

I wanted Mary to be retired and happy, free to put her feet up. She wanted to feel useful. She wanted a daily purpose. She wanted to feel alive.

Mary took the passenger seat for the drive home. As I drove, she spoke in a voice just audible above the spin of the tires. "Mommie told me my daddy died in the war. Whenever I asked my grandmother where I came from, she said a bird flying over had dropped me. I must have been in my mid-thirties when my aunt went to a weight-loss clinic over in eastern Virginia. There's not much to do at a place like that, so you talk. She got friendly with a woman who turned out to come from the same town as my father. He didn't die in the war at all. Went back home where he grew up, a few hundred miles east, married someone else. Mommie was furious when her sister told me. But my aunt thought I should know."

Tires spinning on the hot road again. Mary fell so silent that she might not have spoken at all.

I asked if she had gone looking for her father. Mary fumbled in her bag for cigarettes, cracked the window, lit up, turned her face to the passing scenery. "By the time my aunt learned about him, he had already died."

A devastating blow, I thought. Like losing him twice.

"I traveled over there once," she said. "Turns out he had no children. I was too mad to look, anyway."

"He did have one daughter," I said.

She flicked her cigarette out into the heat.

Mary had searched for her father's Army records on the internet, she said, and stopped when the military website asked her to pay. She said she'd rather search at the town courthouse herself, if she could ever get herself back over to eastern Virginia.

The rigid set of Mary's neck told me she dreaded making that quest alone.

"I could go with you sometime," I said. For decades, she had helped me with my own father. I could help her search for hers.

Mary kept her head turned to the window. "Would you?" she asked.

That afternoon, Mary asked me to help her frost a cake for an upcoming church picnic. She was just a little tired, she said. I jumped at the chance to be useful.

On the kitchen counter, Mary set eggs, butter, sugar, vanilla, and a can of evaporated milk. She handed me a recipe for frosting for German chocolate cake, torn from a cooking magazine. I was to combine the ingredients and stir the mixture on medium heat for nine minutes, until it thickened. When the frosting cooled, I was to add coconut flakes and toasted pecans. Expertly, I thought, I separated the eggs and whipped the yolks, mixed in the other ingredients, and set the pan on the burner.

Minute six, Mary approached to inspect the liquid as I stirred. "Not thickening?" She frowned a little.

"It's only half done," I said, feeling unfairly scrutinized. I shifted my body so that I stood between Mary and the saucepan.

She lingered for another minute in a way I found irritating.

I slid the wooden spoon more slowly around the pan, and

turned the heat up a fraction. Still the liquid didn't coat the spoon. In sauce-making, this is the moment of reckoning. Flour and cornstarch are more dependable thickeners; they act more crudely, almost like glue. To thicken an egg sauce is a delicate process. Too hot, and you create scrambled eggs. Too cool, and you stir and stir and stir.

At minute eight, Mary called over from the sink where she was washing green beans. "Thickening yet?"

I hunched protectively over the pan.

"Careful it doesn't burn," she said.

Minute nine, exactly, she came towards me, reaching for the wooden spoon.

"I'm *doing* it," I said through clenched teeth, tightening my grip. The frosting smelled like it might be scorching, Mary said. I threw down the spoon and stalked out of the kitchen.

Alone in the sunroom, I fumed like a petulant child: Mary had to show me up; she had to prove she was a better cook. I vowed never to share a kitchen with her again. A few minutes later, however, when I heard Mary open the toaster oven for the pecans that had been in my charge, regret flooded me. In storming out on what I took as Mary's bossy intrusions, I'd missed the chance to work side-by-side. I could already see my error. Mary was the professional here. How many frostings had she made? Who was I to resent her oversight? Many of us who grow up in alcoholic families become almost addicted to being in control— a result, perhaps, of all that was out of control in our families. Remembering this, I chuckled. Here Mary and I are, I thought, two women in late middle age, marked by Nina and Roy's drinking: I, at least, was a perfectionist, a classic control queen. It was lucky we were usually on best behavior with each other.

Or not so lucky. Maybe best behavior was our mutual version of walking on eggshells. For decades Mary and I had shared, by unspoken agreement, a politeness and mutual deference that helped us avoid scenes like the one over the cake frosting. On reflection, I sense that with the deference required of Mary in her long-time role in my family, and the ongoing presence of unexamined power differences between us, fighting is a dimension of friendship that we have not felt free to explore. Like the frosting that day in Mary's kitchen, there is a connection between us that does not easily thicken.

The next morning, Mary placed an old shoebox on the sunroom coffee table and lifted the battered top to reveal a tumble of letters and newspaper clippings. Making ourselves comfortable on the sofa, we settled in to examine the documents that Mary had saved from her professional life.

Mary lifted out a sheet of lined paper, penciled in careful, boxy letters. "To Lieutenant C., Mercer County Correction Center, 11/18/91. I just want to thank you for allowing me to call to find out about my son. You are a hardworking, goodhearted person. I'm out of here. Sincerely written, B. G. P."

Mary held the incarcerated man's thank you out in front of us, testimony to her compassion on the job. "I was tough at the correction center, but I was fair," she said. "If you asked me something today and I told you no, you could ask me twenty times the next day and it was always no. And if I said to you, 'I will try my best,' I did. When an inmate's relative died, and I checked out that the family was destitute, I'd drive him to the funeral myself. The other officers didn't like me doing it, but I did."

Next, she retrieved a typed statement edged with now-desiccated scotch tape: "Inmates are not the interruption of our work; they are the purpose of it."

"The officers didn't like this, either. No matter. The sign was on the wall of my office, and it stayed there."

I picked up a glossy, official-looking newsletter, the Mercer County Report for August 1973. A fourth-page photo featured Mary in a dark uniform with metal buttons and a white military-style cap with a dark visor. She was shaking hands with an official-looking white man—bald head, big smile. A large photograph of John F. Kennedy hung on the wall behind his shoulder. The caption read: "The first county correction matron to complete the course for female correction officers at the Officers' Training School."

"You were good," I said.

Mary smiled at this mention of her skill.

"And so beautiful," I added, in the nostalgic way of women looking back.

She shook her head at that, and scrutinized the photograph of herself as if it were a shard unearthed from an ancient city. I thought: Mary was thirty-three when she led the way for Mercer County women into officer training. She hadn't yet married a cruel second husband, her joints probably didn't ache yet. She was entering a career—hard work paying off, all promise. This photo from the past exhibited the very usefulness she longed for now.

A white woman with Mary's intelligence, quickness, and skill would have enjoyed wider opportunities than corrections work. But Mary used the career to free herself from full-time domestic service, a goal for which her mother and grandmother had labored. In corrections, she conducted herself according to her own standards. *I was tough, but I was fair.* Dependable, level-headed, and steady, she rose in a profession that eventually brought her the benefits that, when she retired twenty-five years later, would be hers for life.

"I loved my correction center job," Mary mused. "I'd go in early and stay late. But my stress was at a high level, and, believe me, the wild thing is that the stress was all from the administration and some of my racist coworkers. Not from the inmates, who were supposed to be the dangerous people. If a new inmate came in and said, 'Who's that bitch?' the next day he'd have a black eye. 'That's a lady,' the inmates would say. 'You do not talk about her that way.'"

An article from the *Trenton Times*, August 1991, reported on a local firehouse cleanup that Mary organized as part of her community service and rehabilitation program. Showing me a faded photograph in which she posed with the cleanup crew—two Black prisoners and a white guard, Mary remarked, "These were my guys. They worked so hard for me. The guard was a little racist at first; he had a hard time accepting me as his supervisor. Then he found that I would stand behind him and support him and even go at people to defend him. He turned completely around and couldn't do enough for me." She shook her head and dropped the clipping abruptly to the coffee table. The project collapsed, she said, when the new warden switched her to another department. "I believed in rehabilitation," she said, "which our new warden did not."

Mary's struggles with a new warden in the late 1980s, which she had first told me about at the time, reflected an ominous shift in national corrections policy. Rehabilitation is a sustained effort to help inmates learn coping and work skills that will help them re-enter society. In a reaction against the social unrest of the 1960s—civil rights and anti-war protests, the beginnings of feminism and even gay liberation—influential prison theorists began touting punishment rather than rehabilitation as a goal. The 1970s saw a call for longer and longer sentences even for nonviolent crimes. Over several decades, due in great part to the "war on drugs" instituted by administrations of both political parties, this draconian shift would sweep more and more Black people into prison for nonviolent crimes. Entire generations of Black men would be stolen away: controlled, restrained, kept out of their families, out of their communities, and deprived of essential rights even when they were released.[1]

Even as Mary took her oath as the first female officer, and, later, the first female lieutenant, in the Mercer County Corrections System, her characteristic approach to working with inmates—fair, firm, humane, consistent, and emphasizing rehabilitation—was becoming a relic. The white man who took over the correction center as warden late in the 1980s (Mary would clearly have been a better candidate for the job) subscribed one hundred percent to the new, more punitive approach to incarceration. Through him, a massively harmful, nationwide shift invaded Mary's workplace, poisoned her working conditions, and eventually made her job intolerable.

Knowing this context, I said to Mary, "That warden robbed you of the chance to do all the excellent work you could have done."

---

1 The shift to mass incarceration took place entirely during my politically active adulthood. I continued to trust the mainstream press and, like most of my generation of supposedly progressive white people, remained oblivious to this deadly development. Black scholar and political activist Angela Davis raised the alarm early, writing and speaking about the racist use of American prisons, but I didn't wake up to the injustice until I read *The New Jim Crow*, the 2010 book by attorney and civil rights advocate Michelle Alexander. In 2016, Ava DuVernay's compelling documentary *13th*, further highlighted the immense injustice of mass incarceration. Though the racist restrictions of Jim Crow finally became technically illegal, long-term imprisonment of Black men for nonviolent crimes extended the oppressions of that era right down to the present. Under the guise of "law and order," a term used by US presidents from Nixon to Trump, police departments troll Black neighborhoods, not white ones, and nab Black people for "crimes" that white people commit all the time without getting prosecuted. Law and order: a misguided effort to reduce the crime rate, or a pernicious effort to put away as many Black and brown men as possible.

Mary sat up straighter, adjusted a pillow. "Because I was *good*. Remember I told you it came up from the street that people thought I was the warden, and he thought I was after his job?" She reached into the shoebox and picked up a cartoon on a square of yellowed newspaper. In an office, a secretary asks a visitor: "Would you like to speak to the man in charge, or the woman who knows what's going on?" Another ancient strip of tape across the top showed that Mary had put the cartoon up in her office. "He started right away looking for something I'd fail at. By the end, he had me in a tiny room in the back, doing the shift assignments. Even those, I did perfectly.

"I never kissed butt. I could have made my life a little better, but you struggle all these years, nobody's given you anything, you're really working hard and you know you're doing your job. Why do I have to kiss your butt?" Mary laughed. "There was a sergeant who didn't like me. I used to tell him, 'Mess with me if you want to. I'll get my white mother in Princeton after you. They donate thousands to the Republican Party every year. I'll tell my white mother how you treat me. Go ahead, do it, I want you to.' He stopped harassing me right then."

So, Mary had summoned the clout of my mother's identity to keep a harasser in line. Her words rang in my ears: *"my white mother in Princeton."* For years, I had been invested in keeping Mary's roles separate in my mind. Thinking of Mary as a pioneering woman in corrections sat easier with my feminist politics than thinking of Mary as a domestic worker who moonlighted for my family. Yet here she was at the Mercer County Correction Center, deploying her white mother to ward off a threatening colleague.

Mary laughed. "I prevailed, you see. That warden died soon after I retired. One of my officers went to his funeral and said to me later, 'I just went to make sure the son of a bitch was dead.'" She fell silent, seemed lost in thought. "I do sometimes think I have a multiple personality," Mary said at last. "I was so strong at the correction center, and so passive in Princeton." Mary had never before spoken to me of this competing duality: her toughness at the prison, and the deferential "sweetness" that my parents always lauded in her. I'd always had trouble fitting these "two" versions of Mary into one frame.

"Only one time did your parents ever see me get angry," Mary remembered. "That last Christmas, when your mom was so sick, I got her in the wheelchair, put her in a nice robe and a little lipstick. I rolled her out to see your dad in the living room, where I'd built a cozy fire in the fireplace. Back in the kitchen, I heard her calling me. I went flying to the living room. Your dad had said something mean to her, and she was crying. I was so shocked. 'Why did you do that?' I said to him, real loud, real sharp, and I took her out of there. That's the only time he ever saw me—" She paused, looking for the words. "—the only time he ever saw me different."

Mary, like many domestic workers, selected which aspects of her personality she would allow to show. This selection and self-control, this performance, is a job skill in a line of work where employers require a pleasing personality. That one time, Mary didn't edit how she came across. Her true feelings came through. She spoke angrily to my father and wheeled my mother to safety.

As if to sweep this memory away, Mary reached into the shoebox and drew out an expensively thick, flowery piece of stationery. "Dear Mary," one of my father's lady friends had written in flowing cursive, a week after his death. "I want you to know how very much I have admired you these many months. You have given Mr. Coppedge such loving care. He truly loved you, Mary."

Mary's eyes brightened, as if she had never spoken sharply to my father or wheeled my mother away to safety. "He truly loved me!" she said.

"Of course, he loved you," I said quickly, hoping to hide my uneasy reaction, trying to say what I thought Mary wanted. Since my father died, I'd tried to let the struggles and scars go with him, but Mary's story of Dad lashing out at my dying mother had stirred harsh memories.

I think now of the elegant note, the praise from a woman in Dad's wealthy white world who knew Mary only as a "domestic". Reading the note aloud, Mary seemed so joyful. Yet my father and his friends were condescending about Black people. They made racist jokes. They fixated on ill-founded suspicion and blame. I didn't trust their attitudes. I didn't trust the flowery note. I didn't even trust Mary's joy. But Mary nursed my father into death. Maybe his friends truly recognized the beauty of her care.

Eager to leave the "elegant" note and my complex feelings aside, I grabbed the last item in the box, a small, square piece of white paper, three by three inches. Bold, red letters were stamped across the top: "A BIG Note from Nina."

"Dear Mary," my mother had written, "I have tried unsuccessfully to reach you by phone before we leave for England this afternoon. I wonder if you have had any word about your becoming a lieutenant, and if you will be working different hours."

My mother must have written this note in the early 1980s, when Mary's bid for promotion to lieutenant at the correction center finally cleared the hurdles of official disapproval and delay. I tilted the note away from Mary's view before reading further. I wanted my mother to have wished Mary luck on her long-fought-for promotion, but the reference to hours was not promising. "We are scheduled to return on March 17," the note went on. "If you are free, I would like to have the Blodgets and the Frothinghams for dinner that Saturday. Love and thanks, Mrs. C."

The Big Note from Nina hit my stomach as though my mother had reached out from the past to punch me, diamond rings jutting out like brass knuckles. I felt stunned, and then ashamed: Mom had inquired about Mary's promotion only to enlist her help for a dinner party. "That's a lady," inmates warned the newly incarcerated men. The inmates were so right, I thought, stung by my mother's big, self-centered note. Mary was the lady here, in the truest sense of the word. No question.

On the last evening of my visit, Mary and I gravitated to her formal living room. In a silver-framed photograph of her mother and stepfather's fiftieth anniversary party, Mary went through each row, naming sisters, brothers, aunts, uncles, nieces, nephews, cousins, and friends. She passed quickly over her own face in the last row, saying, with characteristic modesty, that she always looked terrible in pictures (IMHO she doesn't).

Behind the glass doors of a polished cherry cabinet in the corner, Mary kept two neat rows of the books we had shared over the years: colorful paperbacks about women's health, sexual harassment, healthy eating, and many works by Black women written or reprinted in the feminist/womanist 1980s. I opened the glass doors and ran my finger fondly along the spines of these books. *Sula,* by Toni Morrison. *The Color Purple,* by Alice Walker. *Brown Girl, Brownstones* and *Praisesong for the Widow,* by Paule Marshall. *The Women of Brewster Place,* by Gloria Naylor. Moody's *Coming of Age in Mississippi.* A volume by Alice Childress caught my eye, *Like One of the Family: Conversations from a Domestic's Life*. The cover featured a self-possessed and skeptical-looking Black woman, framed against the black-and-white floor tiles of a 1950s kitchen. I pulled the book off the shelf.

In 1956—the year that Mary turned sixteen and came to her first live-in job as a domestic worker—a Harlem actress and playwright named Alice Childress brought out *Like One of the Family*. The novel spins out stories, reflections, and smart diatribes by a character called Mildred, a Black woman who does domestic work for white Manhattan families. The Mildred character nails many of the racist dynamics that Mary must have handled during her summer work for my parents: how they used her first name, while she was to call them "Mr." and "Mrs."; how she wasn't supposed to sit down anywhere but the kitchen or her bedroom; how my father wanted to be sure Mary wasn't a civil-rights "troublemaker"; how my mother claimed that Mary was like one of the family, but did not invite her to eat with us. Had I found this book when Childress wrote it, her excellent send-up could have given me an independent perspective on Mary's work in my family.

Mary took the book from me and leafed thoughtfully through the first several pages. She turned back to page one and looked over at me, as if gauging my readiness for a live reading. I dropped to the seat of a wingback chair to listen. Mary began to read aloud.

> *Hi Marge! I have had me one hectic day.... Well, I had to take out my crystal ball and give Mrs. C. a thorough reading.... She's a pretty nice woman as they go and I have never had too much trouble with her, but from time to time she really gripes me with her ways.*

A striking coincidence, that the "Mildred" character and Mary both referred to their employers as "Mrs. C."

As if handling an explosive that merited sudden caution, Mary paused and studied my face to check my willingness for her to continue. I leaned forward to hear more. Mary hadn't been so energized all weekend.

When she has company, for example, she'll holler out to me from the living room to the kitchen: "Mildred dear! Be sure and eat both of those lamb chops for your lunch!" Now you know she wasn't doing a thing but tryin' to prove to the company how "good" and "kind" she was to the servant, because she had told me already to eat those chops.

Mary chuckled at this. I laughed, too, but nervously. Holding the tale up to my mother like a piece of clothing to check the fit, I realized with a pang that the lamb chop story fit me better. Wasn't I always wanting to come across as the "good" white person, the "kind" one? Didn't I always want to think I was a better "friend" to Mary than my mother had been?

But Mary/Mildred was continuing.

Today she had a girlfriend of hers over to lunch . . . and she says to her friend, "We just love her! She's like one of the family, and she just adores our little Carol! We don't know what we'd do without her. We don't think of her as a servant!" After I couldn't stand it anymore, I went in and took the platter off the table and gave 'em both a look that would have frizzled a egg. . . . When the guest leaves, I go into the living room . . . and drew up a chair and read her thusly: "Mrs. C., you are a pretty nice person to work for,

*but I wish you would please stop talkin' about me like I
was a cocker spaniel or a poll parrot or a kitten."*

At this, Mary held the book out in the air as though it might
ignite her slacks, or the sofa. "Should I go on?" she asked.

"Do you want to?"

"Do you?"

With Mildred's help, Mary and I were entering new territory.
Sassy, confrontational, and truth-telling in ways that might get a
real-time domestic worker fired, the Mildred character vented
truths that Mary had never spoken to me. In what looked at the
time like a dance of permission, Mary was asking if I could handle these truths.

"Definitely, if you do," I said.

Mary read on.

*"In the first place, you do not love me; you may be fond of
me, but that is all. . . . In the second place, I am not just like
one of the family at all! The family eats in the dining room,
and I eat in the kitchen."*

"Mildred can say that again," I said, grabbing a chance to be
good. "Remember you and Mom in Nantucket, eating your
lunch back to back, with the kitchen wall between you?"

Mary paused. "Now that you say it, I do," she said, but before I could enjoy standing with her in the summer kitchen with
the boss on the other side of the wall, she continued with Mildred's emphatic next words.

"Now for another thing, I do not just adore your little Carol."

"Mary loves us!" my mother had always said. "And we love her." I opened my mouth, but Mary went on reading.

> "You think it is a compliment when you say, 'We don't think of her as a servant. . . .' but after I have worked myself into a sweat cleaning the bathroom and the kitchen . . ."

Mary gave a little snort here, and began a dramatic rendering of each task on Mildred's list.

> " . . . making the beds . . . cooking the lunch . . . washing the dishes and ironing Carol's pinafores . . . I do not feel like no weekend house guest. I feel like a servant, and in the face of that I have been meaning to ask you for a slight raise."

Smiling broadly now, Mary flipped to the front of the book and ran her finger down the list of chapter titles like she meant to read more soon.

"Like one of the family," my mother had always said. *Wrong*, I thought. *Wrong, wrong.*

But a conviction began to gather inside me, like a spasm forming, a sneeze or cough I couldn't swallow or squelch. Mary truly was one of our family—I couldn't repress the thought. At the lake house, hadn't Mary called herself the daughter who didn't leave home? At the correction center, hadn't she threatened the insulting officer with retaliation from her white mother in Princeton? Mary seemed to love and fear my mother and father in many of the ways I did. We suffered over their drinking, each in our own way, like siblings in an alcoholic family.

"Don't you think . . ." I began. I realized the wrongness in what I was about to say, felt the words coming on anyway. I shifted to the edge of the chair as if the claim headed out through my lips wouldn't allow me to lean back and make myself at home. "In our case, I mean, I know what Mildred was saying, but in our case, don't you think . . . in a way . . ." I blushed hotly. "You really did become one of the family . . . didn't you?"

Mary thought for a long time, holding the book in front of her as if testing its weight. Finally, she said soberly, "It's a double-edged thing, Wendy. You are one of the family, and then again you aren't. When your mother died, it was the same for me as if I had lost my own mother. None of you seemed to realize that, not your father, or Copey, or you. You were all too busy."

Her reproach devastated me. "I asked you to sit up in front with us at the funeral," I said. My voice sounded whiny and weak. "That was my way of showing that I knew you had lost a mother, too." Today in 2020 I hear this whine and think again of Robin DiAngelo's work on white fragility. DiAngelo's guidance to white people is this: when a person of color gives you feedback that you have done something hurtful or harmful, do not try to explain your good intentions. Say, "Thank you." Say, "I'll try to learn from this going forward."

If you ever doubted that explanations of good intention are a problem, even a further aggression, listen to Mary's guarded response when I harked back to seating Mary in the front of the church. "It was very nice of you," Mary said to me, formal as the furniture. "And I appreciated it."

I am grateful that she didn't stop there. "Your father probably didn't even think I should be *in* the church," Mary went on. "Not that he meant it meanly—he was just a man of his time is all."

"You weren't comfortable sitting up there with the rest of us?"

"I wasn't." Still she held the book between us, her face utterly serious.

Finally, Mary's message landed. Not one of us had treated her like one of the family. As if to mark the seriousness of this revelation, we sat in silence together for some time.

Eventually Mary rose and went to the cabinet, slipped *Like One of the Family* carefully among the other books we had shared over the years, and closed the glass-paned door. She turned off the lights. We would rise early for my train home.

Upstairs in Mary's guest room, I sank onto my old twin bed, smoothly repainted by Mary and Fred, a relic of my old life made pristine again. Despair seized me. Despite clear warning from Alice Childress, despite all the books by Black writers I had claimed to learn from, I'd blurted out the same old thing to Mary. Her energetic reading of Mildred's spirited critiques had taken us forward, but my humbling blurt about her being one of the family had pushed us back. Mary was offering me a chance to know her better. Would I ever live up to it?

In the end, I clung to the step forward. Thanks to Alice Childress and her forthright character Mildred, Mary had told me a new truth. I bungled when Mom died, and now Mary had told me how this hurt her. A door, long barricaded shut by the inequalities that divide us, cracked ajar. Mary and I might deepen our relationship as family to each other, but not through nostalgia, only through sharing—and, for my part, being ready to listen to—more of the truth.

seventeen

Road Trip

MARY AND I ARE IN ELK CREEK, VIRGINIA, IN THE HILLSIDE hamlet where her mother and stepfather raised six children. It is 2004. My parents are long dead, Mary's are still living. Mary has moved back home to keep her aging mother out of a nursing facility. Mary has fixed up a tidy house for herself just a stone's throw up the hill from her mother and stepfather. She has a home in Baltimore, too, across the street from her son and his family. She keeps her small, cozy Baltimore house unoccupied and ready for her return, although, as things turn out, she will spend close to a decade in Elk Creek giving her mother, and then her stepfather, steady care.

Mary takes me on a drive through the tiny hillside communities of her childhood. Every road holds a memory. We stand outside the small, weather-beaten farmhouse in Independence, where Mary grew up with her grandmother, whom she called Mamaw. Mary points to the window of the room where she used to lie dreaming on her Mamaw's bed, listening to the rain on the tin roof. We stand close together on the country road, feeling the heat of the May morning, taking in what a long-ago time that was. She walks me to the overgrown vegetable garden, where blazing sunshine during her noon chores once made her faint dead away. We move quickly by the ruins of the despised chicken coop, site of Mary's most hated farm chore. We drive down the steep mile that Mary used to trudge on her way to and from the school bus, and we peer into the high green banks on either side, half hunting for one of the large black snakes that terrified her as a girl. We stand by the pot-bellied stove inside what is now a small back room of an evangelical Christian church where her female cousin is a pastor—the single room that was Mary's only schoolhouse. She drives me past the ranch house where, as a preteen, she worked Saturdays for a white family. She speeds past the drug store where, in the Jim Crow 1940s and '50s, the racist pharmacist filled prescriptions for Black people but denied them soda.

In the sloped graveyard of the Oak Grove Methodist church, we step among the crumbling, unmarked rocks that centuries-ago mourners dragged from surrounding woods to mark the graves of those too poor for formal remembrance. Mary takes me to her Mamaw's finely carved granite headstone—*Verna Cox Phipps, in loving memory*. We peer in the windows of the small white-clapboard church to the spare wooden pews to which Mamaw mustered Mary and her aunt Dot every Sunday morning, rain or shine. In the grassy area just outside the church, Mary recalls the church picnic where she had her first kiss. Later, in the Elk Creek community cemetery below her mother and stepfather's church, we stand soberly at G.P.'s grave.

We end our tour at the small, wooden house on "the hill," also known as Willow Oak Lane, where Mary's elderly parents are waiting for us—her stepfather Mr. George and her mother, whom she calls Miss Alice. When I ask why "Miss Alice," Mary explains that this is what Black children in the South were taught to call the white ladies for whom their mothers and grandmothers did domestic work. Mary realized early on that her mother had as much class, style and worth as those white women, and deserved as much respect. She began calling her mother "Miss Alice" and has never stopped. We enter the small home built with a bank mortgage made possible by a respectful white businessman after Mr. George returned from military service in WWII to find that housing benefits under the GI Bill were closed to Black veterans like himself.

Mary and I enter the house through the kitchen and find Miss Alice and Mr. George in a tiny, adjoining den. Companionable on twin recliners, they are half-watching TV. Alice Johnson is a slight woman, retired from decades of domestic work for a white doctor in town. She is so soft-spoken that I have to lean over to hear her. She urges me into the spotless living room to view the beautiful nature paintings she created in oils after retirement. Mr. George himself is long retired from the dry-cleaning business. Perched in his recliner, he chuckles a few times at talk that tickles him, and then nods off. Mary natters at them to take their medications and to eat their lunch—like a mother, like a nurse.

On the second day, Mary and I set out at dawn for a dot on the map of eastern Virginia, the town where Mary had learned a few years back that her father lived and died. Mary eases her arthritic body into the driver's seat and drives somberly down the hill, as if we are heading to a funeral.

On the highway, Mary speeds up. She starts tinkering with the cord that plugs her cell phone into the cigarette lighter.

"Making a call?" I ask quickly. "Want me to drive?" I am a

nervous passenger. My hand itches to grab the steering wheel.

"Damn phone went funny on me last month. Sometimes it's charging, sometimes it isn't. Is the light on?"

I check the charge light. "On," I say.

Mary succeeds in freeing the earbud from its tangle of cord and starts trying to get it to stay in her ear. Pick-up trucks and ten wheelers barrel along beside us. We are going eighty. *It's not eighty-five,* I tell myself. *Not ninety. This is Mary's trip. She's in charge. I'm here for support.* Mary has told me that my presence on this journey will give her courage to search for evidence of her father. I hope I haven't come this far to die on the highway. Dad was a lurching driver, a tailgater—gunning the accelerator, slamming on the brakes, cursing other drivers. On this first trip where Mary is truly the boss, I don't want to be in a tizzy about her driving.

Tour buses roar past us on either side.

Mary tosses the phone on the dashboard in disgust and yanks the bud from her ear. "Busy," she says. "My sister better have picked Mommie up on time for dialysis." When she catches me checking the speedometer again, she chuckles for the first time all day. "Used to be, back in New Jersey, I'd be driving to the correction center at dawn with my coffee and cigarette in one hand, putting my makeup on with the other." She looks over, studies my face. "Got pretty good at steering with my knees."

"Got me," I say. "I'll try to relax."

Mid-afternoon, we reach flat farmlands, rich brown earth, many colors of green, and a sense in the landscape of easing east towards the ocean. We pull into the tree-shaded main street of the town we have been seeking. We see a mix of Black and white people walking purposefully from drugstore to bank, from hardware store to library.

Humid heat presses us as we get out of the car to head for the town hall and its repository of records. Mary checks her purse for pad and pencils, locks the car, and gives me a look of adventure and trepidation. Limping and rolling on the car-stiff hips of our late middle age, we head for the town hall. Inside the cool, old building, we enter a room dense with tall, heavy books: military records along one wall, real estate along another, wills and estate documents filling a third, and at the fourth, a coin-operated copy machine. Neither of us has ever done this kind of sleuthing. There is so much living in each of these weighty tomes, so much dying. In the hushed room, I feel almost light-headed with excitement and awe. We may find traces of the man whose absence shaped Mary's life. We divide up the areas between us and begin to hunt.

In one set of records, we find Robert White's induction papers for military service. We learn that he was inducted into the Army in 1941 at the age of twenty-seven, just as the United States entered World War II. He was 5'6" tall then, and weighed in at 150 pounds. His occupation is listed as "farm laborer." Every detail is new and significant. In another volume, we find Robert White's wedding license to a woman from a local family. We find that Robert White shifted to the Air Force and rose to the level of Master Sergeant, one of the most significant promotions for an enlistee, a rise from technical service into operational leadership. He remained in the military for many years, until a random accident with a toppling file cabinet crippled him. We find the inventory of his tiny estate at the time of his death in 1969 at fifty-five.

In three hours of poring over the sources, we find dates,

names, and places, but these are bones without flesh. We find Mary's father's records, but little sense of the man himself. After copying every relevant document on the public copy machine, we walk out of the building that Mary's father must have entered, at the very least, for his marriage license, back when Mary was six.

The records indicated that Mary's dad was buried at Cedar Grove Baptist Church, so we get the address and drive there next. Cedar Grove Baptist is quiet on that weekday afternoon. We stand side by side before the neat brick building that is, Mary observes, in decent shape for a Black church in Virginia. I recall Mary's grandmother's church, and her stepfather's, both simpler than this one, both more rural, more worn. We take photographs—a solemn Mary standing by the large sign on the church's front lawn, the uneven slope of the graveyard out back, me in my skirt and sneakers bending over to pull tangled grasses away from Robert White's gravestone. Like the stones of other men who served in the US military, the stone of Mary's father stands straight, its chiseled letters still readable. *Robert H. White. Virginia. MSgt US Airforce. World War II. October 4, 1914–April 7, 1969.* We have brought no tools to clip the grassy edges, no broom to push away the dried magnolia leaves and accumulated tree litter. We sweep the grave with our fingers.

Over take-out sandwiches in the car, Mary laments that nothing we've found tells us what her father looked like. That's what she most hoped for—she wants to see his picture. We head for the local funeral home, where a friendly receptionist is willing to hunt for the thirty-five-year-old file on Robert White's funeral. The program she hands us feels flimsy and thin in our fingers. There is no photograph.

We drive next out along the town's northern road, where several mailboxes carry the name of Robert's wife's family. We muster the courage to enter driveways, knock on the doors of houses and trailers, and inquire. One helpful neighbor leads us to another.

Over the next two days, we sit on front porches and in living rooms with five different relatives of Robert's wife—all of them old. Mary made this trip not a moment too soon. We learn that Robert grew up not with his birth-family but with a local family who were members of Cedar Grove Church. As an adult, he searched successfully for his mother in North Carolina, and brought her many times to visit. All the children in the family loved Robert White, because he spoiled them, but he and his wife had none of their own. He loved cars, and kept his black Ford Fairlane 500 impeccably clean and shiny. One man tells us that he and Robert used to sit together on "this very porch." I write down all these details on a steno pad I've brought for this purpose, in case Mary wants a record.

Some of the people we speak with say they heard, years ago, that Robert had a child in the western part of the state. They welcome Mary as that child, no questions asked. One person tells Mary she laughs like her father. Another says that she looks like him when she gets a serious look and presses her lips together. Another asserts that Mary looks like her North Carolina grandmother—this seems to please Mary more than anything. The people we meet are universally warm in greeting Mary. "Don't be a stranger," they say, and, "Come on back, sit on the porch, and see who you can meet." They are cooler towards me, a white woman. Over dinner the first evening, in a steakhouse next to our motel, Mary and I talk about how some of the people we've spoken with seem uneasy in my presence. "My white skin and northern accent," I suggest, "this dutiful khaki skirt, my sensible tie-ups?"

Mary smiles. "And all those notes you took?"

"Oh, my God, yes," I say. "They must have thought I was . . ."

We say it at the same time. "A social worker!"

Mary and I cracked up at the time, but there's every chance that the men and women we approached did think I was a social worker. I imagine, now, what expectations this may have stirred. The people we met grew up Black under burdens of Jim Crow that didn't end with the civil rights movement. For many of them, the approach of a social worker may have stirred distrust more than confidence. The social work profession is as susceptible as any to pernicious myths about Black people—that they are needy, insufficient, ignorant, violent, in trouble, unskilled at parenting, in need of "help" or control. A scathing analysis by sociologist Dorothy Roberts, *Shattered Bonds: The Color of Child Welfare* (2002), considers the role that social workers play in taking children away from Black families whom the system deems "unfit" for raising children. Even the most ethical, well-meaning, and diligent of today's social workers must still follow the regulations of a system that is inherently committed to white superiority. If the people we visited did suspect I was a social worker, they were amazingly gracious to me, and understandably more guarded than they were with Mary, due at the very least to my being white.

The second morning over breakfast, after a night spent at the motel, Mary reports on her thinking: Even though my presence may limit what people are willing to say to her, she wants us to keep visiting together. All that day, Mary makes a point of introducing me as her life-long friend who has come "all the way from Boston" to help her search. This makes a difference to us.

At the end of the second day we visit a dim, low-ceilinged living room with an elderly woman who has slipped already into Alzheimer's, and can tell us little. A slight woman, with a still vibrant singing voice from decades in a church choir, she launches into snatches of hymns and spirituals. She nods in our direction, directing us to sing along with her. "Precious Lord," Mary and I sing in wavery, untrained voices, and "Steal Away to Jesus."

Before starting the long drive home, Mary purchases several leafy potted plants at a local nursery. We deliver one to each household.

Mary, who had helped me repeatedly with my own difficult father, allowed me to journey with her in search of hers. Given how long it took me to begin to slough off the toxic effects of my training in white supremacy—to "see" Mary, and to let in truly accurate information about her reality—that she trusted me to accompany her lets me hope that even an imperfect effort matters.

epilogue

Phone Call, November 2020

Mary: We couldn't have said "friend" at the beginning. It took years to get where we are. If you hadn't been a curious person, you still wouldn't know my world. You would just now maybe be trying to figure it out, wondering "what do they want?" If you had been different, we would never have been good friends.

Wendy: If either of us had been different.

Mary: Yes.

Resources for Restorative Reading

Below are works by the precious teachers-in-print mentioned in this book, with original publication dates.

Michelle Alexander, *The New Jim Crow: Mass Incarceration in the Age of Colorblindness* (New York: New Press, 2010).

James Baldwin, *Notes of a Native Son* (Boston: Beacon Press, 1955). (Quotations herein are reprinted with the permission of Beacon Press.)

Katie G. Cannon, *Black Womanist Ethics* (Eugene, OR: Wipf and Stock Publishers, 2006. First published in 1988 by Scholars Press).

Alice Childress, *Like One of the Family: Conversations from a Domestic's Life* (Boston: Beacon Press, 1986. First published in 1956 by Independence Publishers). (Quotations herein are reprinted with the permission of the Williams and Woodard families and SLD Associates LLC.)

Ta-Nehisi Coates, *Between the World and Me* (New York: One World, 2015).

Ta-Nehisi Coates, "The Case for Reparations" in *We Were Eight Years in Power* (New York: One World, 2017).

Combahee River Collective, *The Combahee River Collective Statement*, 1977, https://combaheerivercollective.weebly.com/the-combahee-river-collective-statement.html.

Robin DiAngelo, *White Fragility: Why It's So Hard for White People to Talk About Racism* (Boston: Beacon Press, 2018).

Terrance Hayes, "Antebellum House Party" in *How to Be Drawn* (New York: Penguin Books, 2015). (Quotations herein are reprinted with the permission of Penguin Books.)

Debby Irving, *Waking Up White, and Finding Myself in the Story of Race* (Cambridge, MA: Elephant Room Press, 2014).

Barbara Jensen, *Reading Classes: On Culture and Classism in America* (Ithaca, NY: ILR Press of Cornell University Press, 2012).

Audre Lorde, "The Transformation of Silence into Language and Action," "Scratching the Surface: Some Notes on Barriers to Women and Loving," "An Open Letter to Mary Daly," "The Master's Tools Will Never Dismantle the Master's House," and "Learning from the 60s" in *Sister Outsider: Essays and Speeches* (Berkeley, CA: Crossing Press, 1984). (Text © 1984 by Audre Lorde.)

Peggy McIntosh, "White Privilege: Unpacking the Invisible Knapsack" in *On Privilege, Fraudulence, and Teaching as Learning: Selected Essays 1981–2019* (New York: Routledge, 2019).

Anne Moody, *Coming of Age in Mississippi* (New York: Dell Press, 1968).

Toni Morrison, *The Bluest Eye* (New York: Holt, Rinehart and Winston, 1970).

Toni Morrison, *Playing in the Dark*: *Whiteness and the Literary Imagination* (Cambridge, MA: Harvard University Press, 1992).

Barbara Neely, *Blanche on the Lam* (New York: St. Martin's Press, 1992). (Quotations herein are reprinted with the permission of current publisher Brash Books and Barbara Neely's estate.)

Melvin Oliver and Thomas Shapiro, *Black Wealth / White Wealth: A New Perspective on Racial Inequality* (New York: Routledge, 1995). (Ta-Nehisi Coates quotes *Black Wealth / White Wealth* in "The Case for Reparations"; part of that quotation is excerpted on page 228 of this book.)

Claudia Rankine, *Just Us: An American Conversation* (Minneapolis, MN: Graywolf Press, 2020).

Adrienne Rich, *The Dream of a Common Language: Poems 1974–1977* (New York: W. W. Norton, 1978).

Adrienne Rich, *Of Woman Born: Motherhood as Experience and Institution* (New York: W. W. Norton, 1976).

Adrienne Rich, *Women and Honor: Some Notes on Lying* (Pittsburg, PA: Motherroot Press, 1977).

Dorothy Roberts, *Fatal Invention: How Science, Politics, and Business Re-create Race in the Twenty-First Century* (New York: New Press, 2011).

Dorothy Roberts, *Shattered Bonds: The Color of Child Welfare* (New York: Basic Books, 2001).

Judith Rollins, *Between Women: Domestics and Their Employers* (Philadelphia: Temple University Press, 1985).

Kate Rushin, "The Bridge Poem" in *This Bridge Called My Back: Writings by Radical Women of Color*, ed. Cherríe Moraga and Gloria E. Anzaldúa (Watertown, MA: Persephone Press, 1981). (Quotations herein are reprinted with the permission of Kate Rushin.)

Margaret Walker, *Jubilee* (Boston: Houghton Mifflin, 1966).

Deborah Willis, *Reflections in Black: A History of Black Photographers 1840 to the Present* (New York: W. W. Norton, 2000).

Jacqueline Woodson, *Brown Girl Dreaming* (New York: Nancy Paulson Books, 2014).

ADDITIONAL GUIDES FOR CONTINUING THE WORK

Michael Eric Dyson, *Tears We Cannot Stop: A Sermon to White America* (New York: St. Martin's Press, 2017).

Heather McGhee, *The Sum of Us: What Racism Costs Everyone and How We Can Prosper Together* (New York: One World, 2021).

Ijeoma Oluo, *So You Want to Talk about Race* (New York: Seal Press, 2018).

Claudia Rankine, *Citizen: An American Lyric* (Minneapolis, MN: Graywolf Press, 2014).

Jason Reynolds and Ibram X. Kendi, *Stamped: Racism, Antiracism, and You* (New York: Little, Brown, 2020).

Layla F. Saad, *Me and White Supremacy: Combat Racism, Change the World, and Become a Good Ancestor* (Naperville, IL: Sourcebooks, 2020).

Bryan Stevenson, *Just Mercy: A Story of Justice and Redemption* (New York: One World, 2014).

Becky Thompson, *A Promise and a Way of Life: White Antiracist Activism* (Minneapolis: University of Minnesota Press, 2001).

Isabel Wilkerson, *Caste: The Origins of Our Discontents* (New York: Random House, 2020).

Isabel Wilkerson, *The Warmth of Other Suns: The Epic Story of America's Great Migration* (New York: Random House, 2010).

Acknowledgments

What a joyful list to make!

I am immensely grateful to the many writers, thinkers, and activists of color whose works opened the way for me to understand and inhabit my friendship with Mary Norman—and my whole life—more fully. I have sought to honor you in this book as my "teachers-in-print." I am grateful, too, to the handful of truth-speaking white writers whose work has helped me to imagine that I, too, might break deadly white silences around race and class.

Mary Norman, your friendship and love sustain me. Although this is not the book we imagined forty years ago as we walked the beach at nightfall, your input into every page is the key to whether it will be of use in the world after we go. We have shed many tears in remembering this difficult story. Thank you, more than I can say, for your willingness to go there with me. I love you so much. To your sons, Dennie Norman and Greg Norman: Thank you for reading and embracing this book; your steady faithfulness to your mom teaches me about family.

Polly Attwood, I cannot thank you enough, ever, for all you have given to me in our forty-plus years as lovers and co-conspirators. Your deep commitment to anti-racist teaching helps to inform and ground this book, your faith helps me persevere, and your love—our love—is a daily blessing.

A.J. Verdelle, my extraordinary writing coach, you guided me for so many years, often giving this project time and care that should belong to your own brilliant work. Thank you for your practice of revision as an art form, for your amazing attention to language, and for unfailingly challenging me to honor Mary Norman with keen and informed attention.

While I intend this book mainly for white readers—to raise awareness of realities that Black people in the United States have known painfully for centuries—it has felt important to check my story and analysis with Black writers and activists whose craft and perspective have taught me a great deal. Shay Stewart-Bouley, John Reynolds, and Crystal Wilkinson, thank you for your illuminating comments on many craft aspects of the book, and for weighing in on the authenticity and truth of my portrayal of Black characters, culture and history. You told me honestly where I got it wrong. Thank you for this care. All remaining errors or missteps are my own. Thank you, too, to Reverend Irene Monroe for your years of support as we walked our precious dogs early on, and for the generously honest feedback that, due to my white fragility, I could not always hear.

I wrote this book under what Quakers call a "leading": a nudge from Spirit towards an action that may seem daunting or impossible but that one is "meant" to tackle. A Quaker support circle helped me rise to this leading over all the decades it has taken me to complete the work. Carolyn LeJuste, Joann Neuroth, and Polly Attwood, I am indebted to you for your steady faithfulness, your deep, compassionate listening, your passion for justice, and your love. I am grateful, too, to Beckey Phipps and Tania Burger for your early years in helping me seek guidance.

A special thank you to the generous friends who stuck with this project over many drafts: Kim Bancroft, Marilyn Bannan, Maggy Bartek, Ben Benjamin, Helena Bienstock, Pamela Brooks, Brian Corr, Melody Brazo, Thayer Cory, Alison Dover, Sally

Edwards, Roz Feldberg, Mary Fillmore, Esther Fine, Denise Hart, Miriam Hawley, Jo Ellen Hillyer, Yamila Hussein, Jenny Lawrence, Lysa Leland, Jennifer Leaning, Susan Lloyd McGarry, Nora Mitchell, Dabney Narvaez (d. 2019), Judy Norsigian, Jane Pincus, Julie Rochlin, Kitty Rush, Emily Skoler, Elaine Spatz-Rabinowitz, Dinah Starr, Mary Teachout, Sally Thompson, and Patricia Wild. You have my life-long gratitude, and I love you!

If you are one of the countless kind people over the past 30 years who read and commented on a draft of this book, I can't name you all, but please know that your thoughts and caring are reflected in this text. Thank you!

Thank you to my *Our Bodies, Ourselves* sister-founders, who understand that *These Walls Between Us* continues our work together for justice: Ruth Bell Alexander, Pamela Berger, Ayesha Chatterjee, Vilunya Diskin, Joan Ditzion, Paula Doress-Worters, Miriam Hawley, Elizabeth MacMahon-Herrera, Judy Norsigian, Jamie Penney, Jane Pincus, Norma Swenson, Sally Whelan, and Kiki Zeldes. I remember Pamela Morgan and Esther Rome with love.

Thank you to the many circles of friends and Friends who have sustained my spirit and my work:

- Sunapee Artists and Writers: Jane Pincus, Norma Swenson, Paula Doress-Worters, Hillary Salk, and Mary Fillmore

- Friends for LGBTQ Concerns, my beloved Queer Quaker community, who hosted my first public reading from this book in the 1990s;

- White Privilege reading groups at Friends Meeting at Cambridge (MA) and Red Cedar Friends Meeting in Lansing, Michigan;

- Next Steppers: Andrea Gilbert, Roz Feldberg, Paula Rayman, and Deborah Silverstein;

- My Sunday evening prayer family: Jimmy Seale-Collazo, Deidre Dees, Charlene Desir, Susan Klimczak, and Polly Attwood;

- My fellow-journeyers in faithfulness: Betsy Roper, Jonathan Gilbert, Nancy Bloom, Brian Corr, Jonathan Vogel-Borne, and Minga Claggett-Borne.

Thank you to Debby Irving, author of the ground-breaking *Waking up White*, for your steady encouragement and help. Thank you to Frenchie Blodget (1920–2020), my oldest reader and trusted advisor on my family's life in Princeton. Thank you to Byllye Avery and Sue Gallagher, old friend and new—you each came in towards the end and provided a green light at a crucial moment. Thank you to Richard Curran, my kind and generous co-housing neighbor, for a perfect author photo and wise help with the daunting "author platform." Also in coho, thank you Bob M., Dick, Gwen F., Ileana, Mark, and Jean.

Thank you to my dedicated teachers at Vermont College of Fine Arts, especially Robin Hemley, Christopher Noel, Francois Camoin, and Sue William Silverman. Thank you to my earliest writing guides, Anne B. Shepherd (1917–1996) and Robert Lisle (1925–2011), and to Kathleen Spivack and Julia Thacker, midwives to the earliest drafts of this book.

A huge thank you to Brooke Warner and her team at She Writes Press, and to Ann-Marie Nieves and her team at GetRed-PR—two fabulously strong and smart women who helped bring this book into the world. Samantha Strom and Barrett Briske, you are the greatest!

About the Author

Wendy Sanford grew up in an upper-middle-class white suburban family in Princeton, New Jersey, and attended private schools throughout her life. During the socially turbulent time of the 1970s, she became a feminist, a lesbian, and a Quaker. A founding member of the Boston Women's Health Book Collective, Wendy coauthored and edited many versions of the women's health and sexuality classic *Our Bodies, Ourselves* from 1973 to 2011. In seminary at Harvard Divinity School in the 1980s, she began to read works of women of color as "devotional reading," to remedy her previous exclusive exposure to white and mostly male authors. She served for nearly a decade in campus ministry in the Boston area. In her fifties, she began to reckon with her own white skin and the benefits that came to her through being white. In 2003, she earned an MFA in Writing from Vermont College of Fine Arts. She lives in Cambridge, MA, with Polly Attwood, her spouse of forty-one years.

Ms. Sanford's website is:
wendysanford-thesewallsbetweenus.com

SELECTED TITLES FROM SHE WRITES PRESS

She Writes Press is an independent publishing company
founded to serve women writers everywhere.
Visit us at www.shewritespress.com.

*Redlined: A Memoir of Race, Change, and Fractured Community in
1960s Chicago* by Linda Gartz. $16.95, 978-1-63152-320-5. A riveting
story of a community fractured by racial turmoil, an unraveling and
conflicted marriage, a daughter's fight for sexual independence, and
an up-close, intimate view of the racial and social upheavals of the
1960s.

The Outskirts of Hope: A Memoir by Jo Ivester. $16.95,
978-1-63152-964-1. A moving, inspirational memoir about how living and working in an all-black town during the height of the civil
rights movement profoundly affected the author's entire family—and
how they in turn impacted the community.

Times They Were A-Changing: Women Remember the '60s & '70s edited
by Kate Farrell, Amber Lea Starfire, and Linda Joy Myers. $16.95,
978-1-938314-04-9. Forty-eight powerful stories and poems detailing
the breakthrough moments experienced by women during the '60s
and '70s.

All the Ghosts Dance Free: A Memoir by Terry Cameron Baldwin.
$16.95, 978-1-63152-822-4. A poetic memoir that explores the legacy
of alcoholism and teen suicide in one woman's life—and her efforts
to create an authentic existence in the face of that legacy.

Renewable: One Woman's Search for Simplicity, Faithfulness, and Hope
by Eileen Flanagan. $16.95, 978-1-63152-968-9. At age forty-nine,
Eileen Flanagan had an aching feeling that she wasn't living up to her
youthful ideals or potential, so she started trying to change the world
—and in doing so, she found the courage to change her life.

Uncovered: How I Left Hassidic Life and Finally Came Home by Leah
Lax. $16.95, 978-1-63152-995-5. Drawn in by their offers of refuge
from her troubled family and promises of eternal love, Leah Lax becomes a Hassidic Jew—but ultimately, as a forty-something woman,
comes to reject everything she has lived for three decades in order to
be who she truly is.